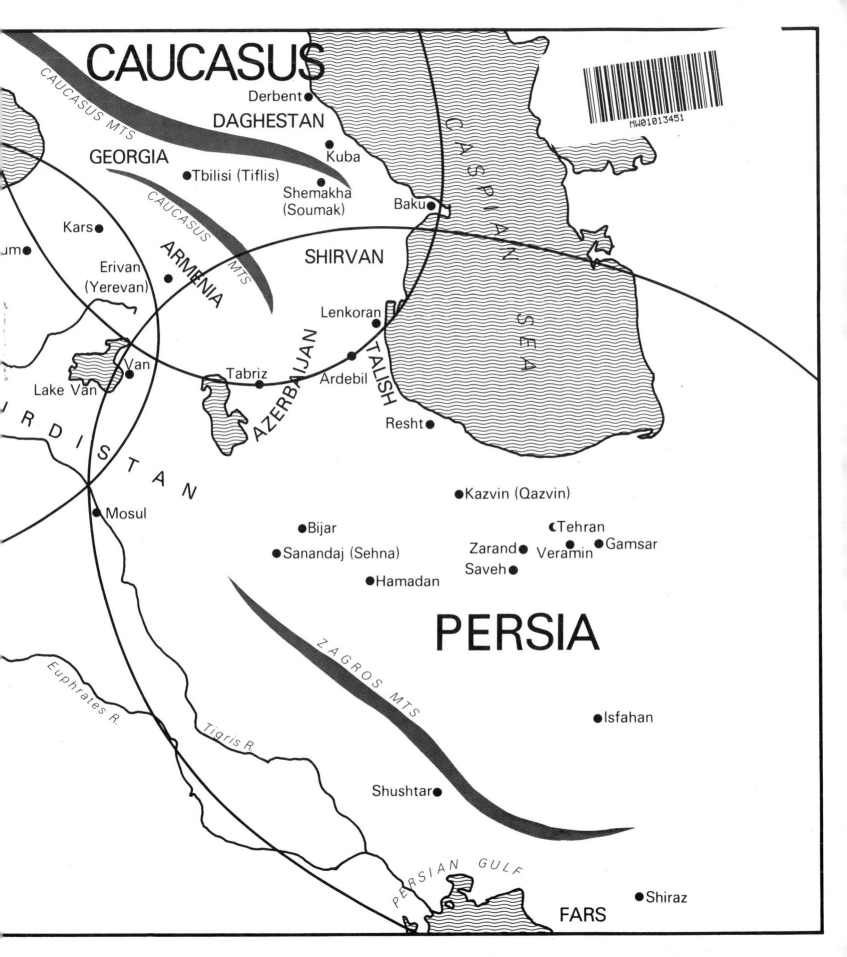

CAUCASUS

DAGHESTAN

GEORGIA

Derbent

Kuba

Tbilisi (Tiflis)

Shemakha
(Soumak)

Baku

CAUCASUS MTS

CAUCASUS

MTS

Kars

ARMENIA

SHIRVAN

CASPIAN SEA

um

Erivan
(Yerevan)

Lenkoran

Van

Lake Van

AZERBAIJAN

TALISH

Tabriz

Ardebil

Resht

KURDISTAN

Mosul

Kazvin (Qazvin)

Bijar

Tehran

Sanandaj (Sehna)

Zarand

Veramin

Gamsar

Saveh

Hamadan

PERSIA

ZAGROS MTS

Euphrates R.

Tigris R.

Isfahan

Shushtar

PERSIAN GULF

Shiraz

FARS

KILIMS

Yanni Petsopoulos

KILIMS

Flat-woven Tapestry Rugs

Rizzoli
NEW YORK

The publishers wish to thank MICHAEL FRANSES for material, photographs and research assembled for this publication.

© 1979, Office du Livre, Fribourg, Switzerland

English edition published 1979
in the United States of America by:

RIZZOLI INTERNATIONAL PUBLICATIONS, INC.
712 Fifth Avenue/New York 10019

Second impression 1982

Library of Congress Catalog Card Number: 79-64336
ISBN: 0-8478-0245-0

Printed and bound in Switzerland

Contents

Foreword

The weft-faced tapestry-woven rugs known as kilims are among the most ubiquitous of rug forms, and among the least understood. Neglected by collectors, undervalued by the carpet trade, unstudied by scholars, and consequently only rarely finding their way to the printed page in the company of respectably intelligent prose, these flat-woven rugs began to benefit only recently from the surge of interest in the weaving of the villages and nomadic encampments of the Middle East; no longer the outcasts of the rug world, they are recognized as occupying a central place in the evolution of carpet styles, and their powerful beauty is able to delight a wide audience.

The first publication to give the kilim equal billing with its more prestigious pile-woven cousins was a curious folio volume entitled *Samples of the Old Turkish Carpets and Kilims,* published by the Sümerbank in Istanbul in 1961. The kilim was given a favoured place at the beginning of the well-known exhibition catalogue *From the Bosporus to Samarkand: Flat-Woven Rugs,* by A. Landreau and R. Pickering, published by the Textile Museum, Washington, DC, in 1969, but that worthy volume lavished proportionately much more attention on the various forms of brocaded rugs. In 1977, an exhibition entitled *The Undiscovered Kilim,* held at the Whitechapel Art Gallery in London, brought the kilim out of the wilderness of inattention, in a beautifully executed catalogue full of magnificent examples of kilim weaving. Around the same time, B. Acar's *Kilim ve Düz Dokuma Yaygılar* (Kilims and Flat-woven Rugs) appeared in Istanbul, and the kilim entered into popularity, prestige, and to prices which broke the hearts of the fortunate few who had collected kilims in the bargain days of the sixties.

Of the leading collectors, dealers, and scholars of this art form, Yanni Petsopoulos stands at the head of all three categories. Gifted with the obsessive energy of the kilim-lover, he has combined resourcefulness, extensive travel, astounding persist-ence, a remarkable visual memory, and a great deal of good luck, in his pursuit of his quarry, the exceptional kilim, throughout the villages of the Middle East and the dark jungles of the rug market. He has seen countless institutional and public collections on many continents, and this overview, a privilege and attainment enjoyed by no other, has given him a lofty perspective indeed. In this undertaking he has been fortunate to be able to work with Michael Franses, another great energizing force in the world of rug studies. This fortunate collaboration has occurred at a time when it has been able to exercise a maximal effect on our knowledge about kilims.

We have arrived at a time in the study of the kilim where there is a strong need for an overall statement, a general hypothesis about forms, techniques, colours, and above all, provenance and stylistic groupings. With its over four hundred illustrations, and with its distilled results of the research of a decade combined with an important photographic archive, this volume presents us with the foundation, the basic groupings, and the aesthetic standards, upon which to build our future understanding of this remarkable art form.

To the reader about to embark upon a journey through these pages, there are two opportunities. The first is the privilege to see some works of art of great beauty, sensitivity, and power, conceived in traditional societies and given form through the artistic abilities of women who poured their expressions and feeling into kilim weaving. The second opportunity, rare enough in books about rugs, is the opportunity to learn from an author whose enthusiasm carries lightly upon its shoulders complicated terms and names of faraway places. The kilim has been discovered, and we are now able to share the story of its changing styles and forms across the Near and Middle East.

Walter B. Denny
Amherst, Massachusetts

Acknowledgments

This book is the product of a long collaboration between myself and Michael Franses. His tireless efforts in the gathering of the photographic material and in our research have made this book a reality. It has been my pleasure and privilege to work with him and to benefit from his insight and his all-embracing knowledge of carpets.

I would like to take this opportunity to thank Prof. Walter Denny for kindly agreeing to write the foreword to this book; Joan Allgrove for her article on the Qashqai; Tamara Dragadze for her ethnographical article on the Caucasian peoples; André Singer for his notes on the Kurds; and Dr Hanna Erdmann and Mrs Van de Wiele for the translation of the book into German and French respectively.

I am most grateful to all the museums in Turkey, Europe and the USA which assisted Michael Franses and myself in our study of their material and in obtaining illustrations. In this context I am particularly indebted to Can Kerametli of the Türk ve Islâm Eserleri Museum, Istanbul; to Belkis Acar of the Vakiflar Hali Museum, Istanbul; to Dr Klaus Brisch and Dr Friedrich Spuhler of the Museum für Islamische Kunst, West Berlin; to Volkmar Enderlein of the Islamisches Museum, East Berlin; to Donald King of the Victoria and Albert Museum, London; to Louise Mackie of the Textile Museum, Washington, DC; to Dr Catherine Glynn of the Los Angeles County Museum of Art; and to the Ethnographic Museum, Ankara; to the Museum of Fine Arts, Boston; to the Kestner Museum, Hanover; and to the Metropolitan Museum, New York.

This book, however, would not have been possible without the generous help of all the collectors and dealers, mentioned alphabetically below, who graciously allowed their kilims to be studied and photographed. In some cases, we were permitted to use their invaluable photographic archives, while in many others we received much beneficial advice, guidance and encouragement. To all of them, my grateful thanks.

Albert and Berj Achdjian
Georges Antaki
Herwig Bartels
Peter Bausback
Raymond Bernardout
David Black

Bert Blitzlager
Rahim Bolour
Jurgen and Molly Brendel
Jim Burns
Robert Chenciner
Cathryn Cootner
Marino dall'Oglio
Alfred de Credico
Amadeo de Franchis
Walter Denny
Charles Grant Ellis
John Eskenazi
Robert Franses
Klaus Frantz
the late Vahan Gumuchdjian
Vladimir Haustow
Eberhart Hermann
Oliver Hoare
Jenny Housego
Jean Lefevre
Clive Loveless
Jim McDonald
the late Joseph V. McMullan
Alan Marcuson
Gail Martin
the late John Martinos
Stavros Mihalarias

Marian Miller
Gary Muse
Paul Nels
Caroline Ogilvie
Herbert Ostler
Kenan Özbell
Helen Philon
David Philpot
Gunther and Ingrid Rapp
Arky and Ginger Robbins
the late Alkis Sahinis
Ulrich Schurmann
John Siudmak
David Sulzberger
Alf Sutton
David Sylvester
Dick Temple
Edouard Totah
Raoul Tschebull
Öcsi Ullman
Neil Winterbottom
Johannes Wolff
Georgie Wolton
Donald Young
Tassos Zoumboulakis
Sami Zubaida

Finally, I wish to thank Gordon Roberton of A. C. Cooper and Peter John Gates who between them photographed the majority of the kilims in this book, often under a lot of pressure; Caroline Ogilvie, who had to put up with me while writing the text; Ian Bennet for his editorial assistance; John Siudmak for his help with the technical section; my publishers for their patience; and last but not least, my wife who, whether she wanted to or not, has been involved in this project from its beginnings many years ago and who, to her eternal credit, stood by me through it all. *London, April 1979*

9

Kilims

Kilim is a Turkish word defined in dictionaries simply as a 'flat-woven rug'. It seems, however, to derive from the Persian form *gilim* which can be traced back to the tenth to eleventh centuries. It appears in a Persian manuscript of the early eleventh century, the *Shah nameh* of Ferdowsi, and in an anonymous geographical treatise of the late tenth century, the *Hudud al-Alam,* or Frontiers of the World. The word is used specifically for flat-woven covers, blankets and garments, as distinct from floor coverings or rugs.

In more recent times, the word kilim, in its widest application, encompasses all types of oriental flat-woven fabrics variously used as coverings and hangings in roles both decorative and functional. The term was, therefore, used rather loosely and indiscriminately for fabrics in a wide variety of techniques such as tapestry weaving of all types, weft-float brocading, Soumak or weft wrapping, warp-faced fabrics, many types of complementary weft- or warp-pattern weaves and various combinations of these. There are, of course, more specific names for many of these fabrics. Here, however, we are faced with a serious problem of classification—one which bedevils the entire field of study: does a given term refer to a technique, a design or to a geographic origin? The answer, except in a few instances, is that we do not know. As a result, these terms are useful primarily as labels and little more.

For example: *Djidjim,* or *Jijim,* is sometimes used to denote weft-float brocaded weavings and, at other times, to denote pieces woven in narrow strips joined together with either brocaded decoration or compound warp-pattern weave. The term *Soumak* is said to be a corruption of Shemakha, a town in the Caucasus; sometimes it is used to mean Caucasian pieces woven in the area by means of weft wrapping and, more commonly, to describe the technique of weft wrapping in general. *Verneh* and *Sileh* are other examples where one does not know whether the term is used in conjunction with design, technique or origin.

The present book, however, is only concerned with kilims in the very narrow sense of the word. We are referring to predominantly woollen, tapestry-woven, weft-faced fabrics. The very same fabrics are sometimes also known by other names such as *gilim* or *gelim* in Persia, *palas* in the Caucasus and *bsath* in Syria and Lebanon. Nevertheless, for our purpose we shall refer to them throughout as *kilims,* as we feel this is the simplest and most widespread term, and one which is understood in most languages.

Geographic and Social Background

Aubusson and Scandinavian rugs, Gobelins and other European tapestries, South American Precolumbian textiles, North American Navajo Indian blankets, Coptic or Islamic fabrics from Egypt, Central, South-east Asian and Indonesian weavings and even Chinese Kossus employ the technique of weft-faced tapestry found in kilims. In some instances the similarity is only structural; in others, however, it extends to designs and, occasionally, to entire compositions. An interesting case in point is the striking resemblance between the Navajo blankets from North America and the 'eye-dazzler' kilims of central and south Persia. Because of such similarities it would be inappropriate to define kilims in terms of structure or design; in fact, the term has a definite geographic overtone, being reserved for oriental tapestry-woven rugs, those made in south-east Europe, the eastern Mediterranean and the Middle East, in areas under the influence of Islamic culture. Their production is focused in the areas known as Anatolia, the Caucasus and Persia; and while they were by no means confined to these regions, being made also in south-east Europe, North Africa and Central Asia, this is certainly where the tradition of their weaving seems to have been concentrated in terms of both quality and quantity.

Anatolia (see map) is the equivalent, more or less, of ancient Asia Minor or modern Turkey. The Caucasus consists of the Soviet republics of Georgia and Azerbaijan, of north-west Iran and of the easternmost parts of Turkey. Persia, finally, comprises most of present-day Iran. The terms chosen are arbitrary historical terms, as it was felt inappropriate to use modern national terms in describing the origins of artifacts made long before modern political entities came into being.

It will become apparent through the kilims themselves, that there are, in fact, no clear limits or geographical boundaries defining Anatolian, Caucasian and Persian kilims. It must be remembered that, in the past, frontiers were not what they are today and that boundaries were constantly shifting. It is not an exaggeration to say that the only frontier guards or customs officials were the local tribal chiefs, potentates or warlords who controlled strategic passes and who extracted right-of-passage

levies from the travellers or commercial caravans venturing into the territories under their control. Therefore, the politically unimpeded movement of peoples, both on the caravan routes and on the paths of seasonal migrations, produced far stronger cultural and commercial bonds among all the peoples in kilim-producing areas than would be possible today. These, in turn, led to a cross-fertilization of ideas and designs. In fact, one of the most interesting aspects of the study of kilims is the manner in which patterns, designs and compositions appear in different parts of the Near East, and how they link, vary and adapt to local tastes and customs.

Although, as mentioned above, there were no serious governmental restrictions on the movement of people and goods, there were many instances where migrations were forced on people as a direct result of politics. It was one of the favourite pastimes of autocratic rulers, be they Byzantine, Ottoman or Persian, to resettle rebellious or potentially rebellious subjects in territories within their realm as far removed as possible from where these people originated. Such movements added to the labyrinthine complexity of the areas' ethnographic make-up, and pose serious problems for those interested in classifying its artistic production either geographically or chronologically. Nevertheless, cultural, social and historical information concerning each and every part of the Near Eastern world is indispensable to our understanding of its artifacts. Unfortunately, it is only recently that ethnographical studies with an art historical objective have been undertaken, and these have, by necessity, dealt mostly with the situation within living memory. Thus their value in assessing kilims made earlier on, which are the subject of this book, is rather limited. Indeed, it may well be that the study of this art has been left until too late, and that we shall never be able to obtain a complete picture of the relationships between the various tribal, nomadic and ethnic groupings and of the impact these relationships had on their weavings.

Given this situation, it has not been our purpose to study and describe the traditions and customs of the weavers of kilims. Yet there is one aspect of local life that deserves a brief

I

mention here, as it bears direct relevance to the production of village and nomadic kilims: the institution of marriage.

Within a tribal, nomadic or rural society, marriage meant much more than the union of two people. The whole economic and social order was reflected in it. Treaties were sealed with marriages, watering rights for animals were acquired, safe conducts to and from summer pastures were secured, commercial agreements were entered into and wealth was consolidated or dispersed. The role of marriage was of an economic and political importance to tribal, nomadic societies comparable to the cult of the dead in ancient Egypt. There, the economic order of the day revolved around the funerary monuments. This was true both in terms of artistic production and in terms of the employment provided for vast numbers of people in the building trade, in the cultivation of the lands forming part of the endowments of the temples and, of course, in providing a livelihood for all those associated with the priesthood. So, it is in the light of marriage as a major social and economic phenomenon that the dowry, one of the indispensable contributions to the sealing of marriage bonds, must be seen and judged. Every bride and her family would endeavour to produce the best and the most their means and their skills would allow. Viewed in this context, the woven artifacts, often kilims, which formed an essential part of the dowry, gain a prominence that their commercial desirability in the oriental bazaars never justified. This is the only likely explanation for all the effort, time and artistic creativity that an entire family would lavish on the production of kilims without any prospect of commercial gain. The position and status of a family was directly related to the quality and quantity of the bride's dowry, and her qualities as a wife were judged by it. Producing a dowry was a labour of love, embodying the girl's dreams and, at the same time, a measure of her quality and of the upbringing she received from her family. Thus, unlike carpets, which from an early date were the product of an established industry and trade, with distribution outlets in many parts of the world, nomadic and village kilims were, instead, always confined to the provincial family tradition, fulfilling a role outside the commercial realities or transactions of the day.

The reason usually put forward in carpet literature to explain the almost total absence of kilims from the oriental rug trade in both the East and the West is their relative lack of durability compared to pile carpets and their often awkward, long and narrow proportions. The validity of this argument is not in doubt; however, it is not altogether convincing if one considers the technical similarities of kilims to Aubusson and other European tapestry-woven carpets, and the fact that many oriental pile rugs of comparably awkward sizes were exported in quantity to the West starting very early. Another and more likely explanation is that it would not normally occur to people to sell the kilims made expressly for their dowry, nor to others to buy items from someone else's dowry. Kilims were treated in the same fashion as household linen and considered as perishable personal possessions which people living in a traditional society would make for themselves rather than buy. As a result, there was no serious commercial interest in them. One has often heard, as an example of the lack of importance of kilims in the East, that they were commonly used as wrappings for other types of carpets. In fact, this shows only the respect in which the carpets were held, rather than any disrespect for kilims. In this instance one could aptly compare the kilims to the priceless silks used in wrapping Qur'ans.

The Study and Classification of Kilims

Attempting to classify the kilims of the Near East and to attribute them to places or peoples is a very difficult undertaking. With few exceptions, the most one can do is define certain groups by placing together those pieces considered to be made by the same people, within a limited period of time, in a specific area, without specifying either the weavers or the area. Unfortunately this vagueness is unavoidable, for there is almost no concrete evidence known to us about the place of origin or the makers of these pieces. This is hardly surprising as, until recently, they were of no special interest to collectors or dealers; their presence therefore went unrecorded. Once again, one can only lament the absence of contemporary ethnographical and anthropological studies with an emphasis on the description of local artifacts.

Given this situation, it has been suggested by some scholars that the only way to sort out these pieces or find out more about them is through exhaustive and detailed field-work, examining and recording the largest possible number of pieces, irrespective of age, in terms of composition, design, structure and materials. There are, indeed, many advantages in this line of research, which we have ourselves followed, though to a limited extent. Almost immediately, however, the pitfalls inherent in this approach became depressingly obvious. To understand this, one must take a look at the present situation and the change in attitude of the weavers towards their work.

In recent times, kilims with their bold and attractive designs have met with a certain commercial success, not unconnected with the fact that they are cheaper to produce than pile rugs. Consequently, local traders have encouraged their production. The net result of this is that pieces are now looked upon as a means of livelihood and no longer as an expression of the weaver's art within the framework of traditional life. The materials are generally of poorer quality, the wool is coarser, the beautiful natural dyes of the past have usually been replaced by cheap synthetic ones with vulgar colours, and designs have degenerated into stiff repetitions (often dictated by consideration of cost and time) of earlier originals. In other words, in modern kilims we find all the evils of low-cost mass produc-

tion, which is understandable on the one hand, but deplorable on the other. Because of this, the modern pieces found in one particular place are of very limited importance to our understanding of the older kilims.

So the task facing the student of kilims is daunting. He has to try to ascertain which of the modern pieces he finds in a particular place are, indeed, the product of that area and have traditionally been made there, and which have only been made there recently at the instigation of some external influence, such as pressures of trade or handicraft organizations. The obvious danger is that older pieces, whose designs are copied in the modern ones, may be mistakenly labelled with the same name in the bazaars of large commercial cities like Istanbul and Izmir.

The structural analysis and classification of kilims can also produce misleading conclusions, because there is limited scope for differences within the medium of tapestry weaving. Consequently, a piece made in east Turkey may have a structure identical to one made in a village on the Aegean coast. The quality of the wool used, provided it is the local hand-spun product, gives a slightly better clue to origin, but even so it is not an absolute criterion and, like the structure, can only be of limited use as one of several indications to be taken into consideration.

Another line of research is is to try to find old pieces during one's field-work. The usefulness of this approach in determining origins is limited, first, by the rarity of such pieces, and second, by the time-honoured mobility of the nomadic and, occasionally, even of the sedentary populations. With the formation of modern Turkey and Iran and the resettling of large numbers of people in areas far removed from their original homes, this situation became even more confusing. To mention but two examples, many old Anatolian pieces can be found today in places like Bulgaria and Greece, while kilims clearly of Balkan origin are found in places like Konya, in the middle of Turkey.

The third approach is to talk to dealers, both in the East and the West. Here one has to be extremely careful of sales-talk, which tends to introduce 'folkloric' terms, and of unconfessed ignorance. It might have been easier one hundred years ago or more, when one could have spoken to those dealers who were crisscrossing the area at the time when local weaving traditions were still strong. Unfortunately, these people were not questioned or, if they were, it was not recorded.

Therefore, having examined all the above possibilites and concluded that what each had to offer was of little use in itself but could be valuable if it was put in the right context, we decided that the most promising method was to look at all the accessible pieces, and to try to make them speak for themselves. This approach is not too dissimilar to that of an archaeologist trying to decipher an unknown ancient language or to that of a child trying to put a jigsaw puzzle together. Thus far we have not, of course, solved the puzzle, but we hope to contribute to its solution. As outlined at the beginning of this section, we have tried to separate the pieces into groups, no mean task in itself, and have illustrated here as many pieces of each group as was practicable, limiting ourselves, however, to pieces we believe to have been made before 1900, because, as explained above, the inclusion of modern pieces would tend to confuse rather than clarify groupings. We have then attempted to explain what led us to determine these groups and, where possible, we have attributed an origin to them, using those indications at our disposal which we felt were relevant and probably accurate.

The Structure of Kilims

Tapestry—the technique of weaving used in kilims—is, in its most basic and elementary form, one of the simplest weaving methods, traceable to antiquity and probably to prehistoric times. It could be argued that its beginnings are not very distant from the invention of the loom. To create a tapestry-woven fabric, two types of yarn or thread are required: the warps and the wefts.

WARPS

These are vertical threads, lying parallel to each other, running the entire length of the kilim. By deciding how many warps are placed on the loom and the spacing between them, the weaver predetermines the width of the kilim. This dimension will remain virtually constant, any possible variation resulting only from unskilled or uneven weaving. The maximum length of the kilim is also fixed by the length of the warp threads, but there is no technical reason why the kilim could not be shorter if the weaver so decides, either because of a change of mind or a miscalculation of the length of the desired composition.

WEFTS

These are horizontal threads which pass over and under adjacent warps, a sequence which alternates between successive

wefts. All the kilims included in this book are weft-faced fabrics. This term means that the horizontal wefts are beaten down on to each other tightly enough to hide from view the vertical warps. Thus the appearance of the surface of the fabric is owed solely to the wefts, and any patterns are the results of combinations of wefts of different colours. Kilims, therefore, usually have polychrome wefts, while the invisible warps are normally monochrome

TEXTURE

The fineness of a kilim is determined by the thickness of the warps and by how closely they are placed, together with the fineness of the wefts and how tightly they are packed. Fineness, however, varies greatly among kilims of different types. Sehna kilims from north-west Persia, which are among the finest ever produced, can have 110 warps per 10 cm. and 450 wefts per 10 cm. At the other extreme, there are the kilims from west Anatolia which have 30 warps per 10 cm. and 110 wefts per 10 cm. Usually, the thickness of the warps is relative to that of the wefts. Among the exceptions are the polychrome kilims of Balıkesir, in north-west Anatolia, where the warps are very thin compared to the wefts and the looseness of the weave, and the Kurdish kilims of the Lake Van region in east Anatolia, where the warps are much thicker than the closely packed, fine wefts.

2

DESCRIPTION AND TECHNICAL FEATURES OF KILIMS

If a kilim is plain and undecorated, or if the decoration is limited to simple, horizontal bands of different colours, it is sufficient to describe it as a *weft-faced, tapestry-woven fabric*. Most kilims however, abound in complex motifs, rendered in a multitude of colours; here, the coloured wefts forming the decoration do not cross the entire width of the kilim but are confined to the width of their respective design. Such kilims are said to have *discontinuous wefts*. Description of weft-faced tapestry weave may be elaborated further according to the technique employed to join designs in the diagonal and vertical direction, that is, according to the means of transition at the place of a lateral colour-change.

SLIT TAPESTRY

With this technique, where there is a lateral change in colour due to a change in design, each colour returns around the last

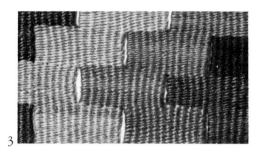

3

warp of its respective colour area. Accordingly, where there is a vertical join, a slit will occur. To achieve a join at an angle,

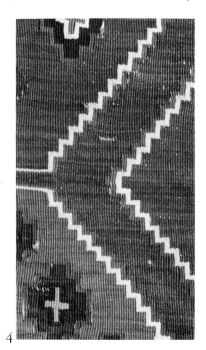

4

a series of offset slits is woven, creating a stepped outline. The narrower the angle, the less noticeable this is; while the wider the angle, the more pronounced the join becomes. Slits,

5

however, cannot be too long or the resulting fabric would be very weak and prone to tear. Thus kilims woven in slit tapestry do not feature designs with continuous vertical lines; where the weaver needs a vertical join, such as when a side border meets the field, he uses a continuous crenellated line.

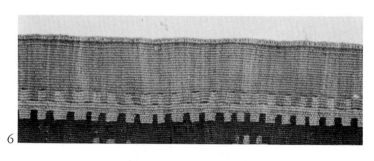

6

7

Slit tapestry is by far the most common type of weave used in kilims. The resulting fabric is usually double-sided, with the exception of some types of Anatolian and Kurdish kilims where, after completing the weaving of a particular area of

8

colour, the weaver leaves the weft thread loose at the back in order to pick it up and use it further on when the same colour occurs again.

DIAGONAL LINES OR 'LAZY LINES'

Normally wefts pass across the entire width of their colour area. However, on some kilims where there are wide and large areas of a single colour (plate 61), the weaver, for ease of execution, only works in small areas at a time. In doing so he returns wefts inside their own colour area, moving laterally one or two warps at a time with each successive weft, to produce an angular out-line. By resuming work on the remainder of the colour area, the first part links up with the rest, the resulting join being a diagonal, or 'lazy line', similar in appearance to the diagonal

lines produced between adjacent colour zones in slit tapestry. These lines are also occasionally used as a decorative feature to produce variations within a solid area of colour and to enrich the texture of a plain field (plate 83).

SINGLE-INTERLOCK TAPESTRY

In kilims using this method to achieve a join between lateral design changes, where two adjacent colour areas meet the respective wefts return around a common warp. Therefore, there are no slits at the vertical joins, and the resulting fabric is stronger and more durable. This method of weaving is

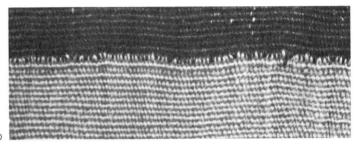

10

seldom found in Anatolian, Kurdish and Caucasian kilims; its use is confined chiefly to central and south-west Persia. Kilims woven in single-interlock tapestry are always double-sided.

DOUBLE-INTERLOCK TAPESTRY

This type of tapestry weaving is used exclusively in Persia, par-ticularly by the Bakhtiari tribes (plates 357 and 360). With

9

11

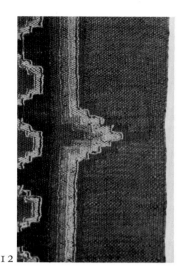

12

13

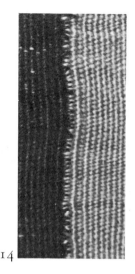

14

this method, one of the wefts of one colour loops around two wefts of the adjacent colour. The resulting fabric has the same appearance on the front as those woven in the single-interlock method, but the back is noticeably different, as two parallel raised ridges are produced at each colour join.

The use of either type of interlock tapestry strongly influences the weaver's choice of designs and compositions. The possibility of weaving vertical lines without weakening the fabric allows for the inclusion of rectangular grid patterns and rectilinear designs using a 90-degree angle.

DOVETAILING

This is yet another technique for linking vertical design outlines. Here, a small number of wefts from each of the adjoining colour zones are grouped together and share one or more common warps. Depending on the number of wefts of each colour sharing the common warps, the join can be described as a 2:2 dovetail, 3:3, 4:4, etc. The join has the appearance of a jagged line, and as the ratio increases, its resemblance to a 'saw-tooth' pattern becomes more pronounced. It should be mentioned that a 1:1 dovetail is, in fact, the same as single-interlock tapes-

try. Dovetailing produces double-sided kilims and is used exclusively in Thrace and north-west Persia.

CORRECTIVE WEFTS

In simple tapestry weave the wefts are horizontal, parallel to each other and perpendicular to the warps. Sometimes, however, either because of the varying thickness of the wool or uneven and occasionally sloppy weaving, the weft line will

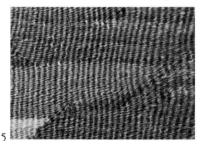

15

slope either up or down. To rectify this defect some extra wefts are inserted in a wedge-like fashion. These inserts are known as corrective wefts and, apart from their remedial function, they are often used for decorative purposes in precisely the same way as 'lazy lines'.

ECCENTRIC- OR CURVED-WEFT TAPESTRY

An extension of the principle of corrective wefts forms the basis of a technique used mainly in Thracian but occasionally also in Anatolian and Persian kilims in order to create curvilinear designs. Such kilims are woven a small area at a time. The wefts, instead of being inserted horizontally, are bent in the shape of

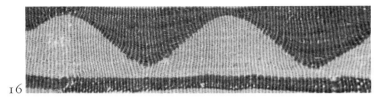

16

the desired design. Successive wefts follow and build up this curve, the shape of which can be altered depending on how tightly or loosely they are packed. At the colour junctions there is no visible structural separation except where the joins are in the vertical direction. The latter are executed in dovetailing

17   18

which, in fact, forms part of this technique. Some of the smaller designs appear as wedged inserts on a background surface that curves around them, while others are complex interlocking motifs whose outlines merge into one another. A skilful weaver can use this method to produce any kind of curvilinear shape, including a perfect circle. To avoid bulges and produce a fabric which lies flat despite the resulting variation in tension of the wefts, requires a high degree of craftsmanship.

Curved-weft tapestry has been used extensively in Coptic, Chinese and Precolumbian textiles and is ideally suited to kilims with flowing naturalistic designs. However, because of the constant use of freely drawn curves and the uneven tension

of the wefts, it does not allow for the precise repetition of geometric designs. It is, therefore, not normally used in kilims with primarily angular, rectilinear patterns that can be more accurately and rapidly executed in slit or interlock tapestry.

These are the main types of tapestry weaves which occur in kilims. They can be used singly, as in the majority of Anatolian and Caucasian kilims that are woven predominantly in slit tapestry, or in combinations, as in many Thracian and Persian kilims.

In addition to these basic means of joining areas of colour there are a number of other technical methods used in the weaving of kilims.

Techniques of Supplementary Decoration

It is common in tapestry-woven kilims for the surface to be enriched with a multitude of decorative devices. The techniques employed for this purpose are varied. The same techniques are often used as the primary means of decoration on compound-weave kilims which are not examined in this book. We are only concerned with them, here, in their secondary role.

WEFT-FLOAT BROCADING

This method is used for brocading small infill designs, often 'S' or diamond shaped, on the finished surface of weft-faced, tapestry-woven kilims. The term 'weft float' signifies that the wefts pass over and under the surface of the kilim, forming the design on the front and floating loosely at the back in the spaces

19

20

between the outline of the design. On many kilims using a double-sided type of tapestry weave, these minor motifs are the only way of distinguishing between the front and the back of the piece.

WEFT WRAPPING OR SOUMAK BROCADING

The technique of weft wrapping is commonly referred to as 'Soumak' after the Caucasian rugs of this name which were executed by this method. Weft wrapping can be used directly on the warps as a method of weaving. In the context of kilims in weft-faced tapestry, however, it is a supplementary broading technique usually unconnected with the structure.

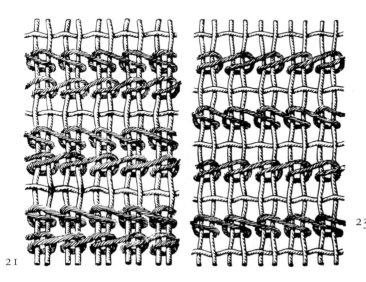

21

Normally, the wefts pass over 3 warps and back under 2, creating a continuous chain wrapped around the warps. This

ratio of 3:2, however, is not necessarily constant; depending on the shape of the desired design it can also be 2:1, or 4:3.

In Anatolian kilims, weft wrapping is chiefly employed to hide the joins and highlight the outlines of tapestry-woven

22

designs. When used in the diagonal direction, one, and more rarely two, rows of wefts are wrapped around the warps at the design junction; when used in the horizontal, the number of rows can be up to four. This process of outlining is usually described inaccurately as overstitching.

TWINING

Although it is often used to highlight and separate horizontal bands of design, the primary purpose of twining is to strengthen the structure of discontinuous-weft tapestry by having occasional rows of wefts passing from one side of the piece to the other. Rows of twining are also often inserted at the beginning of weaving as warp spacers.

23

A single row of twining consists of two wefts, one starting from the back and the other from the front of the warps, which twist round each other as they meet between the warps. By using wefts of different colours a decorative effect can be produced.

Side Finishes or Selvedges

While some kilims finish at the sides with the wefts simply returning around the last warp, most use some means of strengthening the sides, the most vulnerable points in terms of wear. The usual method, common to all Anatolian and

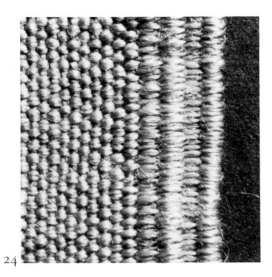

24

Caucasian kilims, is for the last warp, or last few warps, to be made thicker by bunching together two or three warp-threads at a time. In south Persian kilims, the last warp is usually

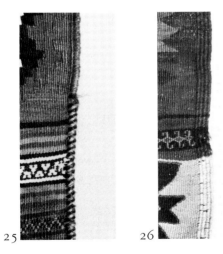

25   26

replaced with a thicker cable, which is very often wrapped in coloured wools forming a barber's pole pattern. In some kilims from the area of Veramin in central Persia there are three or four thick rows of multiple warps or cables. These are normally overcast in dark wool which loops over and under the end warps.

End Finishes

THE FINISH OF THE WOVEN SURFACE

This refers to the treatment of the top and bottom end of the surface of the kilim. In most examples it consists of a narrow plain or striped band between the end of the border and the warps. On some Anatolian kilims, this plain band is decorated

27

with small designs in weft-float brocading, similar to those found scattered in the field. On many Persian kilims, the area between the border and the warps is much wider, and contains one or more narrow bands of supplementary weft, compound

28

29

30

33

Net or web fringe

weave. The latter can be in a variety of techniques producing different patterns, some of which are one-sided, others double-sided. As mentioned earlier, a few horizontal rows of twining may also be used to decorate the end bands of north-west Persian kilims.

THE FINISH OF THE WARPS

The treatment of the warp ends at the top and bottom of the kilim beyond the woven surface (where these are still existing) can often help to identify the origin of a kilim.

Anatolian and Kurdish Kilims

34

Plaited flat fringe and braid

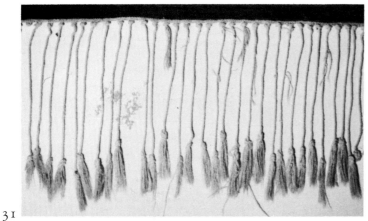

31

Long fringe

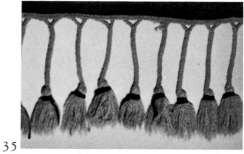

35

Plaited solid fringe and braid

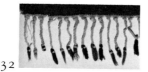

32

Short knotted fringe

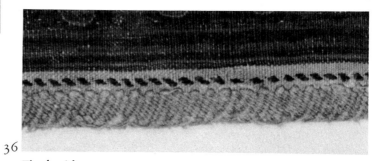

36

Flat braid

37
Flat braid

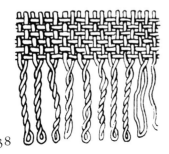

38
Warp loops

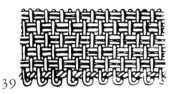

39
Warp loops interwoven with loose warp-coloured wefts

Caucasian Kilims

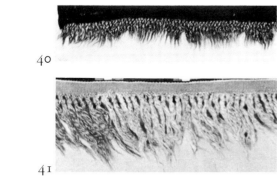

40

41
Net or web fringe

42
Flat braid

Persian Kilims

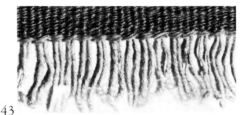

43
Loose warps

44
Twisted fringe

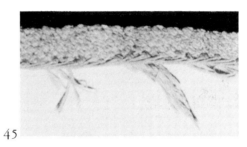

45
Braid

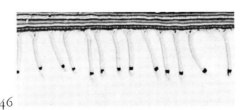

46
Braid and fringe combination

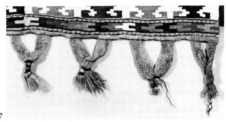

47
Braid and plait combination

Designs, Patterns and Compositions

Over the years, rug literature has been plagued by the lack of standard terms to describe the objects of its study. Vague, ambiguous, and occasionally even conflicting terms are used by different authors to describe the same features, so that it is hard to make comparisons between pieces published in different books with any certainty, let alone accuracy.

In recent years people have become increasingly aware of this problem and large steps have been and are still being taken to remedy it. So far, the most notable success has been in the direction of establishing an accepted terminology for the structural and technical description of rugs, thanks largely to the efforts of people like Irene Emery, May Beattie, Peter Collingwood, Jon Thompson, Kurt Erdmann and Friedrich Spuhler.

It is equally important, however, to aim for some degree of standardization in describing the ornamentation of rugs, from the small individual elements to the overall scheme of decoration. This chapter will therefore define the terms in which the kilims in this book have been described and will attempt to show by means of comparative illustrations how the same principles of decoration are used in kilims woven by different groups of weavers. Because of its vast scope, it is obvious that the subject cannot be examined exhaustively here. Certain important aspects of it have therefore been selected for these comparisons.

DESIGN
Individual element of decoration used either singly, in repetition or in combination with others. Depending on size and importance, the term is used synonymously with ornament and overlaps in meaning with motif, though the latter is more specifically used to describe distinctive features or elements of design.

PATTERN
An orderly sequence of designs; a relationship, or set of relationships between designs such as the arrangement of designs in a matrix or grid.

COMPOSITION
The synthesis or combination of all the constituent parts of the decoration; that is, the term which describes the manner in which the various designs, patterns and other decorative elements are placed to achieve an overall unity.

Description of the Decorated Surface of a Kilim

Direction:

In describing a kilim
terms used for the directions are:

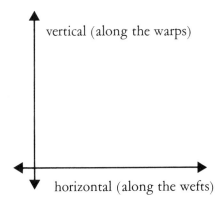

vertical (along the warps)

horizontal (along the wefts)

When a kilim has directional designs, their direction determines the top of the piece. If, however, the composition is symmetrical, the direction of the weave determines the top.

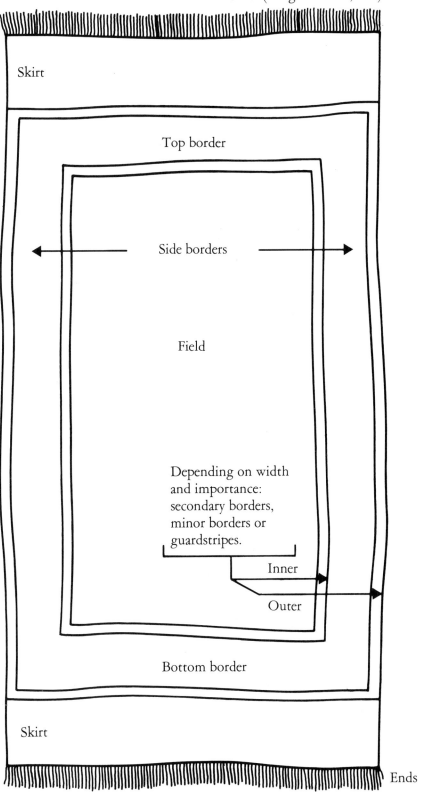

Ends (fringe or braid, etc.)

Skirt

Top border

Side borders

Field

Depending on width
and importance:
secondary borders,
minor borders or
guardstripes.

Inner

Outer

Bottom border

Skirt

Ends

Kilims with a Diamond Grid Pattern

This very simple pattern is ideally suited to the medium of slit tapestry and is used as the basis for a great number of compositions.

In its most explicit form, continuous lines form a trellis (a,b).

More often, however, the diamond grid is implied, being formed by the repetition of diagonally offset designs (c, d).

The same grid pattern can be used to create different compositions according to the chromatic arrangement of the designs (e, f, g, h).

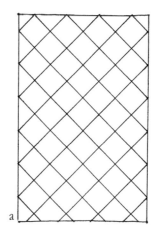
a

b

Persian kilim from Fars, plate 388

c

South-east Anatolian kilim, plate 205

d

West Anatolian kilim, plate 102

e

Central Anatolian kilim, plate 253
Diamond pattern

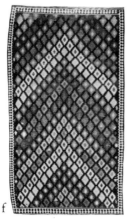
f

West Persian kilim, plate 340
Chevron pattern

g

Persian kilim from Fars, plate 387
Spearhead pattern

h

Persian kilim from Fars, plate 391
Diagonal band kilim

28

a

Endless pattern

b

North-west Persian kilim, plate 341

Different compositions can also be created by taking different sections of the same grid pattern (a, c, e).

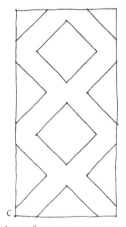

c

Section of pattern

d

Persian kilim from Fars, plate 378

Kilims with a Pattern of Diagonal Bands

In its most explicit form, the field is divided into plain diagonal bands.

The same visual effect is achieved when diagonally offset designs, floating on a field, are arranged chromatically along diagonal bands, e. g. plates 218, 295, 368.

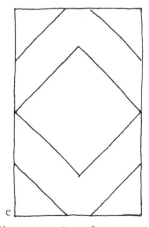

e

Close-up section of pattern

f

West Persian Sehna kilim, plate 351

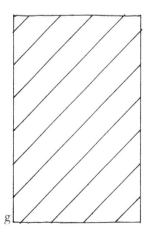

g

h

Persian kilim from Fars, plate 399

Kilims with Patterns Based on the Repetition of Hexagonal Designs

The patterns of all these kilims are generated on the basis of a 60-degree triangular grid.

b

East Anatolian kilim, plate 270

c

Caucasian kilim, plate 301

d

East Anatolian kilim, plate 276

e

Central Persian kilim, plate 372

a

Pattern analysis of plate 270

f

Central Anatolian kilim, plate 158

g

Caucasian kilim, plate 304

30

Kilims with a Rectangular Grid Pattern

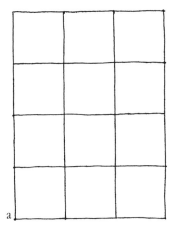

a

Kilims with a Pattern of Concentric Rectangles

f

b

Persian kilim from Fars, plate 411

c

Central Anatolian kilim, plate 251

g

Early Anatolian kilim, plate 63

h

West Persian kilim, plate 362

d

Central Anatolian kilim, plate 175

e

Caucasian kilim, plate 295

i

East Anatolian kilim, plate 245

j

South-east Anatolian kilim, plate 208

31

Kilims with Plain Undecorated Fields

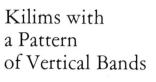

a
North-west Anatolian kilim, plate 91

b
Persian kilim from Fars, plate 382

c
Persian kilim from Fars

d
South-east Anatolian kilim, plate 199

e
West Anatolian kilim, plate 95

Kilims with a Pattern of Vertical Bands

f

g
Central Anatolian kilim, plate 254

h
West Persian kilim, plate 350

i
Persian kilim from Fars, plate 395

j
North-west Anatolian kilim, plate 88

Kilims with a Composition of Horizontal Bands

Possibly the simplest and most common composition found in kilims. Since it follows the direction of the wefts, it allows the weaver to keep regular points of reference.

Band kilims can be divided into four basic types:

1. Major bands with repeat designs separated by narrower minor bands, (b, c, d)
2. Major bands with continuous designs or patterns separated by minor bands (e, f)
3. Minor bands or stripes of the kind used in types 1 and 2 as separating devices, forming the only field decoration (g).
4. Horizontal band pattern implied by the chromatic arrangement of designs floating on the field with no linear separation between them (h).

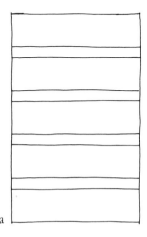

a

b

South-east Anatolian kilim, plate 202

c

Caucasian kilim, plate 312

d

Persian kilim from Fars, plate 398

e

Early Anatolian kilim, plate 65

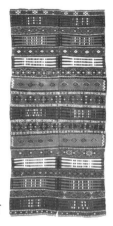

f

East Anatolian kilim, plate 238

g

Caucasian kilim, plate 313

h

Central Anatolian kilim, plate 157

33

Field-pattern Illusion or Figure-ground Illusion

This decorative principle is a typical feature of Islamic art, used with much effect throughout the Muslim world both in architecture and in the arts.

Such an illusion occurs when the outlines and/or the colours of the pattern used to decorate a surface are such as to create a movement of the pattern causing the viewer to confuse background and design by shifting his emphasis from one to the other.

As a method of surface decoration, it underlines the Muslim belief in unity within multiplicity, and the many levels of reality inherent in all aspects of the created world.

c

Detail from central Anatolian kilim, plate 171

d

Detail from border of west Anatolian kilim, plate 120

e

Detail from Caucasian kilim, plate 319

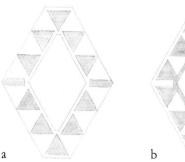

a   b

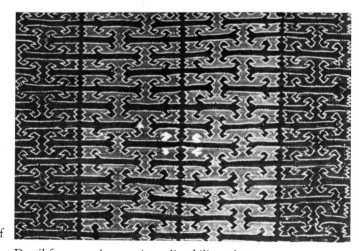

f

Detail from north-west Anatolian kilim, plate 89

34

Interlocking Designs

Two juxtaposed designs are interlocking when their adjacent outlines merge with or overlap one another.

Detail f of the S-shaped designs is the basis for a somewhat more elaborate pattern, variations of which appear in borders of many types of kilims mostly from Anatolia (g to n).

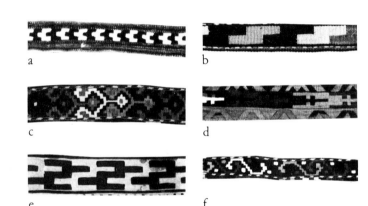

a

b

c

d

e

f

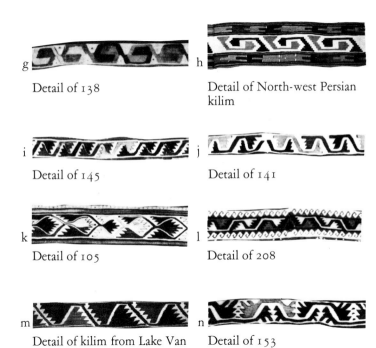

g

Detail of 138

h

Detail of North-west Persian kilim

i

Detail of 145

j

Detail of 141

k

Detail of 105

l

Detail of 208

m

Detail of kilim from Lake Van

n

Detail of 153

An indication as to the origin of this pattern may be found in the last detail shown on this page, where the individual design elements on the side borders are clearly recognizable as birds.

o

p

Reciprocal Patterns

A reciprocal pattern is a continuous sequence of interlocking designs, in any two elements of which, one is the inverse counterpart of the other.

In kilim decoration these are mostly used as border devices or as narrow horizontal bands separating areas of the field.

RECIPROCAL PATTERNS WITH STYLIZED TREFOILS

a
Detail from an Ottoman kilim

b
Detail from central Anatolian kilim, plate 150

c
Detail from a north-west Persian kilim, plate 331

d
Detail from north-west Persian kilim, plate 338

e
Detail from Sehna kilim, plate 352

f
Detail from Shushtar kilim, plate 357

g
Detail from Qashqai kilim, plate 388

RECIPROCAL 'RAMSHORN' PATTERNS

h Detail from side border of Konya kilim, plate 107

i Detail from side border of south-east Anatolian kilim, plate 184

j Detail from guardstripe of south-east Anatolian kilim, plate 197

k Detail from guardstripe of south-east Anatolian kilim, plate 189

l Horizontal version of this design as it appears on south-east Anatolian kilims, e.g. plate 206

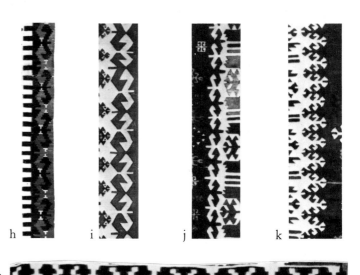

h   i   j   k

l

'LATCH-HOOK' OR 'RUNNING DOG' RECIPROCAL PATTERNS

A linear sequence of 'latch-hooks' is generally known as a 'running dog'.

a   Detail from border of central Anatolian kilim, plate 155

b   Detail from border of north-west Persian kilim, plate 335

a   b

c   Detail from north-west Persian kilim, plate 336

d   Detail from Qashqai kilim, plate 400

e   Detail from south-east Anatolian kilim, plate 184

f   Detail from south-east Anatolian kilim, plate 203

ZIGZAG RECIPROCAL PATTERNS

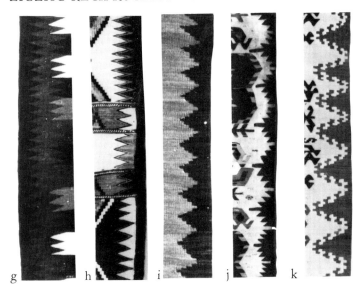
g   h   i   j   k

g   Detail from Qashqai kilim, plate 379

h   Detail from Caucasian kilim, plate 305

i   Detail from north-west Anatolian kilim, plate 91

j   Detail from west Anatolian kilim, plate 135

k   Detail from central Anatolian kilim, plate 153

OTHER RECIPROCAL PATTERNS

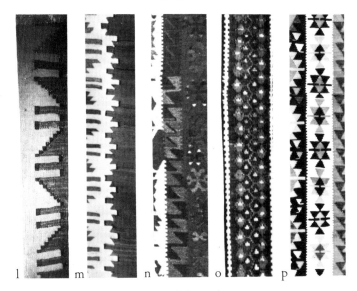
l   m   n   o   p

l   Detail from south-east Anatolian kilim, plate 199

m   Detail from guardstripe of south-east Anatolian kilim, plate 198

n   Detail from guardstripe of central Anatolian kilim, plate 157

o   Detail from inner border of east Anatolian prayer kilim, plate 262

p   Detail from border of north-west Persian kilim, plate 343

Repeat Design Borders

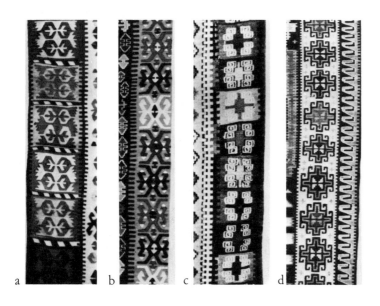

a   Detail from central Anatolian kilim, plate 142

b   Detail from central Anatolian kilim, plate 132

c   Detail from central Anatolian kilim, plate 75

d   Detail from Caucasian kilim, plate 280

e   Detail from south-east Anatolian kilim, plate 186

f   Detail from central Anatolian kilim, plate 223

g   Detail from Caucasian kilim, plate 298

h   Detail from east Anatolian kilim, plate 260

i   Detail from west Anatolian kilim, plate 99

j   Detail from east Anatolian Kurdish kilim

k   Detail from east Anatolian Kurdish kilim, plate 276

l   Detail from west Persian Kurdish kilim, plate 344

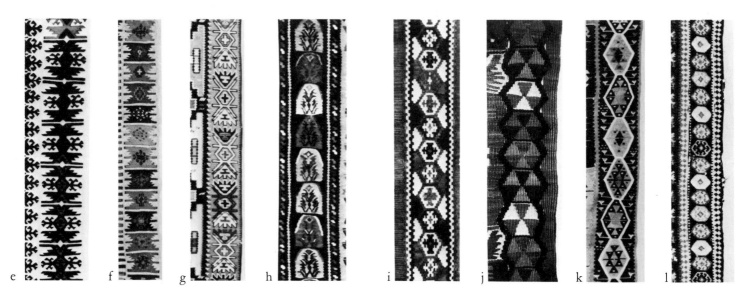

The Bracketed Diamond Design

This design appears almost unchanged in kilims made throughout Anatolia, the Caucasus and Persia. In its present angular form it can best be described as a bracketed diamond. Its lineage, however, can be traced to the knotted Kufic borders of carpets of the eighteenth century in the Caucasus and the sixteenth century in Anatolia (details e and h). In addition it is also a stylization of a well-known design in Islamic art: a knot culminating in four split leaf palmettes, or four such palmettes sprouting from a lobed medallion (i).

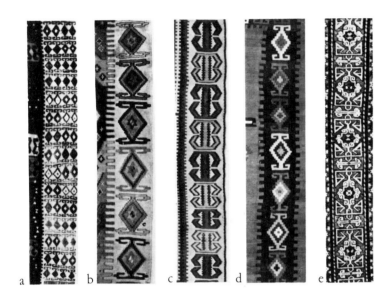

a   Detail from central Anatolian kilim, plate 245

b   Detail from central Anatolian kilim, plate 221

c   Detail from Caucasian kilim, plate 294

d   Detail from north-west Persian kilim, plate 337

e   Detail from eighteenth-century Caucasian pile rug with a knotted Kufic border

f   Detail from north-west Persian kilim, plate 333

g   Detail from south Persian Qashqai kilim, plate 401

h   Detail from sixteenth-century Anatolian pile rug with a knotted Kufic border

i   Detail from sixteenth-century 'chequerboard' carpet with four palmettes sprouting from a lobed medallion

Meandering Vine Borders

The continuous meandering vine with blossoms or leaves sprouting from it is a pattern found in the border decoration of carpets and kilims from very early on.

It takes a more or less naturalistic form in early examples, and gets more rigid and stylized as time passes.

In examples made after the middle of the nineteenth century, the original form and purpose are often unrecognizable. The flowers and leaves are usually no longer connected by stems to the vine and in some kilims from south-east Anatolia and the Caucasus, the flowers and leaves vanish altogether, while the stems remain.

a Minor border, Mamluk carpet, fifteenth century

b Minor border, Anatolian carpet, seventeenth century

c Minor border, Ottoman prayer kilim, horizontal

d Idem, vertical

e Minor border, Ottoman village kilim, horizontal

f Idem, vertical

g Minor border, Anatolian prayer kilim, horizontal

h Idem, vertical

i Top border, south-east Anatolian kilim, nineteenth century

j Top border, south-east Anatolian kilim, nineteenth century

k Side border, Ottoman village kilim

l Side border, Anatolian kilim of the Niğde group

m Side border, south-east Anatolian kilim of the 'Reyhanlı' group

n Side border, Caucasian kilim

o Side border, Persian kilim of the Sehna group

k   l   m   n   o

Floral Designs

The decoration of kilims consists primarily of geometric designs. The following details show some of the types of floral motifs used by various groups of kilim weavers.

a
Detail from Ottoman village kilim, plate 65

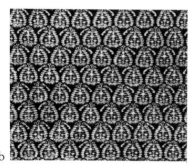

b
Detail from Sehna kilim, plate 348

c
Detail from north-west Persian kilim, plate 366

d
Detail from Anatolian prayer kilim, plate 71

e
Border detail from eastern Anatolian kilim, plate 269

CARNATIONS

The carnation was one of the favourite flowers of the Ottomans, rivalled in popularity only by the tulip. The illustrations below show its use in sixteenth-century velvets, and how it survived in nineteenth-century kilims.

f
Detail from central Anatolian kilim, plate 152

g
Nineteenth-century kilim from central Anatolia

h
Sixteenth-century Ottoman velvet

i
Nineteenth-century kilim from east Anatolia

j
Sixteenth-century Ottoman velvet

k
Fragment of east Anatolian kilim, plate 272

Cloudband or Double-headed Bird Design

This geometric motif appears in a wide variety of nineteenth-century kilims. Curiously enough, it does not appear in contemporary pile rugs, although it can be found on a number of examples from the sixteenth to the eighteenth century.

Its likely derivation is from the cloudband, a Chinese motif adopted by the Islamic world; however, it could also be an adaptation of a double-headed bird.

Arranged in bands, it can be found both as a field and as a border design. Used in conjunction with its mirror-image, however, it can create a variety of field patterns depending on chromatic arrangements.

a

Detail from west Anatolian kilim, plate 98

b

Detail from central Anatolian kilim, plate 145

c

Detail from north-west Persian kilim, plate 368

COMPARATIVE DESIGNS IN PILE RUGS

h

Detail from sixteenth-century Anatolian pile rug

i

Detail from early Anatolian village rug, seventeenth-eighteenth century

j

Detail from early Anatolian village rug, seventeenth-eighteenth century

k

Detail from Caucasian dragon carpet, seventeenth century

l

Detail from sixteenth-century Anatolian rug

d

Concentric diamond grid pattern; detail from plate 205

e

Diagonal band pattern; detail from plate 111

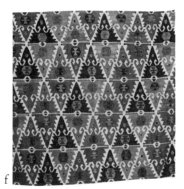

f

Trellis pattern; detail from plate 112

g

Elements floating on a striped background; detail from plate 199

Güls

Perhaps the single most important motif used in the decoration of kilims is the *gül*, i. e. the geometric design usually contained within an explicit or implicit hexagonal outline.

This is the tribal and nomadic ornament *par excellence*, the origins and meaning of which have been the subject of long-drawn-out controversies. Various heraldic, floral and animal interpretations have been advanced, which need not necessarily be contradictory. All of them, however, are far from being fully documented, and great care should be taken to avoid over-generalization.

The following details show two basic types of *güls*, and some of their interpretations by the various groups of kilim weavers.

a Detail from east Anatolian kilim, plate 270

b Detail from Caucasian kilim, plate 305

c Detail from north-west Persian kilim, plate 301

d Detail from south Persian kilim, plate 414

e Detail from south Persian kilim, plate 401

f Detail from west Anatolian kilim, plate 107

g Detail from west Persian kilim, plate 364

h Detail from central Anatolian kilim

i Detail from south-east Anatolian kilim, plate 188

j Detail from Caucasian kilim, plate 311

k Detail from Caucasian kilim, plate 310

l Detail from south-east Anatolian kilim, plate 202

m Detail from east Anatolian kilim

n Detail from north-west Persian kilim, plate 334

o Detail from south Persian kilim, plate 398

HOOKED GÜLS

a   b   c

d   e   f

g   h   i

STEPPED GÜLS

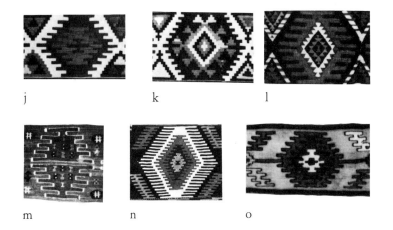

j   k   l

m   n   o

Anatolian Medallions

The following details show the similarities and differences among some of the large primary field medallions found in Anatolian kilims.

a

Detail, plate 141

b

Detail, plate 119

c

Detail, plate 107

d

Detail, plate 138

e

Detail, plate 139

f

Detail, plate 146

g

Detail, plate 143

h

Detail, plate 148

i

Detail, plate 147

j

Detail, plate 150

k

Detail, plate 149

l

Detail, plate 142

m

Detail, plate 129

n

Detail, plate 153

45

Symbolism and Tradition

The role of kilims is twofold; over and above their practical use, they also fulfil a decorative need. As in most forms of art practised traditionally within the Islamic world, function and decoration are inseparable, resulting in what art historians like to term 'minor' or 'applied' arts. Yet in Islam, no such distinction between the fine and the applied arts existed. Art in the abstract, or 'pure' art, was definitely frowned upon. Indeed, artistic expression, whatever its chosen medium, was to be seen as the harmonious blend of form, decoration and function in a perfectly integrated whole.

The decoration of kilims consists of patterns and designs forming elaborate compositions of great sophistication. In some there is a rich complexity of interrelating intricate ornaments, while in others designs are used sparingly to produce highly abstract and seemingly simple effects. Initially, attraction to kilims may be purely visual, as they show an almost infinite variety of designs, some bold and strong, others delicate and subdued. Closer examination, however, and prolonged acquaintance reveal that designs repeat themselves, patterns and compositions recur and that there are a number of distinct compositional types. This is not to say, however, that kilims merely repeat one another; rather they are individual expressions of time-honoured archetypes, each showing its creator's skill while closely adhering to tradition. This strict adherence to originals would be pointless and sterile if the archetypes were no more than meaningless patterns, however beautiful. The opposite is certainly the case. The vocabulary of kilim decoration is rich in symbolism; so much so, that it would not be out of place to talk in terms of an iconography of kilim ornament. Unfortunately, symbolism is a subject fraught with perils and open to infinite subjective interpretations. Yet, in trying to understand kilims, an examination of the role and purpose of symbols within the cultural context of the societies that produced the kilim is both relevant and important.

Universally, symbols are evocative, their meanings implicit and not explicit. Symbolism touches the very essence of Islamic tradition and is to be found in all of man's creations, from monu-mental architecture to the tent, from the exquisite ceramics of the court to the humble household utensils of the peasant, from the king's carpet to the nomad's kilim.

Symbolism is based on the law of correspondence which holds that what is below is a reflection of what is above. This is the cornerstone of all symbolism, for a symbol is the reflection of a higher reality on a lower plane. Beauty, harmony and rhythm are thus elementary and natural derivatives of symbolic art (see also Prayer Kilims chapter).

Through symbolism the order in the natural and spiritual world is recreated by man. It is expressed, however, not according to individual tastes but as a statement of faith. 'There is no God but God...' are the opening words of the Qur'an, implying that everything derives from God and yet everything represents Him.

Symbolic art is a constant repetition of such a statement. Thus, a traditional perspective of the world meant that crafts-men working within their tradition had a fundamentally different approach to artistic achievement from that of modern Western artists. Innovation and creativity for their own sakes were not their concern. The world is eternal; it is created by God and functions according to His will. Living tradition is, therefore, dynamic and never static. It evolves while remaining true to its origins, assimilates without necessarily discarding and provides a continuous unbroken chain of development. Symbols are, on one level, the means of recreating and express-ing eternal and universal truths and not personal or subjective opinions and tastes. Whether they are understood intellectu-ally or not is immaterial, they are a source of intellectual intuition rather than rational analysis. Their significance is accepted, not judged. 'I am the flute, Lord, Thine is the music', Rumi said, thus expressing with poignancy the essence of sym-bolic 'mystical' art and the law of correspondence already men-tioned as defining the relationship between the craftsman and his work.

In the study of kilims, however, the problem can be set in a much narrower perspective. The question is not whether kilim ornamentation can be symbolic or not, since there is no doubt that in traditional art symbolism is ever-present in all methods of expression. Rather, it is a matter of finding out which of the kilims are a true expression of traditional art and which are not, and of finding a key to understanding them. Only when the continuous chain of tradition broke under the strain of external influences, incompatible with its own level of reality, did the time come when the once-obvious symbols became so stylized that they underwent a gradual loss of meaning, which, in turn, led to a rapid and natural degeneration in form. Unfortunately, this process of degeneration acquires an accelerating momentum, and it takes a surprisingly short period of time (often as short as a single generation) to reach a situation where weavers no longer comprehend either the significance or the importance of designs they use. This lack of understanding, deplorable as it may be, would not by itself have been fatal, since symbols, as mentioned earlier, do not have to be understood intellectually in order to be valid. However, by looking upon them merely as decoration, the weavers felt free to alter the size, shape and colour of their designs and to arrange them eclectically in new patterns, creating different compositions, thus disrupting forever the links with the past.

This process of degenerative evolution, which has by now reached all kilim-producing areas, was by no means uniform, nor did it happen simultaneously. Certain areas resisted change longer and more strongly than others. This resistance seems to be directly related to inaccessibility. T. Burkhardt uses the term 'cultural storehouses' for remote places which remained largely untouched by the onslaught of change. It follows that urban centres were the first to sever their links with tradition. It may be argued that with pile carpets this process began as early as the seventeenth century, in the ateliers of Ottoman Turkey and Safavid Persia, with the adoption of court inspired and imposed styles for the execution of large commercial orders. In the case of kilims, however, as the production remained largely in nomad and village hands, it did not start in earnest until the second half of the last century, and did not become widespread before the First World War. As most of the kilims available today date from this period, the problem of ascertaining which of the pieces are the product of a living tradition and which are weakened and degenerate descendants of such a tradition, is a major one. This problem is inexorably intertwined with that of dating kilims, since we have the unfortunate tendency to confuse quality with age and to make misguided assumptions about dating on the basis of aesthetic criteria alone. Thus, even though synthetic dyes were introduced in Anatolia as early as 1870, there were exceptional kilims with natural dyes which employed strictly traditional patterns made in east Anatolia as late as 1930, and which, in the absence of documentary evidence, are often referred to in the trade today as nineteenth-century.

In seeking to understand the symbolic meaning of kilims, it is of paramount importance to understand that the entire composition, and even the structure, is a symbol. The synthesis of patterns and designs which form the composition does not derive from the juxtaposition and combination of heterogeneous and haphazardly chosen elements. In other words, the kilim is not just the sum of its parts. The Islamic belief in unity within multiplicity is ever-present as a decorative principle and becomes the governing parameter of the weaver's artistic expression. All the elements of decoration are harnessed within the overall composition, whether they are individual designs, or sequences of designs forming patterns which in turn create compositions. Certainly, each element has its own place and its role to play. But that role is as part of a totality and should not be seen or judged in isolation. Attempting to understand designs in isolation would be tantamount to removing a word from a well-constructed sentence and expecting its meaning to remain unchanged.

For this kind of understanding, participation in the tradition which used these symbols is absolutely essential, and for most of us, this is a goal beyond reach. Modern man has been largely conditioned by his environment and education to examine the world rationally. The process of intellectual analysis is ill-suited, however, to the task of finding the key to the meaning of symbols. Such a process can only lead to a superficial recording of their appearance and to comparisons of their visual development geographically, chronologically and also in terms of the use they were put to and of the medium of their expression. The dangers of over-generalization and over-simplification inherent in this approach are great, and relationships can be assumed which are totally artificial, such as that a cross found on a kilim might be proof of its Christian origin.

In the study of any traditional art form, symbolic designs used in its decorative repertoire must be examined first and foremost for the meaning they held within that tradition. Only as a secondary consideration is it necessary to extend the search for their meaning further. This second stage only concerns the fuller understanding of the individual symbol rather than the meaning it has within the art form under scrutiny. Where a symbol first appears may well be very interesting. This, however, does no more than satisfy curiosity. While it is in the nature of symbols to have a certain degree of universality, once adopted by a tradition they are assimilated to it and, their origins being forgotten, they become an inalienable part of it. In this process of adoption, symbols which contain multiple layers of meaning may be stripped of some of them and, occasionally, invested with new ones. Sometimes there can also be an important shift of emphasis either upwards or downwards even within the same tradition. This in no way invalidates or contradicts other meanings or values the symbol may have had elsewhere. It only reflects the spiritual beliefs of the specific tradition using the symbol, and efforts should be concentrated on understanding them in that context.

Anatolia

48

49

50

51

52

Early tapestry-woven fragments, showing designs similar to those found in later kilims, Egypt, probably eighth to tenth century AD

50

Early Anatolian Kilims

The Anatolian kilims most people know are those of the nineteenth and twentieth centuries. Kilim weaving was, however, practised in the area much before, and there is some evidence to suggest that production was uninterrupted. Certainly, the earliest surviving large kilims date back only to the late sixteenth or seventeenth century. These pieces are, however, so sophisticated, and show such mastery of the technique, that there is no reason to believe that this is the period when kilim weaving first began. Adding the evidence of the tapestry-woven fragments with geometric designs of latch-hook medallions and stars found in the Fostat excavations, and some weavings of the Coptic period, one can safely assume that kilim weaving was practised extensively in the eastern Mediterranean well before our era.

Exactly how far kilims go back is a question that cannot be answered on present evidence. In the fifth century BC, however, Xenophon, while listing the riches of the court of Cyrus, mentions three types of wall and floor coverings by the names *pilon*, felt rugs, *tapetes*, floor rugs and wall hangings, and *rapta*, stitched rugs. It seems more than likely that among the textiles included in the last two types, some were tapestry-woven kilims. Another early author uses the term *psilotapides*, thin carpets, a reference which seems as close as any to flat tapestry-woven rugs. The existence of kilims in earlier times therefore seems to be beyond doubt, though what they were like, when and where they were made and how they evolved are much more obscure matters.

Surviving examples of early kilims, often in a fragmentary state, are few and far between. Strangely, however, those pieces that have reached us seem to fit effortlessly into distinct categories. But before discussing these kilims we should make a short digression in order to formulate the problems concerning the evolution of kilim designs.

In looking broadly at the textile arts of the eastern Mediterranean basin one thing becomes apparent. Certain groups of fabrics are decorated in a more or less naturalistic manner, that is, they have clearly recognizable human, animal or floral designs in various stages of stylization, while other groups rely strictly on an abstract decorative repertoire of geometric patterns. Whether the latter are simply a further step in the stylization of the former is not the present question. What is more directly relevant, is that tastes in decoration seem to have gone in phases. For example, in the Byzantine, Sassanian, Coptic, Fatimid and Seljuk periods, while naturalism and abstract patterns coexisted, there was a marked shift of emphasis from time to time, with no discernible evolutionary pattern. The Ottomans, on the other hand, developed a marked preference for floral designs in their official or 'court' style to the almost total exclusion of others. Such characterizations of style are, however, relatively simple to make when examining 'mainstream' art or pieces made under the direct influence of the 'court' styles. With kilims and, for that matter, all forms of art made largely in the hinterland, in places cut off from direct and uninterrupted access to the cultural currents and fashions of the day, defining 'style' is a nightmare. It is not just a matter of tracing the origins and discerning the nature of designs; rather it is a case of trying to determine how, when, and to what degree origin and design are interrelated.

The ethnic complexity of the area's population, constant cultural cross-fertilization and the coexistence of conservative and change-promoting trends make generalizations about the development of kilim designs impossible. It would seem, however, that three broad currents of evolution may be discerned. In the first two, there appears a reasonably direct descent; in the third, which is an amalgam of the first two, there are an almost infinite number of descendants, both geographical and chronological.

THE PRE-OTTOMAN TRADITION

There is a large body of kilims with a pre-Ottoman decorative repertoire, of possibly Seljuk origin. The designs of these pieces are of an abstract geometric nature, or of a strongly geometricized animal and floral nature, the stylization and

53

54

56

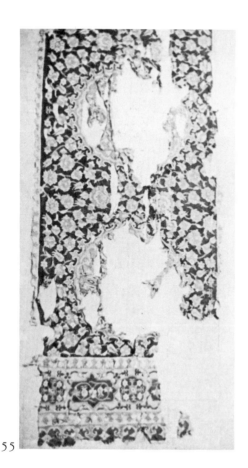

55

57

58

52

abstraction having reached a stage where forms are barely recognizable renderings of nature arranged in geometric patterns. A large number of kilims which can be safely attributed to the nineteenth century (e. g. plates 155 and 158) have a very strict geometric style of ornamentation, parallels of which can be found in pile rugs of the fifteenth century, in the group of fourteenth-century Seljuk carpets found in the mosque of Beyşehir, and in early Islamic textiles found in Fostat (plates 48–52). It would appear that in many parts of Anatolia, a strong local tradition remained undisturbed by the fashions imposed by the Ottoman court in Istanbul, and continued to produce pieces in a much earlier style. That such a style should survive longer in kilims than in carpets is quite understandable given the fact that while the carpets were a commercial commodity, and sensitive to the demands of changing fashions in the commercial centres, kilims remained largely in the places where they were woven for local use, where there was no pressure for them to change stylistically.

THE OTTOMAN STYLE

Classical Ottoman Kilims

Ottoman court art relies almost exclusively on designs derived from flora, either in the form of split-leaf arabesques, palmettes, floral medallions or actual flowers such as carnations, tulips, hyacinths, roses, etc. These designs, which are combined in formal compositions, are themselves quite stylized, though nowhere so highly as the pre-Ottoman designs. Naturalism—recognizable natural forms—is much more prevalent. In many respects, Ottoman decoration shows strong Persian and Chinese influences.

Until very recently, little was known of Anatolian kilims made within the mainstream of the Ottoman court tradition, and this little was based solely on a small fragment found by Riefstahl in the Eshref Oglu Cami in Beyşehir (now in the Mevlana Museum in Konya, plate 53). This situation changed overnight with the discovery of a group of fragmentary pieces in the Ulu Cami in Divriği (plates 54–8). These kilims, which are not particularly fine in weave, are all large in size in varying proportions. Their designs relate very closely to those of Ottoman ceramic tiles, velvets, silk brocades and, especially, embroideries (plate 59). So far, no textual evidence concerning these pieces has come to light. Since, however, in terms of design they fall into the mainstream of fashion-conscious

59

Ottoman art, it is reasonable to assume that they are contemporary with other works of art with similar decorative features. This would date them somewhere between the end of the sixteenth century and the middle of the seventeenth. The clarity of their drawing and the purity of the designs, together with their large size, would suggest that they are the product of workshop looms and that they probably originated in a metropolitan centre.

There is another early group of kilims of which two examples have thus far come to light. One piece (plate 60) in the Kestner Museum in Hanover, has been known for a long time

60

from which sprout pairs of serrated leaves, in the border, are identical to those on one of the borders of the Kestner piece. The technique and texture of these two pieces, the wool and the colours, compare very closely with those of the Divriği group. The drawing of the floral elements, however, and their similarity to certain embroidery patterns suggest a somewhat later dating, somewhere between the middle of the seventeenth century and the beginning of the eighteenth.

The existence of these two groups of early kilims poses an intriguing problem. If 'court' or workshop kilims of high quality were produced in the seventeenth century by the Ottomans as well as by the neighbouring Safavids in Persia (the silk and metal-thread so-called Polonaise kilims), why is it that their production did not continue, all the later pieces being firmly anchored in the village and nomadic tradition? Unfortunately, there seems to be no satisfactory answer as yet to this puzzling question. Nevertheless, there are village pieces which trace their lineage to Ottoman court art and which have survived in reasonable numbers. These, however, are not direct descendants. There must undoubtedly have been a number of 'missing links' between the 'classical' pieces of the seventeenth century and these Ottoman village pieces. It would not be at all surprising if the vast wealth still hidden in the mosques of Anatolia should one day produce these missing links and fill the present gaps in our knowledge.

Ottoman Village Kilims

The natural conservatism of the population of rural Anatolia, producing resistance to fashions and change, seems to explain why Ottoman court-inspired designs were slow to penetrate and be assimilated in the village and nomadic kilim production. Once this resistance was overcome, however (and we have no means of knowing how long this took), such designs were adopted, adapted to local tastes, usually by a process of simplification, and started evolving with their own momentum.

Two clearly distinct but related groups of kilims have reached us from the early stages of this development. Broadly speaking, these postdate the classical Ottoman kilims of the sixteenth to seventeenth centuries and predate those of the nineteenth.

but was, we believe mistakenly, labelled as Balkan, nineteenth century. It was originally a very large piece but has survived as a much reduced and muddled collage of fragments, so that its original composition is difficult to read. This appears similar to one of the Divriği pieces: two borders surrounding a floral field with a central medallion and four quarter-medallions at the corners. The second piece (plate 61) is a recently discovered prayer kilim with an exquisitely drawn and proportioned *mihrab* or prayer niche, in which hangs a lamp on a chain. The roses

61

GROUP A (plates 62–64)

Five pieces are known of this group. Three are illustrated here; the fourth, which is in the Sofia Ethnographic Museum, is published in *Bulgarian Kilims* by Dimitri Velev (Sofia 1960; plate 118) and the fifth is in a French private collection. These kilims are all very large, but they do not have the typical long and narrow proportions of later Turkish kilims. Nevertheless, despite their width they are woven in one piece: generally speaking, a feature common to all early kilims of the sixteenth to eighteenth centuries. Kilims woven in two or three separate pieces date chiefly from the nineteenth century, although there are a number of examples which could be attributed to the eighteenth century.

All five pieces of the group are very loosely woven in slit tapestry and have a coarse, uneven texture. Both the warps and wefts are of the same thick, silky and very soft wool, producing a soft and pliable fabric, unlike in texture to any other known group of kilims. The colours are brilliant, with a wide and contrasting range, predominant in which are white, yellow, apricot, pink, red, purple, light and dark blue, green and black. The exquisite combinations of deep and light colours produce a very striking visual effect. The composition consists basically of a large field surrounded by a wide primary floral border, flanked by secondary borders. The latter have a vine-and-blossom design common to all the known examples of the group.

62   *205 × 311 cm.*

A typical example of this group, displaying the full range of colours found in these kilims. The wide borders contain two rows of leaves or flowers, reminiscent of those found on seventeenth- to eighteenth-century Anatolian pile rugs and embroideries (see J. McMullan, *Islamic Carpets*, No. 80, and Lefevre and Partners, *Turkish Carpets*, No. 3). The secondary borders, containing a vine-and-blossom motif on an ivory ground, are common to all the pieces of the group; their design is once again related to those found on both carpets and embroideries. These secondary borders join the main border and the field by means of a zigzag outline on the sides and a

straight line at top and bottom. The field consists of two parts, the outer being an endless pattern of offset quadripartite hexagons. It acts as a framing device for the inner field, which contains small-scale ornaments in the form of indented diamonds; these are arranged chromatically to form an endless pattern of diagonal lines. The use of different patterns arranged to frame or reveal others contained within them creates a multi-layered effect which is common to all the pieces of this group. The main border of this kilim should be compared with one of the floral bands of plate 68, as it shows clearly the links between the two groups of Ottoman village kilims.

63   *228 × 317 cm. (Detail)*

This piece and the next are both from the collection of the Victoria and Albert Museum in London. This has the same main and secondary border configuration as plate 62. Furthermore, the small motifs in the rectangle framing the central panel are similar to those found on the inner field of plate 62. With the exception of the secondary borders, all the horizontal bands are wider than the vertical ones. The present piece has the same composition and very similar designs to those of the piece in the Sofia Ethnographic Museum mentioned above.

64   *274 × 355 cm.*

The main border-motif found on the last two pieces appears here in the field framing the large multi-layered diamond. This contains at the centre a hooked medallion surrounded by layers of blossoms, some of which look like stylized carnations. The four points of the diamond terminate in trefoils. The side borders have a meandering vine from which stem stylized tulips and leaves. At the top and bottom borders the arrangement of the stems changes to create a pattern more in keeping with the horizontal direction of the flowers. This pattern is one of the typical band designs of the next group of early kilims (plates 67 and 68), and serves as further evidence of the relationship —at least at the design level—between the two groups.

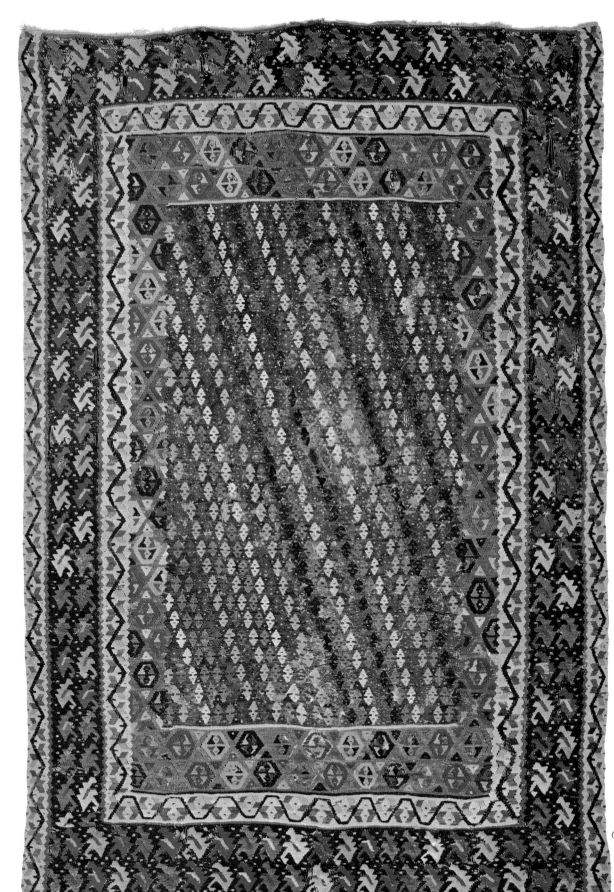

62

63

64

65

GROUP B (plates 65–70)

A rich multitude of small floral designs arranged along narrow horizontal bands is the most distinctive feature of this second group of Ottoman village kilims. Both the warps and the wefts are of wool; the weave is fairly loose and not particularly fine, but not as coarse as in kilims of the preceding group. Most of the individual designs are outlined in a different colour by means of weft wrapping.

All the known examples are woven in one piece. They are, however, much narrower than the kilims in Group A, their width being fairly constant at approximately 160 cm. Their length, however, varies significantly, some pieces being as short as 231 cm. (plate 68), while others can be as long as 430 cm.

Although their decorative repertoire is rich in individual elements, it has a rather limited range of variation. The typical pieces are composed of a series of bands arranged either in a repeat sequence (plate 65) or at random (plate 68). In both cases, however, bands containing floral patterns are not juxtaposed, always alternating with others containing a small-scale complex interlocking and reciprocal pattern. Most of the small floral motifs are recognizable derivatives of the classical Ottoman designs of the late sixteenth and early seventeenth centuries, including the serrated leaves, tulips, carnations, roses and hyacinths so typical of the ceramics and textiles of the period, and of the previously examined kilims of the Divriği group. Here, however, they seem to have undergone a noticeable degree of stylization. The question which arises, since this process was by no means unique to kilims, is where this stylization originates. Are these pieces direct descendants of the earlier kilims, or are they stylistically faithful copies of other stylized textiles or carpets?

The often well-drawn curvilinear flowers give the impression of being somewhat incongruously forced into rectilinear repeat patterns. While it could be argued that it is primarily the bands which dictate this somewhat rigid, axial arrangement, in borders of early carpets and textiles similar ornaments are arranged in a much more fluid manner, displaying a lot of movement and grace. The result of this juxtaposition of bands, each with a multitude of very small elements of decoration, is a total absence of focus in the composition. They convey the impression of a continuous secquence of border patterns, from which they may well be derived. Certainly, all the variants of the floral bands found in pieces of the present group appear as borders in the first group (compare borders of plates 62, 63, 64 with plate 68).

Looking for related designs in knotted pile rugs, we find the closest similarities with Ghiordes and Kula prayer rugs of the late eighteenth and early nineteenth centuries (see Dimand and Mailey, *Oriental Rugs*, Nos. 112, 113, 121, 122, 124, 126, 131, 132). The resemblance goes beyond the shape of the designs to include scale, pattern, arrangement and colour. A suggestion that such similarities may indicate an attribution to Kula or Ghiordes for these kilims is further strengthened by the fact that some of them have coloured warps (plate 65 has light-blue warps and plate 68 primarily yellow warps)—an unusual feature which also occurs on some of the pile rugs of Kula and Ghiordes. The stylization of the flowers and their similarity to those on embroideries of the eighteenth century as well as to those on Kula and Ghiordes prayer rugs of the late eighteenth century, suggest to us that these kilims date broadly from that time. Nevertheless, this chronological attribution is by no means definite. It is quite possible that these Ottoman village kilims could be much earlier. A painting by Albrecht Altdorfer in the Alte Pinakothek, Munich, entitled *Susanna Bathing* (plate 66) and dated 1526 shows what in all probability is a kilim with a composition of horizontal bands and designs directly related to those of the present pieces.

66

At present, eight pieces belonging to this type are known to us:

1 Long kilim with bands, in the Ethnographical Museum in Ankara.
2 Long kilim with bands featuring carnations, from a mosque in Bursa.
3 Band kilim (plate 67), in the Cathryn Cootner collection, Stanford, California.
4 Long kilim with bands, in the H. McCoy Jones collection in Washington, DC.
5 Band kilim (plate 65) which appeared in an auction of Lefevre and Partners, London, 26 May 1978, lot 43.
6 Band kilim (plate 68), in the collection of N. Winterbottom, London.
7 Prayer kilim (plate 69), in the Museum für Islamische Kunst, West Berlin.
8 Prayer kilim (plate 70), in the Ethnographical Museum, Ankara.

65   *152 × 292 cm.*

Placing the kilims of this group in a chronological sequence is difficult, our only clues being the quality of designs and the feel of the piece. On the grounds of quality of drawing and clarity of composition this would appear to be an early example. The composition has an orderly sequence, the bands containing the flowers being alternately red and blue, while the narrower bands with the geometric patterns are alternately on a white or a yellow background. The flowers and leaves in each band are attached to a long, thin, axial stem in a directional manner, all the bands going from left to right with the exception of the bottom band which goes in the opposite direction. Unlike plate 68, where some of the floral motifs float in the bands, here all the flowers and leaves are attached to the stem. This is certainly an indication of quality of drawing if not of age. This kilim shows at its clearest a feature common to all Ottoman village kilims of the eighteenth century and which survives in some nineteenth-century kilims (plates 254 and 274): the filling of empty background spaces with scattered dots in a variety of colours.

67   *no size available*

68   *169 × 231 cm.*

A random arrangement of floral and geometric bands has taken the place of the orderly sequence of plate 65. This piece, which is the shortest known example of this group, has a warmer, lighter colouring. Its charm is heightened by the strong abrashes and by the sudden changes of colour in the backgrounds of the bands. The pattern of serrated leaves in one of the major bands is the same as on the border of plate 62. This piece is the least fine in texture of this group, being much closer to kilims in group A, and has yellow warps.

69   *116 × 164 cm.*
70   *no size available*

Plate 69 is a very early prayer kilim in the Museum für Islamische Kunst in West Berlin. Together with plate 70 in the Ethnographical Museum in Ankara this is the only known prayer kilim belonging to this family of late Ottoman pieces with floral decoration. The simple, plain mihrab of plate 69, with its indented outline, culminates in a well-drawn floral blossom related to the trefoils at the points of the diamond medallion in plate 64. The two elegant leaves at the base of the floral blossom are, in a more stylized, angular form, an almost permanent feature at the tops of mihrabs of later prayer kilims. The mihrab floats on a dark field of leaves, tulips and other blossoms. This field pattern is taken up in the top and bottom major border which looks very similar to the floral bands on plates 67 and 68. The same basic pattern in the vertical borders is handled in a markedly different fashion and scale. The two following kilims, which are later in date, will show the further stylization and degeneration of this floral border ornamentation.

The eight medallions in the main border are similar to those in the bands of plate 67 and in the centre of plate 63. They contain within their unusual lobed outline a purely geometric motif very common in many later kilims. The secondary borders have the same vine-and-blossom pattern as the top band of plate 65 and are a somewhat more elaborate version of the minor borders of plates 62, 63, and 64. Noticeable on this piece is the filling of all the background space between the designs of both field and borders with a profusion of small dots, which is a peculiar and distinctive feature of all these eighteenth-century kilims.

67

68

69

70

71

72

This piece, which is in the collection of the Victoria and Albert Museum in London, is like a tapestry-woven rendering of a well-known type of pile rug. Few other examples have survived, one of which is in the Metropolitan Museum in New York (Dimand and Mailey, p. 217, cat. no. 147). At first inspection, this piece gives the impression of great age. However, comparisons with earlier kilims (plate 69) and pile rugs show that both the primary and secondary designs have reached an advanced stage of development. The triple-arch mihrab would originally have been supported by slender columns with pedestals and capitals. Here, however, through the misunderstanding or reinterpreting of designs, a practice common in later rugs, these columns have been rendered as trees. Both primary and secondary borders appear as more stylized versions of those on plate 69, although the tulips are replaced here by carnations. The main border consists of a vertical stem from which sprout pairs of small stems with carnations. At the top and bottom, instead of the flowers following the direction of the border, as was the practice in earlier kilims and rugs (see plate 64), groups of three carnations stand upright in the same direction as the mihrab. This border composition is quite common in later kilims from many different areas, both in central and east Turkey. The contrast of the vertical main border framed by the meandering vine of the secondary borders is very successful. The present piece is finely woven in wool, but also contains gilt-metal thread and silk. This kilim is related in colour and composition to the white-ground, triple-arch, knotted prayer rugs of Lâdik, while the designs in the spandrels and within the three arches are closer to those of pieces from Ghiordes or Kula. All the evidence, therefore, indicates that it would be unreasonable to date this piece earlier than the second half of the eighteenth century despite its colours and texture which suggest a considerable age.

A mid-nineteenth-century example of the previous kilim to which it is closely related in texture, colour and design. The main borders show a further stylization of the carnation motif. The weaver, in using different colours for each of the petals,

may have been unaware of the meaning of the design. The spandrels of the mihrab are related to those of the previous piece, as is the small diamond at the top of the niche. The central tree has branches which culminate in two leaves which form stylized versions of the ones on the floral motif topping the mihrab of plate 69. The proportions of this piece are very attractive, the stepped mihrab is well drawn and the pale colour range is most harmonious. It is closely related to a kilim in the McMullan collection (in *Islamic Rugs in the McMullan Collection,* plate 106).

The Composite Style

This last aspect of the evolution of Anatolian kilim decoration is especially relevant as it is associated primarily with pieces made after the middle of the eighteenth century and, therefore, with the bulk of the material for the Anatolian section of this book. We have already seen that kilims with Ottoman floral designs were woven in villages (plates 62 and 65). More often, however, instead of adopting the Ottoman style entirely, some of its patterns and designs were picked out of context in order to be included in the existing pre-Ottoman local decorative repertoire and iconography. Such transplants were soon assimilated and, once this happened, they became inalienable and indistinguishable parts of the local style. Thus, we have the birth of the composite style or, more accurately, the composite styles, since this process of blending was by no means an isolated occurrence but seems to span a large area both geographically and chronologically. It goes without saying, of course, that this is a constantly multiplying process, a new composite style being created with each new insertion into a local design tradition which could itself be composite already.

While the purpose of these injections was to enrich the local decorative repertoire, the result was very often to confuse it by depriving it of its cohesion. Eventually, the weavers forgot the overall unity in their designs, patterns and compositions and began to feel more and more free to express their own individual tastes and predilections. This, however, as was discussed in the chapter on symbolism, ultimately sounded the knell for tradition and for all it entailed for kilims. The last hundred years have given us more than ample evidence of this sad process of uninterrupted decline.

Prayer Kilims

Prayer rugs are probably the largest, most prominent and immediately recognizable family of Oriental rugs. From the last century onwards, they have appealed strongly to carpet collectors, partly on account of their small and manageable size but also because of their evocative association with the spiritual tradition of the Muslim world. More recently, the same has been true of prayer kilims.

These kilims were produced in large numbers throughout Anatolia, from the Aegean Sea all the way to the frontiers of Persia. There, however, the custom of weaving prayer kilims seems to have stopped rather abruptly. With the notable exception of a small group of finely woven Kurdish pieces from north-west Persia (plates 344 to 351), which are usually associated with the town of Sehna, and only one known piece from the Caucasus (plate 293), prayer kilims appear to have been made exclusively within the Ottoman world.

A prayer kilim, strictly speaking, is defined as a kilim of small size with a directional composition, usually in the form of an arch or 'prayer niche'. Its function in the act of prayer is to provide a pure surface, a 'sacred space' pointing towards Mecca, upon which a devout Muslim prostrates himself barefoot to perform his five daily prayers. Generally speaking, however, any rug or carpet, irrespective of size, can be called a prayer rug as long as it is used for praying on. In fact, relatively few of the carpets and kilims covering the floors of mosques would be described as prayer rugs if the sole criterion were the presence of a prayer arch. Moreover, rugs and textiles with directional arches or niches have traditionally been used in the Muslim world for wall and floor decoration in secular settings entirely outside the context of prayer (plate 73).

In the case of kilims, there are even some examples where the arch itself is used in a clearly non-directional manner, like the long kilim in plate 258 which has two opposing niches juxtaposed, one the exact mirror-image of the other, and the Reyhanlı kilim in plate 218 which has a large number of small niches decorating the field, arranged in horizontal rows facing towards the centre of the field.

The arch or prayer niche which characterizes prayer rugs is associated with the prayer niche or mihrab of the mosque and is commonly referred to by the same name. The significance and role of the mihrab in Muslim architecture is complex. It is normally placed at the centre of the *Quibla* wall which faces towards Mecca, and it is towards that wall rather than the mihrab that prayers should be directed. The mihrab, therefore, has no specific function or liturgical role in the performance of Muslim ritual. Its initial appearance seems to have been in a secular, rather than in a religious, context as the focal point of a palace's throne room, at the place of the throne. This honorific association with kingship, which was inherited from pre-Islamic traditions, was then transposed to a religious setting. As a feature of mosque architecture, it first appears in Medinah, on the mosque built by the Ommayad Caliph

73

al-Walīd in AD 706 on the site of the Prophet's house. Most scholars agree that its role was to commemorate the place Muhammad occupied when addressing his disciples and leading their prayers.

Almost immediately, however, the mihrab became a standard and inalienable feature of mosque architecture, and its form was directly associated in the minds of the faithful with religious worship, becoming in fact a symbol of it. With the passing of time it grew in importance and in size, and acquired diverse geometrical forms in keeping with local styles. Gradually, its symbolism became more complex, with new layers of meaning being superimposed on the original thus elaborating on it and, at the same time, leading to a shift in emphasis and a clouding of the mihrab's original purpose.

Small rugs with directional designs first appear in fourteenth-century Persian paintings. Whether these arches necessarily represent mosque mihrabs or simply associated decorative motifs is open to question. The large number of miniatures showing textiles with arches used as wall coverings in buildings, tents and even outside courtyards would seem to indicate, if not a change in meaning, at least an important shift from the notion of the mihrab as commemorative of the Prophet's place in his house in Medinah. It is very likely that the arch in Islamic art inherited all the complexity of meaning invested in it by the various pre-Islamic religions, like Judaism and Christianity, both of which used it as a symbol of worship. This would explain the fact that, often, the arched or pointed designs of prayer rugs have shapes and outlines entirely unknown in mosque mihrabs, such as the multiple superimposed arches of plate 115 and the triple arch with columns of plate 71. The latter is a well-known design of doorways and windows in Muslim architecture, and it probably gives the best indication as to the symbolism of the 'mihrabs' of prayer rugs.

The doorway is a universal symbol shared by most traditions in both East and West. The arched part of the doorway corresponds to the dome of the universe, the world of the spirit, while the vertical sides or columns relate to the earth and the material world. It could be described as the two-dimensional equivalent of a temple, church or mosque, whose shape is basically a cube surmounted by a dome. The door or window is variously described as the celestial gate, the door to Paradise through which appears unattainable perfection, the door to the realization of the inner self pointing to the path, the Way a believer must follow.

In prayer rugs, the decoration used within the arch to convey this meaning is a stylized abstraction of the ideal world achieved through a variety of floral and animalistic designs, representing Paradise, usually in the form of a garden. Similarly, the sky is also represented on the rug as a reflection of the world above, a microcosm of Heaven seen through the sacred gate. The Tree of Life, another common decorative device, suggests both the hierarchical order in the natural world and also the stages of realization the believer must go through before reaching nearness to the Creator. The same symbolic meaning appears to be implied by the use of superimposed arches that, once again, represent hurdles or stages one must overcome before achieving a state of grace. Furthermore, the door or window may open on to the inner self and reveal the divine light of God. This last aspect is iconographically represented by a lamp hanging within the prayer arch symbolizing the Quranic passage: 'God is the light of heaven and earth; the similitude of this light is as a niche in a wall, wherein a lamp is placed and the lamp enclosed in a vessel of glass; the glass appears as it were a shining star. It is lighted with the oil of a blessed tree, an olive neither of the east nor of the west; ... God will direct unto this light whom He pleaseth.' (Sūrah 24, Light, Verse 35)

As with symbolism in general, the question arises whether such meanings were understood rationally at the peasant and nomadic level, or whether they were repetitions, or even variations, of traditional archetypes. It is the nature of symbols, however, to exist on many levels of reality and to be true to themselves independently of their creators. The precise meaning of the designs on a specific prayer rug depends both on the weaver's intention or artistic intuition and the viewer's interpretation. Rarely do both have the same perception, especially if the latter is conditioned by the modern, rationalistic way of thinking.

The shapes of mihrabs in prayer kilims are very varied. As already mentioned, some are fairly realistic renderings of architectural forms such as the triple-arch doorway supported by columns (plate 71) and the minaret (plate 80). Others are reminiscent of Turkish tombstones covered with a turban (plate 231). It has been suggested here, however, that such kilims were not used for prayer but were instead shrouds for wrapping the dead before burial.

In general, however, most kilim mihrabs are pointed arches of rather abstract shape. The simplest type can be described geometrically as a triangle superimposed on a rectangle (plate 83). The proportions of the resulting niche vary widely; they can be short and wide as in plate 123 or tall and narrow as in plate 76. The arches of these niches have just as diverse shapes and outlines. Some have an elaborate and complex lace-like form as those in plate 109. Others have a geometric stepped arch (plate 259), and in others still, the arches are outlined with a row of continuous reciprocal 'latch-hooks' (plate 255). The latter can be of two types: those where the latch-hook pattern is drawn in a colour distinct from those of both the mihrab and the spandrels, creating an independent pattern joining and separating one from the other (plate 163), and those where a latch-hook outline is created, where the mihrab and the spandrels blend and interlock into one another (plates 181 and 256).

In looking at individual prayer kilims, their diversity of origin must be remembered. There are, in fact, hardly any families or types of Anatolian kilims that do not include examples of them. Such prayer kilims display all the features of structure, texture, colour and ornamentation characteristic of their respective group of origin, so they can be identified in the same way as all other compositional types.

74   *137 × 198 cm.*

75   *no size available*
76   *110 × 175 cm.*

These two kilims belong to one of the many groups produced in central Anatolia. The inner borders and the outlines of the long mihrabs are similar to those found on Obruk kilims (plates 162 to 166), while the designs on the outer borders relate to those found on 'Yürük' kilims from the area, such as plates 175 and 177.

77   *no size available*

78   *145 × 209 cm.*

This small kilim is not directional in composition and, therefore, strictly speaking is not a prayer kilim. It belongs to the same type as colour plate 74 with which it shares colours and texture. The common Anatolian pattern found on the end borders is drawn identically on both pieces.

79   *102 × 137 cm.*

This charming prayer kilim probably comes from the region of Niğde in central Anatolia. The field is almost entirely covered with a repeat pattern of diagonally offset hexagons. It is only at the top that the pattern changes to allow for a larger directional motif which implies a prayer niche. This piece is a somewhat coarser version of the large and very fine kilim on plate 158, yet the seeming imprecision of execution in no way diminishes the strength and harmonious balance of the composition.

80   *105 × 160 cm.*
81   *118 × 158 cm.*
82   *130 × 152 cm.*

The traditional nature of kilim designs and their adherence to time-honoured archetypes, while showing the creativity of the weaver, is well illustrated by these three examples from three different areas.

Their unusual prayer arches are of the same generic type, which is reminiscent of the architectural form of the minaret, a feature most clearly seen on plate 80. The latter is probably from the Aydın region of west Anatolia and should be compared with the larger kilims of the area (plates 131 and 133).

Plate 81, which appears to be the oldest of the three, is also from west Anatolia though its wool is softer and the colours deeper and mellower. They include apricot, strong tomato red, purple, light and dark blue, green and yellow, relating closely to the pile rugs of Melas. The border surrounding the mihrab on both plates 81 and 82 contains at the sides a series of designs which are occasionally referred to as 'ramsheads', but which are more likely to derive from Ottoman tulips (compare with plates 268 and 269.). Both kilims have bold multiple crenellated guardstripes at the joins of the vertical bands.

Plate 82 has the same type of mihrab as the other two, particularly plate 80. It has, however, the texture and colours of a central Anatolian kilim of the Kayseri-Kırşehir region with the characteristic tomato and burgundy reds, green, yellow and deep blue. The floral decoration of the inner border, together with the two floral medallions at the lower part of the mihrab, are related to those of eighteenth-century kilims like plates 63, 65 and 67.

74

75

76

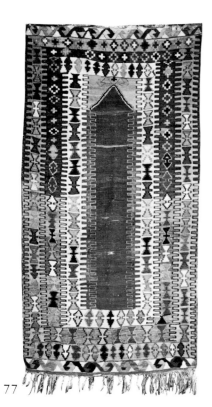

77

78

79

80

81

82

83

84

85

86

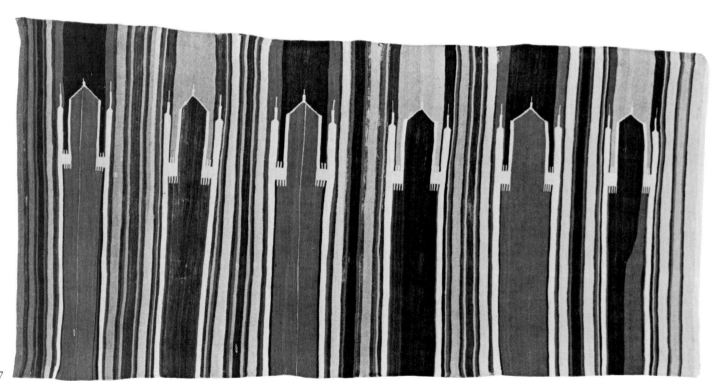

87

83 *130 × 160 cm.*

One of the oldest known prayer kilims, this piece probably dates from the eighteenth century. The border motifs are similar to those on some eighteenth-century pile prayer rugs of the Konya region, while the loose texture and the colours, especially the pink of the mihrab and border and the green of the spandrels, are related to those of other eighteenth-century kilims (plates 62 and 63). The trefoil motif at the top of the mihrab should be compared with those on the central medallion of plate 64.

84 *112 × 173 cm.*

This simple and elegantly drawn prayer kilim, containing in the mihrab one of the most recognizable renderings of the Tree of Life, has all the texture and colour characteristics of Kars kilims (plates 273 and 274). The large medallions forming the border pattern, however, are more commonly found in the band kilims of Malatya.

85 *123 × 189 cm.*

This crisp-looking prayer kilim comes from the Konya region of central Anatolia. Kilims of this type were produced in large numbers towards the end of the last century and well into the twentieth. The drawing of the arch of the mihrab is rather unusual as is the less-emphasized opposing arch at the base of the mihrab.

SAFS

Although the overwhelming majority of prayer kilims are of a small size and contain one mihrab, there are some large pieces, usually long and narrow, that have a series of juxtaposed mihrabs. These are referred to as 'safs' and are evocatively described as family prayer kilims (plates 86, 87, 247 and 248). They usually have three or seven mihrabs, but there are many exceptions to this rule. Kilim safs are relatively few and are far less varied typologically than single-arch prayer kilims. Judging from the surviving examples known to us, it appears that they were made exclusively in Anatolia and that they were more favoured in the east than in the centre and west of the country.

86 *153 × 395 cm.*
87 *165 × 340 cm.*

The two multiple mihrab prayer kilims shown here are unusual; until recently nothing was known about their origin and various locations had been suggested as their source, including North Africa, Syria and even Afghanistan, where patchwork hangings of similar design are common. It had also been mentioned that the architectural form of the 'mihrabs' suggested the entrance to a Persian mosque flanked by minarets. However, careful examination of their structure and colours led us to attribute them to Anatolia and possibly to the western-central part of the country. In 1978, a later example with only three mihrabs was discovered and purchased in Nevşehir in central Turkey thus strengthening this attribution.

Plate 86 is in the collection of the Islamisches Museum in East Berlin. It has only three colours, white, red and blue, and is extremely fine in weave. Plate 87 differs from it noticeably, although it has some similarities in the drawing of the mihrabs. It is much more colourful, and the field, which is uniform on plate 86, is divided into bands of different colours. The mihrabs extend to the edge of the piece and there is no border. The weave is much looser and the white warps end in a multilayered braid along the end of the piece, typical of western Anatolian kilims, especially those of the Balıkesir and Helvacı groups. Those of plate 86, on the other hand, end in a most unusual and complex arrangement of knots. The more recent piece mentioned above has the texture of plate 87 but the drawing of plate 86, its blue, red and white colours being replaced by pale green, red and white.

The composition and the type of mihrab of these safs show a distinct relationship with a fifteenth-century pile saf in the Türk ve Islâm Eserleri Museum in Istanbul which is published in Kurt Erdmann, *The Early Turkish Carpet* (Oguz Press, 1977, plate III).

North-West Anatolian Bergama-Balıkesir Kilims

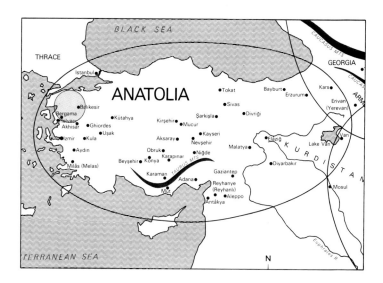

From the fifteenth century onwards, carpet weaving was widely practised in north-west Anatolia, the products of which have traditionally been attributed to Bergama. This, however, should be thought of more as a generic term than as a precise definition of origin.

The passing of time brought relatively few changes to the designs and compositions of Bergama rugs. They developed naturally in a pattern of evolution common throughout Anatolia: simplification followed by stylization and abstraction. Yet there are nineteenth-century examples with clearly recognizable patterns attributed to the 'Holbein' group of sixteenth- to seventeenth-century Bergama pile rugs. Unfortunately, no kilims of that early period have survived, and it is now probably impossible to ascertain whether any were made or not.

There are, however, large numbers of flatwoven pieces dating from the beginning of the nineteenth century onwards which can safely be attributed to the area. These are mostly brocaded kilims made in the weft-float technique on a warp and weft faced uniform dark ground, decorated with archaic and traditional interlocking geometric patterns harking back to

those found on Seljuk carpets. The combination of their designs and the subtle sophistication of the resulting composition is such that it is most unlikely that they developed in the nineteenth century or that they were transplanted into the region at that time.

Tapestry-woven pieces are less common. They appear to fall within one family which is generally attributed to Balıkesir, a town located halfway between Bursa and Bergama.

The major designs and compositions of Balıkesir kilims are unusual and exclusive to them. They consist of diverse arrangements of interlocking 'latch-hook' motifs combined with vertical wavy bands to give field-pattern illusions, the viewer never being certain which is the background and which the design. It has been suggested, however, that the archetypal Balıkesir composition (e. g. plates 88 and 93) should be read as three blue (or blue and green) Trees of Life floating on a red ground.

With few exceptions such as plate 93, Balıkesir kilims are woven in one piece and are relatively shorter and wider than most Anatolian kilims. They have the quality of wool and the colours of eighteenth- to nineteenth-century Bergama pile rugs. Their warps are usually of white wool and usually terminate in a combination of a braid along the edge of the kilim and a plaited fringe. Some pieces have this arrangement at both ends and others only at the bottom, the top having a loose fringe.

The limited colour-range, which relies primarily on reds and blues, is probably their most distinguishing feature.

The designs of Balıkesir kilims have only diagonal and horizontal outlines, vertical lines being totally absent. As a result, the slits are so small that they are not noticeable. They are further obscured by the highlighting of these outlines with weft-wrapping or overstitching which is usually done in white cotton and occasionally in red or blue wool.

Although all Balıkesir kilims share a set of common technical features and design compositions unique to them, they can be divided into two types.

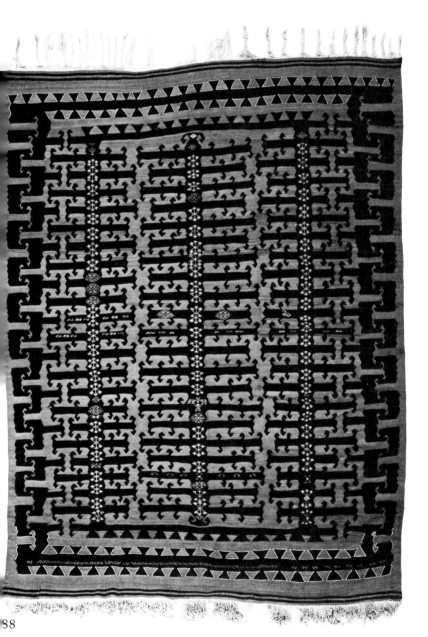

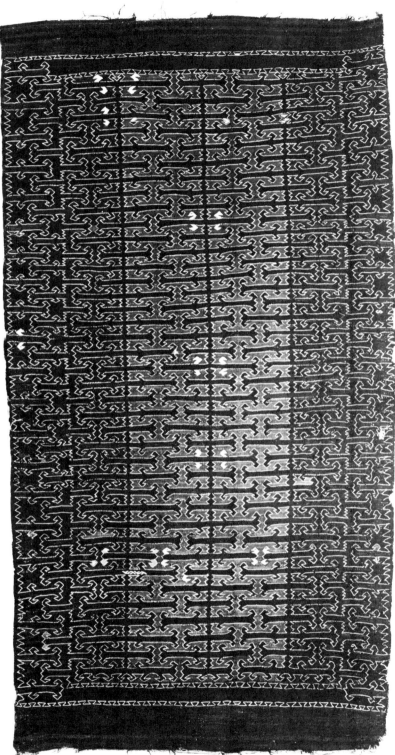

88

89

90

91

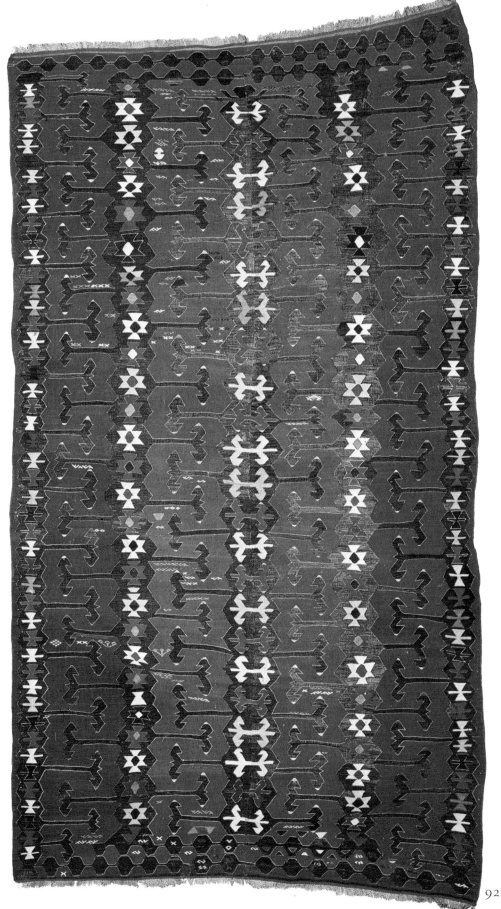

92

93

94

The Red and Blue Type

The patterns of these kilims are executed solely in these two colours, with the possible inclusion of white for the outline of the designs. The reds are made of madder and are of various tones such as oxblood and tomato. On later examples the red used is cochineal. The blues also vary from deep blue to light, sky blue. The patterns are very simple and bold; the only minor, infill motifs are executed in weft-float brocading. The weave of this type of kilim is one of the finest in west Anatolian.

88   *171 × 221 cm.*
89   *no size available*

Two related examples of this red and blue type of Balıkesir kilim. The pattern, though simple in concept, has a hooked outline of great complexity. The only infill decoration here consists of small brocaded motifs. The wavy lines at the ends of plates 92 and 93 here have the shape of a series of angular wedges. The field contains three 'trees' flanked by broad meandering lines. The main difference between the two kilims lies in the fact that plate 89, which seems to be the older of the two, has a two-tone red field like plate 92, while plate 88 has a uniform tomato-red ground.

90   *134 × 220 cm.*
91   *132 × 186 cm.*

The later pieces of this group have become much simplified in design. On plate 90 the hexagons and the bands of the field contain a single decorative ornament, a double-sided hooked motif. The plain border at the sides joins the field with an interlocking stepped pattern. Notice the alternation of colour in the border. The blue bands have a red border, the red bands, blue.

Plate 91 is a very simple, yet strong and attractive Balıkesir kilim, the plain tomato-red field contrasting successfully with the deep peacock-blue border.

All Balıkesir kilims of the red and blue type have a distinctive end finish, consisting of a series of narrow red and blue stripes across the width of the field. This feature does not seem to appear on pieces of the polychrome type.

The Polychrome Type

Balıkesir kilims of this latter type are more loosely woven than those of the former, resulting in a much heavier fabric, and their patterns are drawn on a larger scale. The predominant colours are still blue and red, to which green is occasionally added as a major colour at the centre of the composition: in earlier examples this is either bottle green or bluish green, while on more recent pieces it is olive green.

The minor designs are more prominent here than in the red and blue type, and are of a type common to all west Anatolian kilims. They are executed in slit tapestry in a variety of colours such as white, green, apricot, red and yellow, a feature which gives their distinctive colouring to these kilims.

92   *183 × 330 cm.*

One of the oldest and most powerful of Balıkesir kilims, this piece, which is woven in two joined halves, shows clearly the field-pattern illusion. The composition can be read as four vertical, red, angular, meandering bands floating on a blue field: the two outer ones in deep oxblood red and two inner ones in tomato red. Alternatively, it can be seen as a two-tone red field on which are placed stylized blue trees with horizontal branches culminating in pairs of latch-hooks. The designs are outlined in white, yellow and red wool. The woollen warps are of the 'salt-and-pepper' variety.

93   *172 × 280 cm.*
94   *175 × 275 cm.*

At first glance, the similarity of these two Balıkesir kilims is striking. Closer examination, however, shows a number of differences in the choice of the minor ornaments and variations in the arrangement of the hooked motifs. The overall appearance of plate 94 is somewhat simpler and more rigid than plate 93, as the central branches of the latter have two pairs of hooked motifs, whereas in the former they only have one. The only difference in colour is in the centre of the field, where plate 94 is light olive green and plate 93 is a deep sea-green.

West Anatolian Plain-field 'Manastir' Kilims

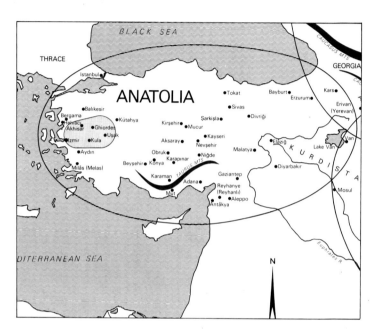

Few examples are known of this group of sparsely decorated west Anatolian kilims, most of which appear to be of considerable age. They are unsophisticated tribal pieces whose attraction lies in the simplicity and boldness of their designs and in the strength of their contrasting colours, most prominent among which are a deep tomato-red, a brilliant yellow and a mid-blue. The wool is thick and lustrous and the weave uneven, producing a textured surface which is further emphasized by the prominent abrash (variation in shade) of the colours. The unusually thin warps are of white wool and terminate in a braid and fringe arrangement similar to that of Balıkesir kilims. The decorative repertoire is very limited, consisting of large and small medallions with multiple serrated outlines. Large areas of the field, which is either blue or yellow, are left totally undecorated.

These kilims are reputedly woven east of Izmir in the region bounded by Akhisar, Uşak, Alaşehir and Izmir. A number of them have found their way to the markets of Izmir, Istanbul and the island of Lesbos, just off the Turkish coast. In the trade they are referred to as Manastir kilims.

95   *170 × 305 cm.*

The composition of this west Anatolian kilim, which consists of a plain field flanked by wide, decorated skirts, is more commonly encountered on the kilims of south-east Anatolia (plates 198 and 199). Apart from this feature, however, no two groups of Anatolian kilims could be more different. In appearance the present piece is reminiscent of some Kazak pile rugs from the Caucasus. The series of bold geometric hexagonal medallions is flanked by a large-scale 'running dog' pattern. The eccentric weft lines in the plain red field, combined with the abrash effect of the wool, add to its charm.

96   *160 × 305 cm.*

This is a more complex version of colour plate 95. The colour range, however, is the same. The 'running dog' motif of the last piece is replaced by a pattern of interlocking polychrome lozenges more often seen on the kilims of Aydın. The narrow black stripes containing crosses, which separate the bands, are a distinguishing feature common to all the kilims of this type.

97   *105 × 174 cm.*

This small prayer kilim is closely related to the two previous pieces, both in quality of wool and in coarseness of weave. The saw-tooth edge joining border and field and the serrated outline of the polygons are also characteristic of these kilims. The impression of a mihrab is suggested by a pointed arch floating on a sparsely decorated, deep yellow field. The colours are identical to those of colour plate 95.

95

96

97

Helvacı Mixed-technique Kilims

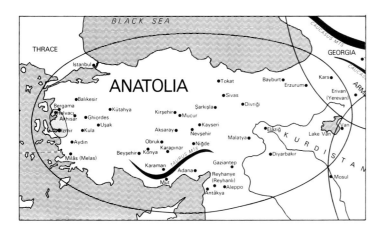

Another group of west Anatolian kilims is made near Aydın and known under the name of Helvacı. Kilims of this type are usually made in mixed technique, combining slit-tapestry weave with weft-float brocading; examples made purely in slit tapestry, such as plates 98 and 99, are rare.

These and the band kilims of Malatya (plates 238 to 244) are the only Anatolian flatweaves where, normally, two techniques are used with the same degree of emphasis. Their study can further our understanding of kilim designs, as the change they undergo in the adaptation to a different technique gives a better idea of the concepts behind these designs.

Helvacı kilims are immediately recognizable by the prominence of light pastel colours such as greenish yellow, pale green, sky blue and pink. Dark maroon, black, deep blue and red are also used, but it is the pale tones which give these kilims their distinctive appearance.

98   *102 × 444 cm.*

Those kilims of the Helvacı type that have a band composition are the only examples of the group that are always woven in slit tapestry. They have the characteristic range of pale colours typical of this group. All the designs are very simplified and stylized versions of motifs found in many Anatolian kilims, and the somewhat stiff way in which they are rendered here points

to the lateness of the Helvacı kilims, relatively few of which are devoid of chemical colours—a further proof of their lateness.

99   *110 × 158 cm.*

A colourful pattern of small hexagons surrounds the pale green field, on which, together with a variety of small field ornaments, there floats a pointed arch which lends a directional element to the composition. This form of implied mihrab is most unusual and known only on west Anatolian kilims. The large designs at the base of the mihrab and in the spandrels coincide with the position of the hands and the feet of the believer in the position of prayer but should not be seen as a stylization of them. The border pattern relates to that of plate 131, with which the present piece also shows strong colour similarities.

100   *109 × 145 cm.*

The bold, slit-tapestry linear border contrasts strongly with the busy decoration of the field. The designs of this piece are brocaded versions of the ones on plate 99; these include the large motifs in the mihrab, which are repeated in the spandrels, and the two ornaments at its base. In common with the two previous kilims, the top and bottom of this piece is defined by a narrow stripe of two-colour twining.

101   *172 × 223 cm.*

An example of a large Helvacı kilim, this piece is woven in two halves. The border is similar to that of plate 100, as is the deep maroon, tapestry-woven, weft-faced ground. The decoration here consists of large and small diamonds with multiple outlines. The colours are the typical pale ones associated with this type of kilim: yellow, light blue, light green, tomato-red and white.

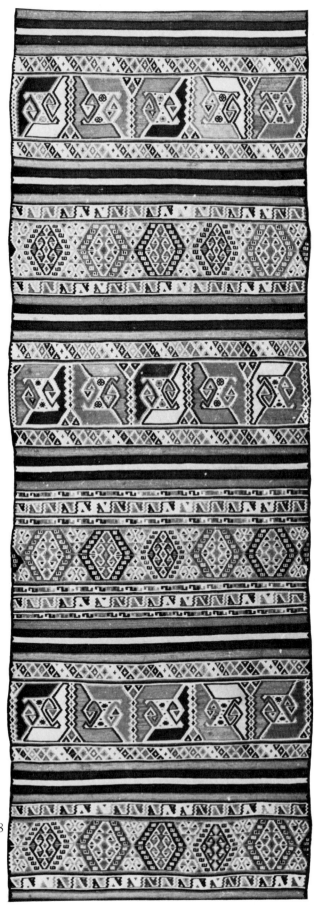

98

99

100

101

The Kilims of Mut

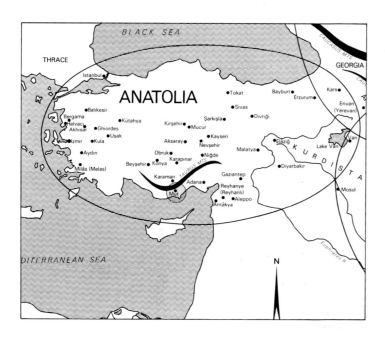

102   *160 × 300 cm.*

This kilim with chromatic similarities to the Mut pieces belongs to the group of 'Manastir' kilims, plates 95–97.

103   *130 × 197 cm.*
104   *132 × 200 cm.*
105   *190 × 414 cm.*

The mountainous region south of Konya, known since antiquity as the Taurus range, is sparsely inhabited by semi-nomadic shepherds. This inhospitable area was the home of many kilims. The pieces illustrated here are characteristic of kilims woven in a place called Mut, a large village about 80 km. south of Karaman.

These pieces share an uneven thick texture and very simple bold designs executed in brilliant and contrasting colours against a bright tomato-red ground.

Plates 103 and 104 are identical in almost every detail of weave and design. By sheer coincidence these two kilims happened to appear on the London market within a month of one another from two entirely different sources. At the top, their warps end in a flat braid, while at the bottom they form loops.

Plate 105 is unusually long for this type of kilim and lacks the narrow saw-tooth border of plates 103 and 104. Its texture and colours relate this piece to the prayer kilim in plate 117, which could also have the same provenance.

Mut kilims often have dark warps, sometimes of natural brown wool and sometimes of goat hair.

102

103

104

105

West Anatolian 'Karaman' Kilims

106   *177 × 207 cm.*

107   *155 × 350 cm.*
108   *158 × 363 cm.*

These typical west Anatolian kilims were probably woven within the same small area and at approximately the same time. The composition is common to both pieces: a conjoined hexagonal field pattern, flanked by double-sided animal forms related to those found on colour plate 135. The characteristic feature of this group is the border configuration: at the sides, a band containing a black and red reciprocal pattern joins the field by means of a stepped outline. This border is abruptly halted at the top and bottom ends by the skirt pattern of large repeat ornaments. Many such pieces can still be seen in the bazaars of Konya and Istanbul.

109   *138 × 208 cm.*
110   *115 × 195 cm.*

This is a somewhat unusual type of prayer kilim. The outline of the mihrab and the large border designs are not directly related to any other Anatolian prayer kilims. The colours and minor infill designs are typical of this family of kilims from the Konya region.

Both pieces have the same outer reciprocal border pattern in red and black, so common in kilims of this group (plates 107 and 112). The basic difference between the two pieces is primarily one of proportion and scale. On plate 109 the mihrab dominates the composition, while on plate 110 it is much smaller, the large independent border designs taking precedence. Both kilims have a brick-red mihrab with light green spandrels surrounded by a white border. Small quantities of cochineal red can be found in the minor designs.

111   *165 × 362 cm.*
112   *167 × 305 cm.*

The basic repeat-motif forming the grid pattern of both these kilims is a very archaic Anatolian design which can be found on a large number of village pile rugs of the seventeenth and eighteenth centuries. It is one of the most popular kilim designs, being used extensively throughout Anatolia, especially in the south-east (plates 205 and 210), see Designs, Patterns and Compositions. The triangular motifs are arranged in bands here, although the gaps between these motifs form a triangular lattice-like grid. The variations in the chromatic arrangement of each piece, however, create different field patterns. On plate 111 the pairs of superimposed triangular motifs—one the mirror image of the other—share the same colour, thus forming lozenges. The colour sequence of these lozenges forms a pattern of diagonal bands lying across the field from left to right. On plate 112 the triangular motifs are not the same colour as their mirror image; instead, the colours follow a diagonally offset formation from right to left, resulting in a triangular pattern in which the white lattice is visually predominant. The two pieces, which have an identical range of colours, originally had the same reciprocal red and black side-border pattern. On plate 111, however, the borders have been cut. Both pieces have a common type of end border, which also appears on plates 118 and 119.

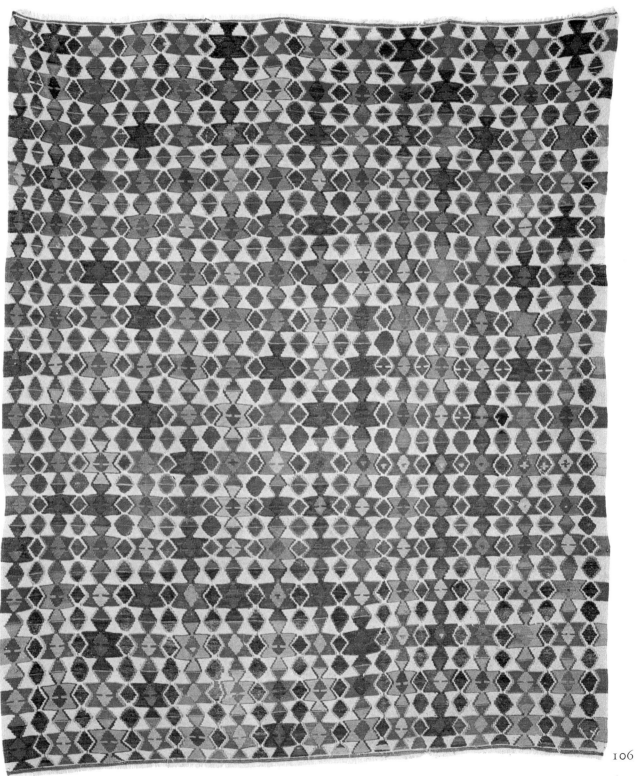

106

107

108

109

110

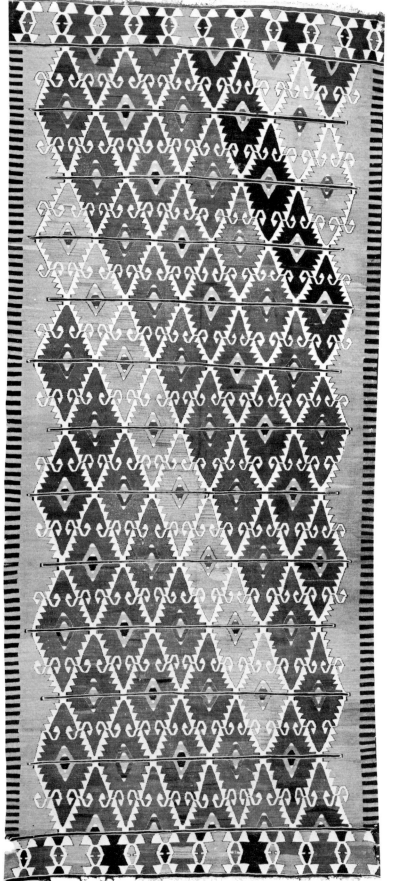

III

112

113

114

115

116

117

118

119

120

113   *135 × 191 cm.*

114   *140 × 173 cm.*   **116**   *114 × 178 cm.*
115   *133 × 181 cm.*   **117**   *139 × 200 cm.*

The four examples illustrated here are all variants of the most common type of west Anatolian prayer kilim of the Konya family. Such pieces were probably woven in a number of villages and, indeed, there are enough differences in both style and structure to suggest a different origin for each piece. A basic composition of multiple superimposed arches is common to all four.

Plates 114 and 115 appear to be the oldest of the four. The weave is finer, the colours mellower, and the drawing more elegant. Similar but more recent examples of plates 116 and 117 can be found with some synthetic dyes. The form of the arches of plate 117 occurs more commonly on weft-float brocaded kilims of the same area.

118   *150 × 250 cm.*

A powerful west Anatolian village kilim with a simple and direct appeal. Its pattern can be seen either as a series of elongated hexagons flanked by pairs of hooks, or as a series of hexagons into which large spearhead motifs protrude. The boldness of the field decoration is accentuated by the small-scale border motif of the most simple and elementary type, an angular stepped line which is most commonly seen as a guardstripe joining borders to fields (see plate 107).

119   *185 × 327 cm.*
120   *154 × 310 cm.*

Both kilims are of the same basic type as colour plate 118. Indeed, plate 119 is so similar in both colour and design that it was probably made in the same village. The only difference is that the hexagons are less flattened and, as a consequence, there are fewer of them, although the length of the two pieces is similar. Plate 120 is somewhat finer than both plates 118 and 119, and the drawing more elegant. The conjoined hexagons forming the field pattern contain facing pairs of large hooks, similar to the ones flanking them, instead of the multiple-hook hexagons of the previous two examples. On both these kilims, the bands of the two end-skirts have the same repeat motif creating a field-pattern illusion, though the drawing differs noticeably on each.

Multi-panel Kilims without Borders

The absence of borders, and a field divided into three or more panels separated by horizontal bands, represent a composition encountered with great frequency on kilims from many areas of west, central and south Anatolia. There are several versions of this composition, each displaying considerable variation in minor ornamentation, a fact consistent with the diverse origins of these kilims. Unfortunately, there is not enough specific information presently available to permit precise attributions; therefore, these kilims have been grouped here as a compositional type.

121   *166×303 cm.*

Each panel of the tripartite white field contains a rectangular medallion flanked by two half-medallions. On the kilims of this type which appear to be the oldest (the present piece being an example), the edges of the central medallion jut outwards while those of the side ones are indented, almost as if they were meant to fit into one another but had been forcibly separated. On more recent examples (plate 128) this feature is less prominent, the medallions becoming almost rigidly rectangular, and the only vestige of a connection between the medallions being suggested by the thin, hooked arms projecting out of the central medallion, and equivalent 'gaps' penetrating from the field into the side half-medallions.

The infill decoration of this finely woven piece is rich and varied, and it contains an astonishing number of colours, sixteen in all. A peculiarity of this kilim is that one half is wider than the other by about 20 cm.

122   *109×147 cm.*
123   *109×149 cm.*

These two curious prayer kilims are closely related to plate 121

in structure, minor designs and colour range. They are thought by many to come from the region around Adana in south Anatolia, and should this be the case, it would help to attribute plate 121 to the same region. This seems a likely attribution as the latter was found in the bazaar of Antâkya, (ancient Antioch), and there are a number of kilims with a more rigid version of the same composition that belong to the Reyhanlı group of south-east Anatolia (plate 191).

The unusual proportions of the field, greater in width than in length, are emphasized by the equally rare composition of a small mihrab floating on a much larger ground. On plate 122 a pair of arms terminating in floral forms appears at the top of the mihrab. Strangely, the same pair of arms is found also at the bottom of the mihrab of plate 123, a feature not found on any other Anatolian kilims.

The large-scale skirt pattern is commonly found on west Anatolian kilims like plates 107 and 108. The colour range of the latter two pieces, however, is altogether different and their texture much looser. These two examples probably date from the second half of the last century, plate 123 appearing to be slightly older than plate 122. The field colour of both is a deep rose red, and the borders are a dark inky blue.

124   *157×370 cm.*

The composition of this handsome kilim is similar to plate 121. The proportions are different, however, this piece being narrower and longer. The minor infill ornaments are also larger in scale, and the piece is less finely woven. The drawing of the medallions is more stylized, the interlock of the medallions being much less noticeable. The merit of this kilim lies primarily in the quality and warmth of its colours.

121

122

123

124

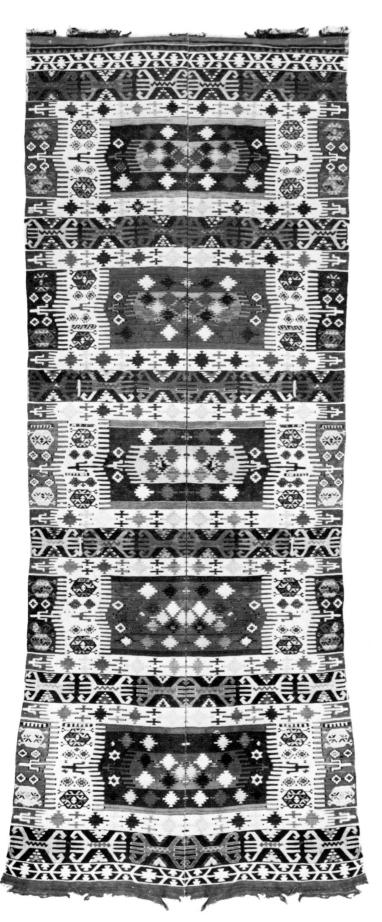

125

126

127

128

129

130

125   *142×361 cm.*

This is yet another variant of this composition: a finely woven kilim, which unlike plates 121 and 124, has a white cotton field, the three panels of the previous pieces being replaced by five. The colour range is delicate, harmonious and cool, with many shades of red, blue and green. The minor elements of decoration differ from both those of plates 121 and 124, and relate somewhat to central-south Anatolian kilims like plate 159, which also have the same colour range.

126   *no size available*

This kilim from the collection of the Türk ve Islâm Eserleri Museum in Istanbul belongs to the same group as plate 125. The texture and colours are identical, and the bands decorating the field have the same pattern as those dividing the field of plate 125 into panels. Though there are a number of types of Anatolian kilims with a band composition, few pieces have come to light with this pattern of alternately facing and opposing 'hands'.

127   *(Detail)*
128   *(Detail)*
129   *(Detail)*
130   *(Detail)*

Numerous examples of these very long kilims are known and many still appear in the rug trade, some of which contain synthetic dyes. The colour range is limited and quite sombre, the emphasis being on red, blue and dark brown.

Plates 127 and 128 have the same basic composition as plates 121 and 124. However the bands separating the panels are much wider, and there are more of them between each panel. The designs are repetitious and stylized, and arranged somewhat rigidly. Plates 129 and 130 also have a field divided into panels by a series of narrow bands. Here, however, the rectangular medallions of the previous pieces are replaced by striking, bold medallions of a complex hooked form, flanked by contrasting designs which are simple and firmly rectilinear. A very similar piece appeared at an auction in London (Sotheby Parke-Bernet, 29 March 1978, lot 75), bearing the date AH 1230 (AD 1815).

Aydın Kilims

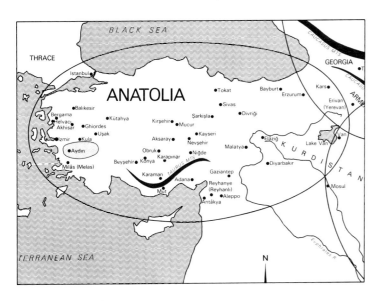

A number of kilims from west Anatolia are known by the name of Aydın kilims after a town off the Aegean coast, south of Izmir. These are among the largest Anatolian kilims, some of which are woven in two halves like the majority of those from west Anatolia (plate 132). More usually, however, they are woven in three parts (plates 131 and 133), a wide central panel being flanked by two narrow strips which form the borders. The reason for weaving kilims in this fashion is not clear; it certainly has nothing to do with the width of the loom. It may be that local weavers found it easier and quicker to weave the border patterns (which in any case were different from those of the field) separately and continuously, building a rhythm unbroken by the need to keep both border and field designs simultaneously in their minds. But there is also a functional explanation. In the mosques of Konya, kilims were hung as portières; In one such instance, a piece woven in two halves had been sewn together at the middle but the borders had been cut at the sides. The borders and the top were secured to the door frame; the field, acting as a loose flap, was pushed forward and backward by people going in and out of the mosque. In fact, by joining and cutting in this manner, the equivalent of a three-part kilim had been created. Thus it is possible that tripartite kilims were made to be used specifically as portières, although the first explanation appears the more likely one.

In common with west Anatolian kilims in general, the colours of Aydın pieces are bright and strong, their combination creating bold contrasts of light and dark. The weave is tight and the resulting fabric is fine by west Anatolian standards, although not as fine as some central and south-east Anatolian kilims. Aydın kilims have distinct end finishes: the border designs are followed by a series of narrow multicoloured stripes and a single row of twining; the white warps are gathered together in groups, knotted and then twisted to form a short fringe of about 5 cm. A further knot is then tied and the resulting strands left to form a tuft.

131 *155 × 425 cm.*
132 *153 × 407 cm.*

These are two representative examples of west Anatolian kilims of the Aydın type, which have almost identical field decoration in different colour combinations. The composition creates a field-pattern illusion: plate 131 can be seen either as a series of blue hexagons, each flanked by a pair of blue hooks on a white ground, or as a series of white hexagons, flanked by large trefoils pointing inwards, floating on a blue ground. Similarly, on plate 132 there is either a series of white hexagons flanked by pairs of hooks on a blue and red ground, or a series of red hexagons flanked by large blue trefoils floating on a white ground.

Plate 131 is woven in three parts, the two side-strips forming the borders. The designs of these borders should be compared with the bands flanking the skirts of plate 96 and with the border of plate 99. At both ends there are wide skirts containing an enlarged version of the border pattern.

Plate 132 is woven in two pieces. The deep salmon-red border has simple hooked ornaments and is flanked at the top and bottom by a wide band containing large hooked motifs similar to those on plates 135, 143 and 147.

131   132

133

134

133   *145 × 366 cm.*
134   *145 × 390 cm.*

Two more Aydın kilims woven in three parts. The side borders of both pieces consist of a series of juxtaposed rectangular compartments containing designs. The wide bands at the top and bottom of both kilims contain a very archaic reciprocal border design known from knotted Anatolian village rugs of the seventeenth to nineteenth centuries, in the latter century especially examples from Melas. The tapestry-woven plain white field of plate 133 is decorated with a variety of small brocaded ornaments. The borders flanking the field are divided into rectangular compartments of many colours with crenellated outlines, each containing a hexagon. The border compartments of plate 134 have a saw-tooth outline and contain hooked motifs similar to those found in the field. The large field-medallions with multiple, concentric, hooked outlines are of a type found on west Anatolian kilims in general, and are one of their distinctive characteristics. The treatment of the field and its division into compartments, however, is peculiar to Aydın kilims.

West and Central Anatolia: Kilims of the Konya Region

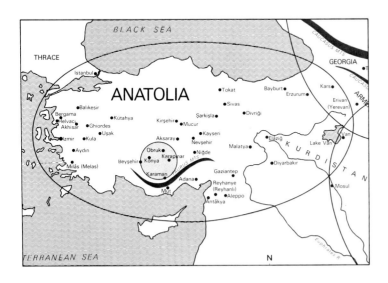

Among all Anatolian kilims, a place of honour is deservedly given to the white-ground kilims of west and central Anatolia, which are commonly attributed to the Konya region. There is little evidence that these kilims were woven in Konya itself, though large numbers of them appeared in its bazaars and some were found in the local mosques. They bear some relation in colour to the Konya pile rugs, though these do not usually have the white ground so prominent in the kilims. The term Konya should be understood to refer to the large area whose centre is the city of that name, as these white-ground kilims are related both to those of the Aydın region to the west, and to those of Aksaray and Niğde to the east. It is arguable that 'Karamani', their old trade name, is the generic term that describes these kilims best. In older times, Karaman not only denoted the city south of Konya, but also the whole area of central-south Anatolia whose administrative capital was Konya.

Konya kilims are easily recognizable. They are made entirely of wool, none of them having any cotton. They are not particularly fine and the weave is loose. They are woven in slit tapestry and most of the designs are highlighted with weft wrapping. The colours are strong and deep, and their combinations create powerful contrasts. None of the older examples has any cochineal red, or even a madder-dyed red of 'cochineal' hue. The ground is usually white, though occasionally red or blue grounds also occur. The majority are woven in two halves, while there are examples woven in three pieces and others in one. Small kilims are not common; pieces usually vary from 2.5 m. to 5 m. in length.

135   *173 × 411 cm.*

This is one of the most beautiful kilims. The colours are of high quality and their combinations extremely harmonious. The bold and powerful pattern is drawn in an irregular, almost naive manner; an impression strengthened by the presence of the strange long-bodied and two-legged animals. The overall effect is charming.

The plain wide blue band forming the basic pattern is highlighted by the narrow bands of red and yellow which flank it. Woven in two halves, it is unlikely that this kilim would have had a main border at the sides; instead, it is edged by a bold red reciprocal pattern with a serrated outline, the same border concept as occurs on plates 137 and 153. The end border configuration should be compared with that of plate 147. Large numbers of more recent kilims with the same overall composition contain double-sided variants of the long-bodied animals found on this piece (plates 107 and 108).

136   *190 × 414 cm.*

While the blue lattice is basically the same as those on the more finely woven kilims of Aydın (plate 131), its proportions are different. The repeat motif on the end skirts is similar to those on plates 135, 143 and 144, though here it is drawn on a much smaller scale. Possibly the most striking feature of this kilim is the bold, wavy, mauve, blue and maroon border which flanks the field; no other west Anatolian kilim with such a border solution has been observed.

137   *139 × 365 cm.*

Plate 137 is comparable to colour plate 135 not only for the drawing of the pattern, but also for the exquisite colour range which the two pieces share. The lattice on both is of an unusual form; instead of creating a continuous hexagonal pattern, joining the end borders with a complete or a half hexagon, on these kilims it culminates at both ends in forms that resemble pairs of outstretched arms, thus creating a finite pattern. Whereas the sides of the field are often filled either with many minor designs (plate 131) or with animals (plate 135), on plate 137 as on plate 136 we find smaller versions of the central hexagonal medallions. The side borders also relate in type to plate 135. Here, however, the reciprocal red angular pattern has a hooked outline, while on the former it had a serrated edge. A similar red border appears on yet another early piece, plate 153.

138   *164 × 400 cm.*

The quality and mellowness of the colours, together with the almost complete corrosion of the black parts of the designs, give this finely woven piece the appearance of great age. The basic pattern is the same as that of plate 137; two angular blue bands forming hexagons flanked with pairs of hooks are placed on a deep tomato-red ground. Here, however, the hexagonal medallions, both inside and outside the blue field pattern, are much larger and more prominent than on plate 137. Further-

more, they have a hooked outline whereas on plate 137 there is a serrated one.

This kilim has a very narrow reciprocal side border, which is a small-scale version of the ones on plates 108 and 110. The cartouches in the skirts are common to west Anatolian kilims. The end bands, however, have an unusual pattern of interlocking 'S' forms which is known only on a few early pieces. (Compare the pattern with that of plate 8 in *The Undiscovered Kilim.*) It appears to be a rare variant of the common west Anatolian pattern found on plates 141 and 142.

139   *168 × 409 cm.*

The composition of this kilim is of the same type as those of the last four pieces. The texture, however, is much heavier and looser, and the colours deeper. Six large hexagonal polychrome medallions float on a deep indigo-blue field which is surrounded by a brick-red border. Close comparison should be made with plate 132 which has similar basic colours and patterns.

140   *168 × 380 cm.*
141   *188 × 417 cm.*

The basic feature of both these kilims is the series of large, multi-layered, hooked hexagons in the middle of the field. On plate 140, however, the hexagons are conjoined and contained within a continuous blue and white outline. The field flanking the hexagons is divided into panels of different colours, the colour change occurring at the base of the hexagons. On plate 141 the medallions float independently on the uniform white ground.

The two kilims share a large variety of small infill ornaments and the bands of continuous interlocking 'S' forms at the ends; the borders, however, are of a different type, although both are common to west and central Anatolian kilims. Plates 139, 140 and 141 have the same loose and heavy texture and share a common chromatic range, albeit with variations of emphasis on individual colours.

135

136

137

138

139

140

141

142

143

144

145

146

147

148

149

142   *185 × 422 cm.*

The boldness and freedom of the composition, combined with the exquisite colours, make this one of the most exceptional kilims of the Konya type. The five abstract medallions are of a form not seen on any other piece, with the possible exception of early central Anatolian village pile rugs. Woven in two pieces, the white field is surrounded by a border consisting of a continuous series of small rectangular compartments, which contain interlocking geometric motifs, more often found on kilims of the 'Aksaray' type. The end borders are flanked by skirts decorated with a section of an endless pattern of carnation or animals motifs, commonly found on kilims of the Konya-Niğde type (plates 153 and 156). The narrow band at the two ends, containing a continuous interlocking 'S' motif, is a common feature on many types of west and central Anatolian kilims but does not seem to occur so often on pieces made further east.

Kilims with Angular Hooked Medallions

The composition of an angular lattice with large hooked motifs on a white field appears to have been very popular among the weaving villages of west Anatolia. While this composition was common to a large number of kilims, it differs in style and proportions from piece to piece, and the minor infill ornaments were used in various interchangeable ways. Nevertheless, kilims are often found which are so similar that they were probably made in the same place and within a very short time (plates 143 and 144, 145 and 146). Kilims of this group, when examined in quantity, allow all sorts of chronological and geographical sequences to be built through the relationships of individual ornaments, colours and textures. Absence of hard evidence, however, makes such sequences largely conjectural.

143   *163 × 344 cm.*
144   *no size available*

Comparing very closely related kilims in terms of both similarities and differences is possibly the best means of gaining an insight into their designs and compositions. These two pieces are a case in point. Both kilims have three large medallions with a bold three-layer outline, floating on a white field and separated from each other by means of a row of small hexagons. On the red border float small hooked ornaments separated by lines. This is an intermediate stage between the separate rectangular compartment border of plates 134 and 142 and a repeat motif border like that of plate 141. The skirts at the two ends are of the same type as those of plates 132, 135 and 147. The difference between the two pieces lies in the choice and arrangement of the minor infill motifs and in the nature of the guardstripes. On plate 144 a brown crenellated stripe joins field to border, while on plate 143 a stepped outline is formed by the overlapping of field and border.

145   *165 × 400 cm.*
146   *155 × 396 cm.*

Another two almost identical kilims, although both appear more recent than the two previously illustrated examples. However all four are related in terms of composition, and almost certainly have a common ancestry. The large independent hooked ornaments of plates 143 and 144 are here conjoined into a continuous series. The hooks are increased in size, but their outline is slimmer. The repeat border cartouches are those seen in the end borders of plate 135, and the overall border configuration is similar to plate 149. The guardstripe pattern is common to the Konya-Niğde kilims plates (151 and 152) and even more so to the south-east Anatolian kilims of the Aleppo group (plates 192 and 197). The chromatic range is limited; the most prominent colours are the red and blue which form the outline of the medallions, and the whole of the field, which is of white cotton. Both the presence of cotton and the colours indicate a relationship between these two kilims and those of the Konya-Niğde group (plates 150 and 151).

147   *155 × 425 cm.*

An unusual kilim, this crisp and well-drawn piece is woven in three parts, a central panel with two narrower border strips. The end skirts have the common repeat motif found on many west Anatolian kilims (plates 132, 135 and 144). The outer reciprocal guardstripe has a pattern encountered on seventeenth-century west Anatolian 'large pattern Holbein' rugs.

Five large hooked motifs float on the white field; each of them consists of a small hexagonal medallion from which sprout four pairs of hooked arms. The outline of these arms forms a secondary hooked pattern on the white ground, resulting in a field-pattern illusion. The narrow multicoloured stripes at the ends of the kilim are similar to those on plate 148, and the short fringe relates this piece to the kilims of the Aydın type.

148   *163 × 408 cm. (Detail)*

The large ornaments of this kilim are of the same type as those of plate 147. Here, however, the central hexagon is much larger and the hooked arms are shorter, giving an altogether different appearance to the design. The borders have different designs of an interlocking type, but, again like plate 147, they are woven on the separate side-strips which flank the field panel. It is interesting to note that, whereas plate 147 has a reciprocal guardstripe at the outer edge of the side borders, here a reciprocal guardstripe of a different and more complex pattern is between the border and the field, a more usual position on three-piece kilims (see plates 151 and 152).

149   *129 × 220 cm.*

Small pieces of this type are very unusual. The single, large, hooked ornament in the field is a variant of those seen on the last few kilims. The side borders are the same as on plate 145, but the end skirts have a combination of the patterns on plates 145 and 147. The inner guardstripe is like the one on plate 148.

Central Anatolia: Konya-Niğde Kilims

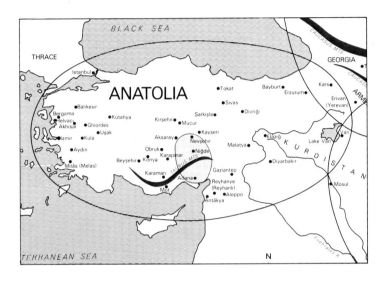

GROUP A

The following three kilims are closely related to each other. Though they have archaic patterns, none appears to be earlier than the middle of the last century. They are all woven in three pieces and have the same border design at the sides, which consists of an angular zigzag band filled on each side with hooked motifs. This type is among the oldest generic types of Anatolian kilim border designs and can be traced back to the beginning of the eighteenth century and possibly earlier (see chapter on designs, patterns and compositions). Examples of other variants of the wavy-line border appear in plates 157, 158 and 160.

The colour range of these three pieces is that shown on colour plate 152. The weave is even and flat and of medium fineness, producing a fabric common to most good kilims of west and central Anatolia. An interesting feature of tripartite kilims is that the guardstripe separating the field from the border is always drawn on the side pieces, never at the edge of the

wide field panel. At the actual joints the border strips and field panel have the same colour, that of the field background.

150   *156×417 cm.*
151   *150×375 cm.*

The differences in these two almost identical kilims are minimal. Plate 151, which belongs to the collection of the Islamisches Museum in East Berlin, has somewhat fatter medallions than plate 150, which has an extra end border containing long cartouches. The guardstripes of the two pieces are also different: plate 151 has the same one as plate 152, while plate 150 has the one found on plate 157, an earlier kilim of the same family. The reciprocal hooked guardstripe motif of plate 151 is commonly found on south-east Anatolian kilims (plate 192) and, drawn on a larger scale, it appears as a border design on another group of west Anatolian kilims (plates 107 and 108). The large medallions with the red and blue outlines should be compared with those on plates 143, 145 and 149. Plate 150, the more finely woven of these two kilims, has a white field, made of cotton and wool.

152   *168×402 cm.*

The field consists of bands of floral motifs which are angular stylizations of the carnation motifs found on sixteenth- to seventeenth-century Brusa velvets. Unlike most other kilims of this type, where the designs are directional, this piece can be viewed from both ends, as the bands of carnations are arranged symmetrically along a central band containing a double version of the design. The end borders are decorated with a repeat of a very old design traceable to Seljuk architectural ornament, and should be compared with those of plates 157 and 161.

150

151

152

GROUP B

The pieces illustrated in the next five plates belong to one of the oldest and most refined groups of central Anatolian kilims, which were probably woven somewhere in the region between Konya and Niğde. They all seem to date from the second half of the eighteenth century to the beginning of the nineteenth, an inference supported by the elegance of the patterns and compositions in conjunction with the antiquity of the designs and the exquisite quality of the colours. The carnation pattern of plate 157 is a stylized derivation of a classical Ottoman textile design. The large hexagonal medallion, surrounded by small diamonds on plates 154, 155 and 156, and by leaves on plate 153, can be traced back to fifteenth-century Turkey, Byzantium and Sassanian Iran. The border designs, the drawing of the small motifs and the colours, link these pieces to a number of other kilims from central Anatolia, some from the north (like the Aksaray group), some from the west (plates 135 and 142) and some from the east (plates 185 and 197).

153   *141 × 442 cm.*

This is probably the earliest example in the group and displays its typical composition: a field of white wool with two rows of large floating hexagonal medallions which is framed by a narrow border and flanked by skirts of astonishing width. No other kilim known has such wide skirts. The main border is like that of plate 180, which is from the same general area. The narrow end borders have an unusual version of a typical Anatolian border design which also appears on plate 178. The colours are sober, cool and harmoniously balanced. Predominant among them are purple, green, blue, red and white. Unlike plates 154, 155 and 156, where the medallions are surrounded by small diamonds, here their place is taken by 'leaves' of the same type as those flanking the carnations on plates 152 and 157. It is these leaves, together with the skirt pattern, the colour range, and the texture which determine the attribution of all these kilims to the same family.

154   *140 × 374 cm.*

This bold and simple kilim shows another variation on this composition. The medallions, simpler and more stylized, float on a white cotton ground. This creates a sharp contrast with the bright and deep colours. Although this piece and plate 153 have the same range of colours, the change of emphasis in their combination brings about a totally different effect. The border pattern, floating on a tomato-red ground, appears to be the precursor of those found on Aksaray kilims (plates 171 and 172).

155   *143 × 400 cm.*
156   *87 × 426 cm.*

In two more variants of this large medallion composition, the white fields of plates 153 and 154 have become the brilliant, deep tomato-red of plate 155 and the deep blue of plate 156. Unlike the other two kilims where the skirts were placed outside the borders, here the skirts are contained within them. The end borders on both pieces have the same pattern. On plate 156 this is the normal horizontal version of the side border design which is common to the next group of kilims (plates 158 and 159), but the side borders of plate 155 have an elegant reciprocal wavy line, which also appears in early Anatolian architectural decoration and on north-west Persian kilims (plate 335). The skirt patterns are of the same general type. Those of plate 155, however, together with the pointed design joining the skirts to the field, are similar to the borders of Aksaray kilims (plate 171), while those of plate 156 have the carnation design seen on the field of plate 157, with which it is also linked by similarities in colour and in the side border.

157   *164 × 448 cm.*

The archaic carnation pattern and the beauty of the colours make this a truly magnificent kilim. It is closely related to plate 152, sharing with it the basic field pattern, the end border designs and a similar side border pattern. The drawing of the field, however, is much more elegant. Here, the carnations all point in the same direction and are contained within a striking, terracotta red border. The white field is mostly wool, but in parts is a combination of wool and cotton, a feature not uncommon on kilims from this part of Anatolia.

153

154

155

156

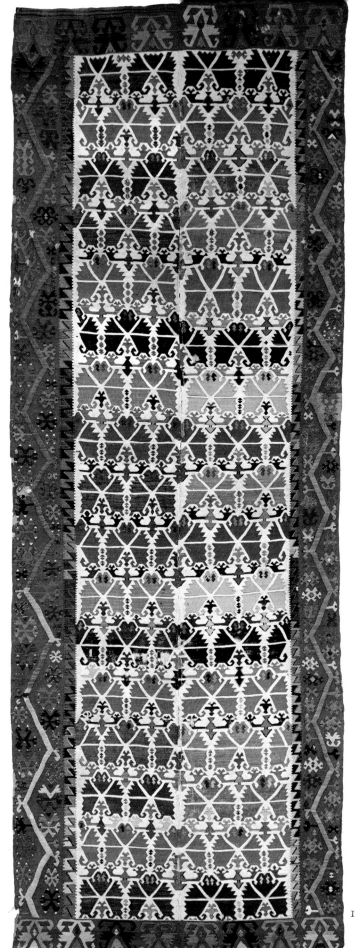

157

GROUP C: NIǦDE-ADANA

The kilims shown in the following three plates are from the same general area of central Anatolia, woven probably somewhere in the region between Niǧde and Adana. Their distinguishing characteristics are floral borders and geometric field patterns. They lack the freedom of the pieces in the previous group. They compensate, however, by a precision of drawing and execution, producing attractive, crisp and clearly defined compositions, in which the strictly geometric field patterns interact harmoniously with the flowing floral motifs in the borders.

158   *167 × 337 cm.*

The warm red border makes a powerful contrast to the cool colouring of the field, as does the continuous flowing, floral border decoration to the austerely geometric field pattern. The hexagonal medallions are diagonally offset on a 60-degree grid, but the rigidity of the pattern is broken by the change in colour of the background.

The medallions of this kilim are simplified smaller versions of those of the previously illustrated group. Many late examples of this type of kilim exist, but they lack any movement and elegance, the drawing of the designs being much more degenerate.

A bold linear pattern of horizontal stripes, bisected by a vertical stripe, effects the transition between the field and the border and appears superimposed on both. The floral border design occurs on a number of early kilims from the end of the eighteenth century, such as plate 156, although a stiffer version survives well into the twentieth. However, pieces made after the middle of the nineteenth century all seem to have a white ground border, dark colours such as the red of the present piece vanishing quite early.

159   *162 × 451 cm.*
160   *168 × 406 cm.*

These two powerful kilims share the same composition of complex abstract medallions placed on a blue field, which is surrounded with the floral border common to all the kilims of this type. The colours are deep and strong, and the vocabulary of designs richly varied. Among the minor designs in the field are the small hexagons that formed the field pattern of plate 158.

Plate 159 has a row of five large medallions, and plate 160 has four. The guardstripe patterns joining the borders to the field are different, and so is the choice, scale and arrangement of the minor and infill designs. The unusual hooked motif contained within the hexagons at the centre of the large medallions relates to pile rugs attributed by Erdmann to sixteenth- to eighteenth-century Anatolia *(700 Years of Oriental Carpets,* plate 121), and can be seen on south-east Anatolian kilims of the 'Aleppo' group (plate 188). In more recent times the composition of these attractive kilims was copied in many places in Anatolia, even as far east as Lake Van near the Persian frontier. Such later pieces, however, lack the strength of design and the quality of these older examples. Plate 160 is published in colour in *The Undiscovered Kilim.*

161   *148 × 365 cm.*

Like plate 219, this kilim has a wide range of designs which connect it to a number of other groups from central and east Anatolia, a fact which suggests an attribution to the same general area as the last three pieces. The floral side borders are of the same type as those on plates 158 and 160; the guardstripes, similar to those on plates 157 and 183, and the end border designs are stylized variants of the ones on plates 152 and 157. The floral trellis pattern in parts of the field relates this kilim to the south-east Anatolian Reyhanlı kilims (plate 210) and is also found in the spandrels of east Anatolian prayer kilims (plate 259). Finally, the hooked motifs in the remainder of the field are common to prayer kilims from Obruk (plate 166) and Sivas (plate 255). The warmth of the colours, however, indicates a more western provenance and, together with the reasons given above, strengthens its tentative attribution to the Niǧde region.

158

159

160

161

The Kilims of Obruk

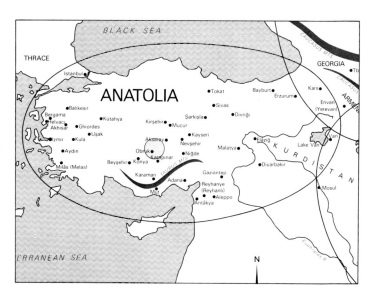

162	*145 × 172 cm.*		**165**	*122 × 172 cm.*
163	*126 × 180 cm.*		**166**	*120 × 178 cm.*
164	*128 × 182 cm.*		**167**	*135 × 439 cm.*

Obruk kilims are among the most easily identifiable Anatolian flatweaves. Almost all are prayer kilims. Large numbers of them were made, most of which date from the latter part of the nineteenth century up to the present time.

Few of the older pieces have survived, and they differ markedly from the later pieces both in fineness of weave and in quality of colour. Designs, however, remain fairly constant. The main colours are sober and cool, consisting mostly of different shades of blue, green, mauve, red and white; apricots, yellows and red are used in the small infill designs of the early examples. The colour repertoire changes drastically in more recent examples, the emphasis being on bright light tones, most of which are derived from synthetic dyes.

The repertoire of designs is limited and repetitive. Prominent in the decoration of the borders is a section of an endless cruciform pattern, the best illustration of which appears on plate 163. Patterns of this type can also be seen on the kilims of the Sivas-Malatya region (plate 245) and on some Persian kilims of Fars (plate 410). The mihrabs are usually well-proportioned and have a pointed arch which blends with the sprandrels by means of a bold reciprocal latch-hook pattern. The top of the arch culminates in a stylized tree motif which is then repeated in the spandrels. The field of the mihrab can be plain, as on plate 165, or decorated, as on plates 163 and 164. These last two examples are among the oldest kilims of this group; the simplicity of their decoration and the elegance of their proportions are most attractive. The repeat designs of the outer border of plate 166 are not characteristic of Obruk kilims but typical of the neighbouring kilims of the Sivas region (plate 255). Plate 167 shows an example of a long and narrow type of kilim also attributable to Obruk.

Painting by Edward Lear (1812–88) showing an Obruk kilim.

162

163

164

165

166

167

Aksaray Kilims

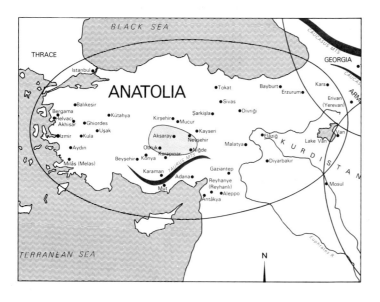

The following five kilims are known in Turkey under the name of Obruk or Aksaray, both towns located east of Konya on the road between Konya and Kayseri. There is, however, an established kilim-weaving tradition in Obruk producing prayer kilims (see plates 162 to 166) that are noticeably different in both texture and design from the present pieces. Furthermore, the latter are related by similarities of major and minor designs to the kilims of Kayseri and of south-east Anatolia. It is more reasonable, therefore, to attribute them to Aksaray, which is about 75 kilometres east of Obruk.

168   *no size available*

This powerful kilim is tentatively attributed to this group because of the colours, side border designs and some infill designs in the field. The end borders and the major field ornaments, however, indicate a more westerly origin. No other closely related piece has come to light. It is just possible that this is one of the problem pieces, the result of a weaver who moved with marriage or migration, and used designs from her

place of origin combined with those of her place of adoption, and the latter's available materials.

169   *158 × 379 cm.*

By comparison, this is a more easily recognizable Aksaray kilim. The border is characteristic of the group and so are the large hooked medallions. The latter, of course, together with the infill designs, are also found on the south-east Anatolian kilims of the Aleppo group. The drawing and scale of these designs and their combinations of colours place this kilim firmly in the present group.

170   *105 × 368 cm.*

Though well drawn and finely woven on a dark blue ground, this is a late version of this type of kilim, containing a red colour of possibly synthetic origin. The infill motifs of both field and border relate this piece to some others belonging to a neighbouring group, the 'Rashwan' kilims of central Anatolia (plate 223).

171   *152 × 358 cm.*

This is a relatively early example of an Aksaray kilim. The large ornaments floating on the white field are elegantly proportioned and combine with the white ground to form a field-pattern illusion. The designs on the side borders are similar to those on plates 169 and 172, and can be read in two ways: either as pairs of hands alternately facing and opposing each other, or as a section of an endless pattern of offset star-shaped polygons. The noticeably wider end borders are decorated with a series of designs of the same general type as those of the side borders; such designs are common in many groups of Anatolian kilims. In western pieces they usually appear in side

68

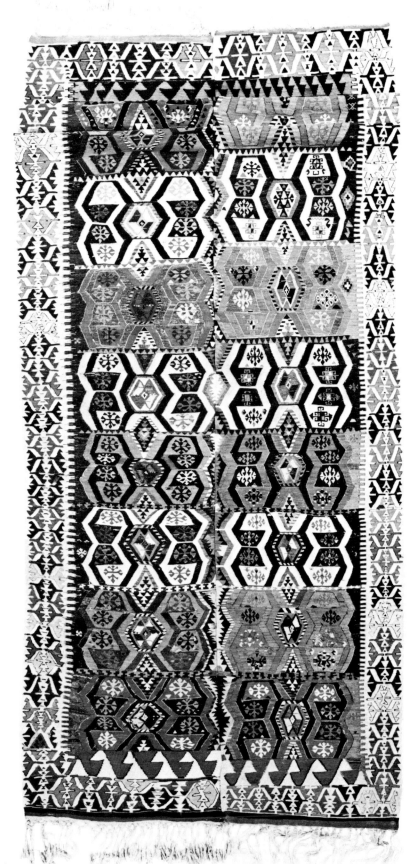

169

170

171

172

borders (plates 140 and 142), while on central and east Anatolian kilims they appear as both field and border ornaments, but on a much smaller scale (plates 245 and 247). Of all the known kilims of this type, this is the only example with three rows of large designs instead of the usual two or one.

172   *147 × 407 cm.*

The merit of this piece lies in the variety and excellence of its strong colours. Their wide range and the quality of the materials indicate that this is one of the earliest pieces of the Aksaray group. Both field and border designs are very close to those of plate 171, as are the designs on the side borders. The borders of the two pieces, however, should be compared, as they show different variations on a single theme, i.e. combinations of the same elements to form different patterns. The weavers of Aksaray kilims did not seem particularly concerned about matching the designs on the two halves of the kilim. There does not seem to be any correspondence in the infill designs in the centre of this kilim, nor was there any attempt to match the large ornaments in the middle of plate 171. The end borders on both pieces match well, however, the overall length of each half being the same.

Central Anatolian Yürük Kilims

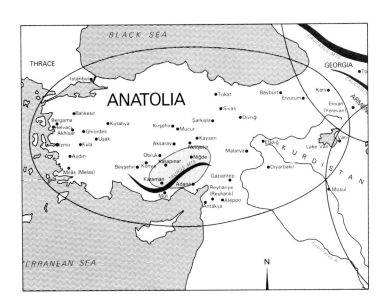

These simple village kilims from central Anatolia are grouped together because of their common colour range, texture and similarities in design. They seem to be related to the Konya group of kilims, to those of Aksaray and to those of south-east Anatolia. Furthermore, their similarities in colour with Yürük pile rugs would suggest an origin somewhere east of Konya and south of Kayseri.

175   *no size available*
176   *no size available*

There is hardly any difference between these two kilims. They both have a field divided into rectangles of different colours, joined together by means of black horizontal stripes and vertical crenellated lines. The chromatic arrangement of the rectangles forms a pattern of two large diamonds. Both pieces have thirteen rectangles along their length and five along their width. The design within the rectangles is an archaic motif which can be traced back to rugs appearing in fifteenth-century Flemish paintings by Hans Memling and, more recently, in vil-

lage rugs and kilims from both Anatolia and the Caucasus (plate 280). The version found on these two kilims is an interesting variant of the design (plate 173).

173

Detail from pile rug in a painting by Hans Memling, fifteenth century.

174 Detail from kilim

Instead of angular hooks coming directly from the body of the stepped medallion, floating black 'S' forms surround it, creating the same effect. This type of motif, on a much smaller scale, is a common infill design on south-east Anatolian kilims, but this is the only group on which it appears as a major field ornament.

177   *no size available*

The field designs of this kilim are the same as those of the last two pieces. Unlike them, however, it has a random chromatic arrangement of the rectangles, and the designs are woven more loosely, lacking their precision of execution. Furthermore, it is surrounded by a white border decorated with the same design as the centre of the stepped medallions.

178   *170×380 cm.*
179   *152×375 cm.*

These two pieces have a most unusual composition which is very rarely seen on kilims; it is reminiscent of some Yürük pile rugs, to which they are also related in terms of colour. Plate 178, which is the finer of the two, has the same border and infill motifs as plate 177. The white band at the top and bottom contains a very archaic variant of a common Anatolian end border; it appears in the same version on plate 153 which is from the same general area, and in its more normal form on plate 141 and 142, both of which come from further west.

Plate 179 retains the side border designs of plate 178. The field, however, contains different infill designs, such as six-pointed stars with *yin-yang* interiors, but mostly small hexagons with 'H' motifs. In common with plate 178, plate 179 has border designs at the ends which differ from those at the sides. The 'running dogs' of the former are here replaced by rectangular compartments containing hooked designs. This type of border is more common on kilims from further west, such as plate 147. The colours of these kilims are chiefly dark and light blue, light green, apricot, tomato red, brown, yellow and white.

175

176

177

178

179

Adana-Gaziantep Kilims

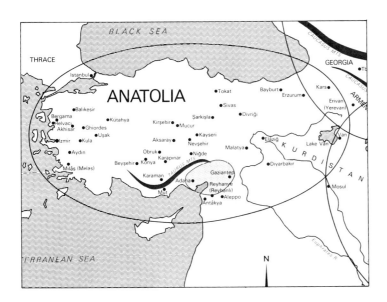

Central Anatolia is a region rich in kilim production; many distinct groups were woven there, although often pieces are found which combine characteristics of more than one group. The present kilims are of a most fascinating and important type. They are made in the southern part of central Anatolia, somewhere in the Adana-Gaziantep region, and date from the beginning to the middle of the nineteenth century. Their importance lies in the fact that they are prototypes for the well-known and numerous south-east Anatolian kilims of the Aleppo region. These latter pieces all date from the middle to the end of the nineteenth century.

180   *161 × 475 cm.*

An early example, this well-drawn kilim contains the full repertoire of minor ornaments associated with this group of kilims, especially the six-pointed star, the small stepped diamond, the *yin-yang* and the 'latch-hook' diamonds. The large designs are

180

181

182

183

184

185

common on south-east Anatolian kilims of the nineteenth century but there they are placed on a ground of vari-coloured bands. Here, the latch-hook diamonds in between the main designs are indented, merely implying the division of the plain white field into wide horizontal bands. This piece should be compared to plate 153 for the reciprocal side border and to plate 198 for the reciprocal end pattern and the field decoration.

181   *122 × 197 cm.*

Prayer kilims of this group are rare. The drawing of the mihrab is forceful and well-proportioned. The multitude of small *yin-yang* in the spandrels adds to the cerulean effect of the top of the piece. The colours have the subdued harmony typical of this group.

182   *101 × 147 cm.*

The colours of this small kilim are closely related to those of the prayer kilim plate 181. Prominent among these are green, mauve, cochineal red, salmon pink, madder red and blue. The border should be compared with those of plates 181, 223 and 245, all from the neighbouring areas.

183   *164 × 394 cm.*

This is the most recent of the six pieces illustrated, dating from the second half of the nineteenth century. The minor designs are, nevertheless, clearly those of this group. The guardstripes are similar to those on the kilims of Nigde (plate 150). The repeat border motif and the major field designs should be compared with those of Aleppo kilims (plate 201).

184   *146 × 372 cm.*

This is yet another example which demonstrates the similarities and strong relationships this group of kilims has with the south-east Anatolian kilims from Aleppo. The field decoration has the same pattern of large 'capped hexagons' as plates 192 and 193. Like plate 180, however, they are not placed in bands, the usual arrangement in Aleppo kilims, but are on a plain white ground. The colours and minor infill designs are typical of the present group. The piece is superbly highlighted by a 'double latch-hook' reciprocal border of pale green. The same pattern appears (usually in black and red) on west Anatolian kilims (plate 107) and as a guardstripe pattern on Aleppo kilims (plate 192).

185   *153 × 427 cm.*

A simple and most attractive composition consisting of a series of conjoined white diamonds with a multiple inner and outer outline. The row of diamonds floats on a maroon field decorated with ornaments that should be compared with those of the Niğde kilims (plates 155 and 156), of which these are minor versions. The repeat border design contains at the centre the *yin-yang* motif; its form, however, also appears on Yürük kilims (plate 179). Though at first sight the composition is similar to 'Rashwan' kilims, there the diamond forms differ in outline, covering the entire field instead of floating on a plain field. The minor infill designs are also different and, of course, so is the chromatic range.

South-east Anatolian Kilims

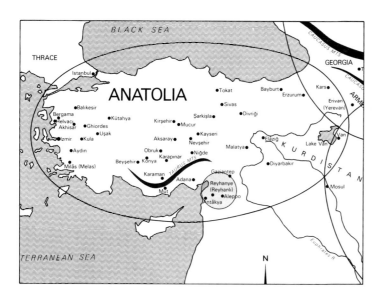

GROUP A: ALEPPO

This is one of the most prominent and easily identifiable groups of Anatolian kilims. They were made in south-east Anatolia, in the region whose administrative capital during the Ottoman period was the city of Aleppo in north Syria. Many of them are still found there, often being used as curtains and door-hangings in old houses. Local accounts suggest that every house had a few of them in the past, and it is likely that they were woven for these specific purposes. However, they do not appear to have been custom-made, as many were too long and had to be folded at the top before being hung.

These functions may explain why they were always woven in two pieces, something that has long puzzled students of kilims. The reason often given is that they were made by nomads, constantly on the move, who used narrow looms which were easy to transport. It seems unlikely that this could be the only explanation. In the first place, not all the kilims were woven by nomads, and secondly, many of the weavings they did make were in a single piece much wider than half a

kilim. Furthermore, a nomadic loom usually consisted of no more than two poles pegged in the ground; thus the problem of transporting a large loom was not of paramount importance, expecially as weaving was not practised while on the move. Finally Aleppo kilims, through their sophistication and precision of drawing, appear to be the work of settled people, and therefore the width of the pieces reflects their function rather than practical problems of manufacture.

The pieces grouped together here were all made within a relatively short period of time, most probably in the fifty-year period between 1850 and 1900. This dating is corroborated by two kilims: plate 190, which does not look any older or newer than most other pieces in this group, was acquired by the Victoria and Albert Museum in London in 1884, probably within a few years of manufacture. Plate 191 is another typical south-east Anatolian kilim, which bears an Armenian inscription and the date 1860 at the top of the plain red field.

Aleppo kilims are finely and beautifully woven, and the differences between colours are subtle. They do not display the bold contrasts found in west Anatolian kilims, and rely instead on softness and flow of design. The variety of compositions is considerable, and prayer kilims aside, they cover almost the whole range of patterns known to exist in kilim-weaving throughout the Middle East. Their most striking characteristic is the predominance of burgundy red (as it appears on plate 186). This colour, called cochineal, is extracted from the insect *Dactylopius cocus Costa,* and, depending on the concentration of the dye or the way it is mixed and mordanted, many shades and hues can be obtained and are indeed found in pieces of this group. For example, in the kilim illustrated on plate 187, four different colours are achieved through the use of cochineal.

The borders of these pieces are always white, made of wool or cotton, or, occasionally, of a combination of both (plate 187). The design that appears on this white ground is a repeat element in various colours. It may vary in size and elaboration from piece to piece but always retains its generic characteristics; one can often see more than one variation of it on the same piece.

The form in which it appears most often is:

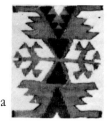

a

it becomes more ornate in:

b

and more simplified in:

c

Another important feature of this group is the separation between the field and the side border. This is achieved by means of a reciprocated pattern, which can take three forms (for details of reciprocals, see the Symbolism and Tradition):

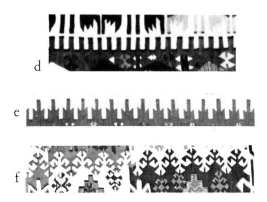

d

e

f

At the top and bottom, the borders are very interesting. They can have the same design element as the side borders (plate 186), or a variant of it (plate 192) or even sometimes, one half of another variant (plate 187):

g

h

i

At the top left corner, in a few cases, the reciprocal pattern changes from one type to another for about 30 to 40 cm.: from rectilinear to angular (plate 187); from simple curvilinear to angular (plate 192); from complex curvilinear to rectilinear (plate 189). This is a very strange characteristic, found only on this groups of kilims, and its significance, if any, is not apparent.

At either end, the field is usually terminated abruptly; however, it sometimes culminates in reciprocal forms differing from those appearing on the sides by being more horizontal in direction.

j

k

l

186   *180 × 330 cm.*

This very fine example displays the colours of Aleppo kilims at their most typical, together with a wide cross-section of the finely drawn and executed motifs for which this type of kilim is renowned. The large conjoined medallions in the shape of flattened hexagons have an outer stepped and hooked outline in white, which is reciprocated by an inner outline of the same form. The resulting lacework effect is very successful. It is worth noting that a number of small infill motifs are drawn in such a way as to create a field-pattern illusion. The complex and refined reciprocal guardstripe at the sides provides a harmonious transition between the strong border and the field.

187   *170 × 403 cm.*

The colours of this piece are subdued and delicate, with four different hues of cochineal red, ranging from pale pink to deep burgundy, and two tones of blue. The main ornament of the field consists of a pair of hooked motifs flanking a small hexagonal medallion; such ornaments are also found on kilims from Obruk and Aksaray. The side borders, with the angular rectilinear version of the border motif, contrast with the top and bottom borders which contain halves of the border designs of plate 195. Notice the change in the guardstripe pattern at the top left-hand corner.

188   *163 × 386 cm.*

The side border design is identical to that of the previous piece. The contrasting top and bottom borders contain another variant of the motif, one that is also found on plate 193. At the lower right-hand corner the motif of the end border continues at the side. The archaic field ornaments are arranged in superimposed horizontal rows, and the colour distribution is symmetrical along the horizontal axis. The ornaments themselves are elegant hexagonal hooked medallions, the points of which interlock to create a field-pattern illusion depending how they are viewed. The same type of hexagonal medallion can be seen on kilims from central Anatolia (plates 159 and 160).

189   *170 × 340 cm.*

Unlike the two previous examples, this kilim has the same border motif all around, and the guardstripes at the sides have the most complex version of the reciprocal pattern; notice again the change to a simple, angular, crenellated motif at the top right-hand corner. The field pattern contains three rows of vertically superimposed hexagonal medallions which are a late, and probably misunderstood version of those on plate 155. The gap between the hexagons is filled with a profusion of the small ornaments common to all kilims of this group, but their arrangement is somewhat unsuccessful; the overall effect lacks both definition and a point of focus.

186

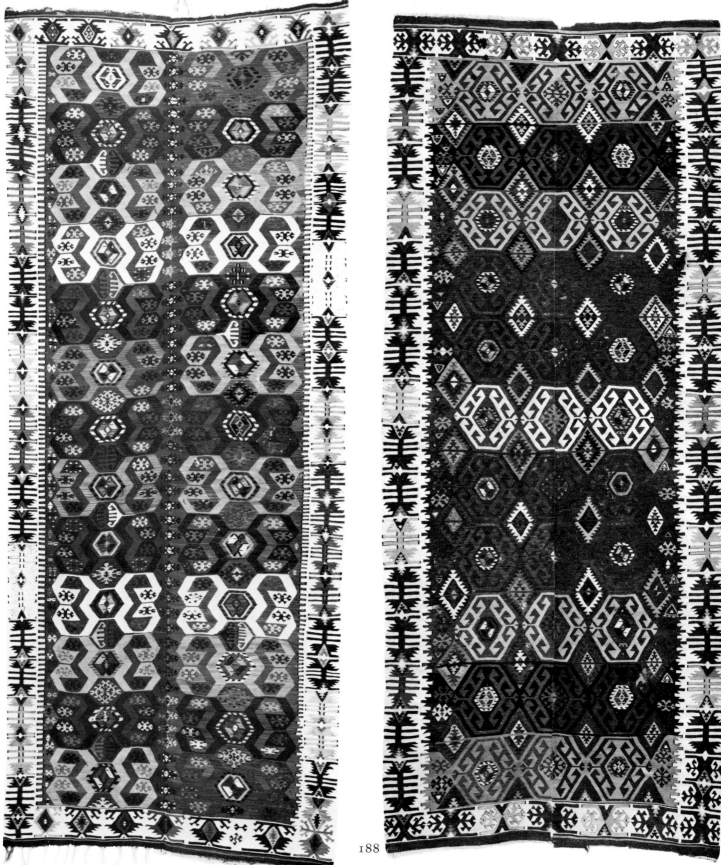

187   188

189

190

191

192

193

194

195

196

197

198

199

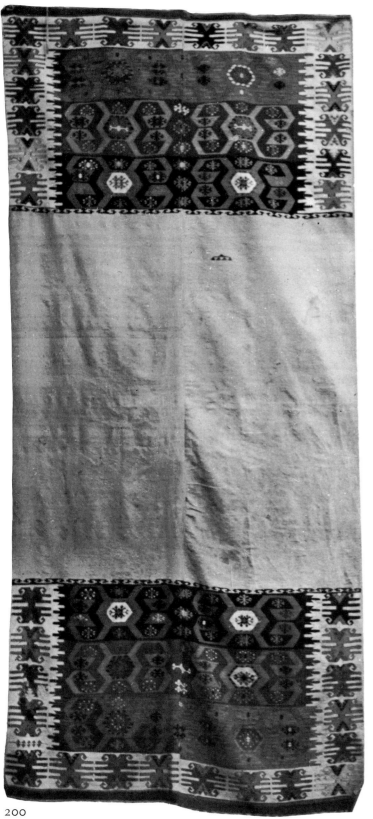

200

201

190 *160 × 360 cm.*

This kilim, which belongs to the collection of the Victoria and Albert Museum in London, has a deep cochineal-red field composed entirely of the minor ornaments of this group, displaying their full repertoire. Unlike the previous piece, however, the effect here is harmonious and contrasts well with the border patterns.

191 *no size available (Detail)*

Detail of a kilim bearing an inscription in Armenian.

192 *152 × 320 cm.*
193 *162 × 357 cm.*

The two very finely woven pieces shown here are examples of the most common composition found on Aleppo kilims. Plate 193 appears the older of the two. Horizontal rows of bracketed diamonds are contained within bands of different colours which blend into one another by means of a small reciprocal hooked design; the simple side border has been seen at the top and bottom of plate 188. Note the different end border pattern consisting of a meandering vine with flowers in the gaps. In some earlier pieces of other groups made at the turn of the eighteenth to nineteenth century, these flowers grow directly from the meandering vine, a feature never encountered in Aleppo kilims.

Unlike plate 193, in plate 192 the bracketed diamonds are placed on the uniform, deep red field. Here, the infill ornaments are more complex, intricate and prominent, a feature common to the pieces woven in the last quarter of the nineteenth century. Note the change in the border design at the sides and end of the piece and also in the reciprocal guard-stripe pattern at the top left-hand corner.

194 *92 × 136 cm.*
195 *106 × 175 cm.*

These are two rare examples of small kilims belonging to this group. It is interesting to note that, though the pieces are of small size, the scale of the individual ornaments is the same as on all the large kilims of the group. The series of small indented hexagons in plate 194, separating the bands containing the large bracketed diamonds, are an unusual detail for this type of kilim. The composition of plate 195 is similar to that of plate 171 from Aksaray and creates a visual confusion as to which is the pattern and which the background.

196 *134 × 334 cm.*

Yet another piece with a bracketed diamond field pattern is shown here. This is a late example of the design, probably made around 1900. Though very finely woven with a profusion of delicately and precisely executed small infill ornaments, this piece has a somewhat more rigid appearance than plates 192 and 193. The colours are much deeper, and the dark red field contrasts strongly with the sharp white cotton border.

197 *152 × 365 cm.*

The composition of this piece is also commonly found on 'Rashwan' kilims from central Anatolia in the Kayseri-Malatya-Sivas area (plate 223). The four large concentric medallions set in the field have the outline of an indented star-shaped polygon alternating with that of a diamond. The bright, yet deep, red field has an unusual tone for this group of kilims. However, the border design, the reciprocal guard-stripes, the small infill ornaments and the texture place this kilim firmly in the Aleppo group. The larger infill designs of the field, which were also seen on plate 186, are variants of a major field motif found on central Anatolian kilims (plates 155 and 156).

198 *160 × 373 cm.*
199 *156 × 370 cm.*

The unusual composition of a plain undecorated field flanked by two wide skirts at the ends and surrounded by a border, mainly occurs on kilims from south-east Anatolia. Several pieces have come to our attention: five with a red field, one with a blue field, and one (plate 200) with a camel-coloured field.

The skirt pattern of plate 198 consists of large diamonds conjoined with smaller ones above and below. The side borders, similar to those of plates 187 and 188, run the entire length of the piece. The composition of plate 199 is somewhat different; the white side borders only flank the skirts. The plain red field has a green reciprocal angular pattern at the sides and a 'running dog' motif at the top and bottom ends. The pattern in the skirts is an endless repeat of a very old Anatolian design found in kilims from the Aegean coast all the way to the frontiers of Persia. Both these and the previous piece have the vine-and-blossom end borders already seen on plates 193 and 194.

200   *no size available*

This piece, in the collection of the Türk ve Islâm Eserleri Museum in Istanbul, is the only known piece of this type having a plain field with a colour other than deep cochineal red or blue. Instead, the field is in camel-coloured wool As in plate 199, the white border only goes along the three sides of the skirts; however, in this example, the plain field extends to the very edge of the piece. Furthermore, the border motif is the same at the sides and ends of the skirts, whereas the two previous examples have the vine-and-blossom border pattern at the end borders. The piece is attributed to the Konya area by the museum; for many reasons, however, this seems unlikely. It has the same colouring and texture as pieces of the present group, especially plates 186 and 187. The latter also has an identical pattern in the field. The narrow reciprocal band at each end of the plain field is the same as that on plates 192, 193 and 198, with which it also shares the reciprocal guardstripes at the sides. Lastly, the warps, twisted in groups to form a long fringe, are typical of the Aleppo group of kilims.

201   *152 × 367 cm.*

A very fine and old example of another composition common to Aleppo kilims. The field pattern of large diamonds with smaller conjoined diamonds above and below has already been seen in the skirts of plate 198. This piece, which is symmetrically arranged along the horizontal axis, has at the sides of the bands three different versions of reciprocal guardstripe patterns. Notice also the heavier concentration of minor infill motifs to the right of the piece. The major ornament of this kilim and the one seen on plates 192, 193 and 194 are the most common major designs of Aleppo kilims. It is interesting to note that whenever these 'three-diamond' motifs appear, they are arranged in three vertical rows, while the bracketed diamonds are in four rows.

GROUP B

This group of kilims is very closely related to both those of the previous group from Aleppo and to the next from Reyhanlı. However, though this group belongs to the same large family there are specific features which distinguish it from the others.

The present pieces are among the oldest kilims from southeast Anatolia. Those from both Reyhanlı and Aleppo continue to be made well into the twentieth century, but no examples of this group seem to have been made after the third quarter of the nineteenth century.

The overall ornamentation is simpler; these pieces lack the dense concentration of minor infill designs so noticeable in both Reyhanlı and Aleppo kilims. The elaborate reciprocal guardstripe patterns seen on the previous group are absent, their place being taken by a simple, angular, crenellated line. The border design elements are less elaborate, somewhat smaller and purer versions of the ones seen on Aleppo pieces. Furthermore, unlike the latter which always have a white ground border, often of cotton, the present pieces have either blue, yellow, brown or ivory borders, always made of wool.

The chromatic range is also somewhat different. The colours remain delicate, refined and subdued, but instead of the predominance of many shades of red that is found on Aleppo kilims, the repertoire here is wider and warmer with much yellow, green, blue and apricot. The colours are more akin to those of the next group, the Reyhanlı, yet softer and mellower.

202   *150 × 290 cm.*

The colouring, border design and texture are typical of this group of kilims. However, with the exception of the border, the composition and the individual large field designs in the shape of stepped, indented hexagons are reminiscent of some kilims from the Caucasus (plates 311 and 312).

The narrow bands dividing the field contain a 'double anchor' motif commonly found in Kurdish pieces woven between Malatya and Lake Van.

203   *152 × 375 cm.*

Though very similar to plate 201 in both composition and design, this kilim belongs to the second group of the south-east

Anatolian family of kilims. The main difference is in the colour range and the handling of the individual inner design elements such as the border motif, and the two-layer reciprocal 'running dog' pattern separating the bands in the field. This example, dating probably from the beginning of the nineteenth century, has delightful colours which include yellow, light green, pale and dark blue, apricot, red and white. The central band in white cotton contrasts well the natural ivory-white of the border.

204   *Fragment, no size available*

Only about two thirds of this piece remain. The colours are very similar to those of both plate 203 and colour plate 202. The main field design is very similar to that of plate 195 and somewhat related to that of plate 187.

205   *180×340 cm.*

Despite its poor condition this piece still retains all the characteristics and strength of an early and beautiful south-east Anatolian kilim. At the ends, the typical border motifs of this group (as seen on plates 203 and 206) are on a maroon ground. The side border designs, though related to those of this group, are also akin to those found on the compartment kilims of the Sivas-Malatya region (plate 245).

The field consists of diagonally offset ornaments arranged chromatically to create multiple patterns of large diamonds. It should be noticed that the weaver has not defined her motifs by the use of a linear grid; instead the skillful repetition of the designs suggests a trellis-pattern. The overall impression, however, is of designs floating on a white ground.

206   *175×333 cm.*
207   *146×395 cm.*

These pieces share the same composition and colour scheme. The border designs, typical of this group, are placed on a mid-blue ground; the deep red field consists of an endless repeat pattern of diagonally offset small lozenges contained within a white diamond lattice. The small motifs inside the lozenges are placed in a sequence which creates patterns of larger diamonds. At both ends, the field joins the end borders by means of a 'T-shaped' reciprocal pattern. This pattern, already seen on pieces

of the Aleppo group (plates 192 and 193), is drawn on a noticeably larger scale. The principal difference between these two very finely woven kilims, which probably date from the first half of the nineteenth century, lies in the handling of the borders. Plate 206 has narrow borders which join the field by means of a vertical crenellated guardstripe. On plate 207, however, the blue borders jut into the field and are separated from it by the outer edge of the white lattice. One of the small motifs placed in a lozenge of plate 207 contains an inscription.

GROUP C: 'Reyhanlı' Kilims

Within the large family of south-east Anatolian kilims, a prominent place belongs to a group of pieces known as 'Reyhanlı'. The name refers to kilims coming from Reyhanye, a village near Antâkya, the ancient Antioch, only a few miles from the present Syrian border. At the time when most of these kilims were woven this village lay within the administrative region of the Ottoman Empire whose centre was Aleppo, a fact that explains why many of them have been found there. They are reputedly woven by Circassians who settled there in the mid-nineteenth century and established a cottage industry, producing a distinct type of kilim which was, and still is, highly regarded by Eastern dealers and collectors because of its fineness and precision of execution. This was especially so in the recent past, when purely nomadic pieces were disregarded as coarse and 'unsophisticated'.

No Reyhanlı kilim seems to predate the middle of the nineteenth century, while most are probably from the second half of the nineteenth and early part of the twentieth. The older examples are extremely tightly and finely woven; more recent examples, however, have become relatively coarse in weave and degenerate in drawing.

Most Reyhanlı kilims have a crisp symmetrical appearance, and are drawn with great clarity, a feature in keeping with the fact that they were virtually made to order for use in the sophisticated environment of town houses.

There, until recent times, they hung as curtains and portières, their designs relating closely to those of the carved wooden doors of the Middle East. Unlike most Anatolian kilims, which were made for use within the weaver's household, these pieces were produced for the market.

202

203

204

205

206

207

In common with two other groups of kilims from the area, Reyhanlıs are long and narrow, woven in two halves, with the exception of the very small pieces, some of which are prayer kilims. They also share similarities of colour and design. There are, however, certain features which are peculiar to Reyhanlıs by which they may be recognized: they are very finely woven, profusely ornamented with small-scale designs, and display an astonishing precision of execution. The warps are of white wool. The wefts are of wool, although undyed cotton is always employed for the white areas of the designs, and generous use is made of silver and gold wrapped threads. Occasionally, silk, bits of cloth, feathers, human hair and straw are woven into the pieces.

Almost all Reyhanlı kilims have, as a standard feature, a series of two to five narrow borders framing the field. Some of these have a continous meandering design, while others display a sequence of small ornaments such as flowers, rosettes or latch-hook medallions:

a   b   c   d   e

The most typical composition in Reyhanlı kilims is known in Anatolia as 'sandıklı' from the word *sandık* which means coffer or chest. In such examples the field enclosed within the multiple borders is divided into panels or compartments. At the centres of these panels are windows opening on to further layers of design. This composition is also found in kilims earlier than the Reyhanlıs; such older pieces are shown in the Sivas-Malatya compartment group (plates 245 and 249). The latter also have a similar sequence of multiple borders, which is so typical of Reyhanlıs, though they contain different decorative motifs.

208   *142 × 290 cm.*   **209**   *168 × 366 cm.*

This is the most commonly encountered type of Reyhanlı kilim. The three narrow borders surround the tripartite field. Each of the three field-panels is decorated with flowers, the stems of which form a trellis pattern. The centres of these panels contain windows into another layer of design, forming an endless repeat of a very old Anatolian design. On both pieces the guardstripes separating the borders and the panels have double crenellated outlines in the vertical direction that become reciprocal 'running dog' patterns in the horizontal. Note the different types of 'running dog' on each piece, together with the difference in the motifs employed on the border decoration of the two pieces. Plate 209 appears to be the older kilim, being richer in colour and somewhat less rigid in design.

210   *145 × 360 cm.*

Little if anything distinguishes this kilim from the previous two. The meandering vine motif appears in its most complete but elegant form. It should be noticed that on most Reyhanlı pieces, the meandering vine border only appears at the sides, being replaced at the ends by a repeat motif, a compositional feature which is consistent with their relatively late date.

211   *148 × 340 cm.*   **212**   *155 × 390 cm.*

These two kilims have a very similar border configuration. The outer and inner borders, both of which contain a zigzag vine interspersed with small hooked ornaments, flank a narrower border with a variety of small ornaments. This vine border seems to be a stylization of the floral border found on plate 69.

Plate 212 has three large conjoined lozenge-shaped medallions on a deep blue field, strewn with a profusion of small decorative motifs. On plate 211 there are two vertical rows of more elongated lozenges, placed in pairs on a tripartite field. However the infill designs in the lozenge medallions of both pieces are very similar. Given the wide range of rich and mellow colours, and the transition of the vine motifs from the sides to the ends, one is inclined to consider these two kilims among the earliest Reyhanlıs. It is also worth mentioning that this type of lozenge-shaped medallion does not seem to survive in pieces with synthetic dyes made after 1900.

208

209

210

211

212

213

214

215

216

217

218

213   *150×330 cm.*

Two vertical rows of lozenge-shaped medallions appear to float on the white cotton field of this piece. The medallions are less elongated than on the last two examples, and the hooked motif within them appears more compressed and rigid. The field here is surrounded by four narrow borders instead of the customary three, their decoration alternating between repeat motifs and a continuous vine pattern.

214   *152×365 cm.*

In an interesting and unusual variant of the lozenge medallion composition, the tiny diamonds at the top and bottom of the lozenges are much larger here than on the three previous pieces, creating two continuous vertical rows of large and small conjoined diamonds surrounded by a prominent white hooked outline. These enlarged diamonds are on the same scale as the minor infill designs in the field. Unlike most Reyhanlı kilims, this piece has three identical borders.

215   *no size available*
216   *165×374 cm.*

The composition of these two kilims is related to that of the plain-field Aleppo pieces (plates 198 and 199), with two wide skirts flanking a large field panel. Here, however, the field is not plain, but the decoration is nonetheless more sparse than in the skirts. The hooked skirt designs of plate 215 are related to those of plates 195 and 204. On close examination however, an interesting field-design illusion appears, the background appearing to form star-shaped polygons. The large multiple diamonds at the centre of the kilims are similar to those on plates 198 and 201.

217   *99×167 cm.*

Small Reyhanlı kilims in general, and prayer kilims in particular, are rare. Plate 217, which compares in fineness with Sehna kilims, is an example. A series of twelve narrow borders surrounds a white cotton field containing a tall mihrab, the unusual shape of which is exclusive to Reyhanlı kilims. In the spandrels, two well-drawn ewers face the top of the prayer niche. The minor infill motifs scattered within the red mihrab are the ones found on all Reyhanlı kilims.

218   *133×342 cm.*

The composition of this piece, while common enough on Reyhanlıs, is totally unknown on any other group of kilims. Small versions of the mihrab on plate 217 cover the entire field of the piece. These niches are arranged symmetrically in horizontal rows on either side of a central band containing a double-sided interpretation of the same design. Whether such a piece can be considered a multiple-mihrab prayer kilim (saf) is debatable. The scale of the mihrab and the lack of directionality would argue against it. It would seem more likely that the small mihrabs are used here purely as decorative motifs.

219   *165×350 cm.*

This colourful central Anatolian kilim displays an interesting repertoire of designs which links it with almost all known types of Turkish kilims. The designs in the three central panels are closely related to Reyhanlı kilims from south-east Anatolia (plates 208 and 210) and so is the overall composition. The two narrow bands with interlocking elongated 'S' motifs next to the outer border at the top and bottom are also seen in west Anatolian kilims (plate 138). The outer side borders are similar to those on plate 228 which is from central Anatolia, while those on the inner border are found on the prayer kilims of Obruk and Sivas. Lastly, the repeating motif in the horizontal bands separating the three field panels is typical of the Malatya-Sivas group of compartment kilims.

219

Central Anatolian 'Rashwan' Kilims

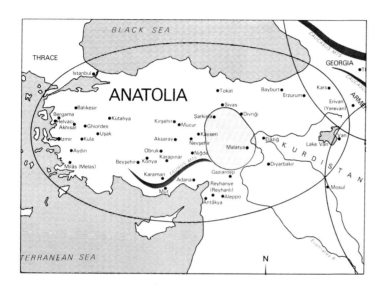

The inhabitants of the area between Kayseri and Malatya in central Anatolia, both Turks and Kurds, produced large numbers of kilims. Their repertoire of designs was limited, as were their colours and composition. As these are among the most common types of Anatolian kilims it was felt necessary to illustrate a number of them, in order to show the subtle and numerous variations on a single basic theme. Two typical examples are shown in colour plates 223 and 228. In general, the earlier pieces have muted, balanced and warm colours as displayed on plate 223, while later pieces, like plates 225 and 226, have a smaller repertoire of cold and hard colours, mainly deep blue, cochineal red, bluish green, and white, which is often of cotton.

The composition, although somewhat repetitive, demands considerable skill on the part of the weavers. They have to execute a large number of parallel diagonal lines, some with a straight edge, others with a serrated or stepped outline. The final result depends on their ability to weave such lines successfully, while filling the gaps between these diagonal lines with an unending repetition and alternation of small ornaments. These skills are recognized in the East, where such pieces are treasured much more than in the West, where they are considered to lack the imagination and strength of their western Anatolian counterparts.

The warps are always of undyed white wool and are usually twisted in groups at the ends to form a long fringe. The wefts are mostly of wool, with gilt-metal and silk threads appearing in some of the later examples. Undyed cotton, natural ivory wool, and occasionally a combination of both, are used for the white areas of design. It has not been possible to designate with any precision the exact locations where such kilims were woven. It is safe to assume, however, that they were made throughout the area, as there are many examples using the same basic composition yet with noticeable variations in fineness of weave, precision of execution, colour, size and material. The variation in texture is quite remarkable, ranging from the very fine (plate 223) to the very coarse (plate 224). Such differences cannot be attributed solely to the relative skills of individual weavers since, on examining many of these kilims, similarities and affinities emerge which suggest localized weaving habits within a larger area. In the bazaars of Turkey today these pieces go under many names such Kayseri, Şarkişla, Malatya, Elâziğ, etc.; in Syria, where many of them are found, they are all referred to as Rashwan kilims. The Rashwans were Kurds living in central and east Anatolia, many of whom migrated eastwards and have now settled in Persia, east of Tehran. The generic nature of this term makes it preferable as a label for these kilims, as it does not suggest a precise provenance.

TYPE A

220   *178 × 427 cm.*

A crisp and clearly drawn piece, indicating it is one of the more southern examples of this type of kilim. The sharp border-designs are similar to those found on Aleppo kilims (plate

201). The serrated outline joining the field to the borders is unusual and harmonizes with the serrations of the border motifs; its colouring, noticeably a medium green, distinguishes this piece from the mainstream of the group.

221   *116 × 180 cm.*
222   *125 × 203 cm.*

Small kilims of this family are much less common than long pieces. Both these examples have the same top border which differs from the side borders.

Plate 221 has a bold 'bracketed diamond' border design which is reminiscent of the 'knotted Kufic' border design so prominent on earlier Anatolian pile rugs. The field ornamentation is more restrained than on plate 222. The outer layers of the medallion of plate 221 do not follow the broken outline of the inner ones, as they do on plate 222, an uncommon treatment of the design. The bottom border of plate 222 and the section of design appearing at the two top corners of the field of plate 221, together with the latter's fringes, link these two kilims to those from the Aksaray region (plate 172) and define them as western examples of this type.

223   *147 × 370 cm.*

One of the most finely woven pieces of the type, this rug displays the full range of colours of the group. The drawing of the infill designs, the repeat border motif and the double-sided 'running dog' at one corner connect this piece with some south-east Anatolian kilims (plates 204 and 205).

224   *173 × 285 cm. (Detail)*
225   *173 × 320 cm. (Detail)*

Two more variants of the same type, each handling the basic composition with marked differences in design and scale. The elements of the end borders are segments of those in the side borders. These two kilims are later and somewhat degenerate versions of the type, each having lost in its own way the elegance in the drawing of plates 220 and 223.

226   *160 × 300 cm. (Detail)*
227   *151 × 335 cm. (Detail)*

These two are also among the later examples of the group. The diagonal lines of the previous pieces are replaced here with a stepped outline. Plate 227 is somewhat brighter and less rigid than plate 226. Its medallions seem to float on a uniform ground, while on plate 226 they expand endlessly to cover the entire field. The drawing of plate 227 indicates that this type of composition is a derivative of that on plates 1 and 197. It is interesting to note that while plate 226 chromatically resembles the preceding two pieces, plate 227 relates more to the following three kilims.

TYPE B

228   *185 × 340 cm.*

This kilim and the following two belong to a distinct type of Rashwan kilim of which we know four more examples. They are immediately recognizable by their apricot border and end finish which is braided, or knotted in a web-like fashion. Though the individual main field medallions remain basically the same, here the continuous row they formed in the previous pieces is broken, each medallion being separated by means of a narrow band; on this piece the latter contains a reciprocal double-hooked repeat motif common in south-east Anatolian kilims (plates 193 and 206). The border motifs are also different from those on the previous examples.

229   *81 × 124 cm.*

A small example of this variant with a composition of expanding diamonds. Although the diamonds themselves increase in size, their 'heads' at either end remain constant. Some of the smaller motifs on the field are executed in gilt-metal thread.

230   *160 × 418 cm.*

This very long kilim is more elegantly drawn than plate 228, with better proportions and spacing of the designs. Again the medallions are separated; this time by a narrow section of an infinite cruciform pattern which also appears on Obruk prayer

220

221

222

223

224

225

226

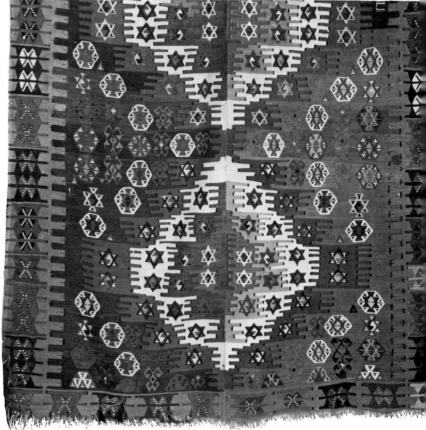

227

228

229

230

231

232

233

234

235

236

237

kilims (plate 165), on Sivas-Malatya compartment kilims (plate 245) and on some kilims from south-west Persia (plate 410). It is worth noting that, with the exception of small pieces, all the kilims with apricot borders and separated medallions examined have four medallions in the field, while all the previous pieces with white borders and continuous medallions have only three, irrespective of their length.

TYPE C

The last seven illustrations belong to yet another distinct type of the Kayseri-Malatya area, Rashwan family of kilims. They share the typical medallions of this family and some of its minor designs, but they are also related to the following group, the band kilims of Malatya. Their texture and some design elements, however, while closer to the latter, place them in a distinct group of their own. Their woollen warps are very wiry and harsh in feel. At the ends, they are either knotted into a narrow fringe or plaited into a narrow braid, and occasionally both.

An identifying characteristic which appears on many of them is the peculiar two-layer border in which a white diamond lattice floats on a ground of plain horizontal stripes; a serrated outline separates this border from the plain-coloured edge. The weave of these kilims is often peculiarly uneven, varying considerably in thickness within the same piece and producing an unusual type of coarseness.

231	*71 × 152 cm.*
232	*82 × 122 cm.*

The principal difference between these two pieces lies in the proportions of the mihrab and the borders. The infill designs are very similar, though plate 231 shows a greater number of combinations. The hooked ornaments scattered in the field of both kilims are related to those in the centres of the medallions of plate 234.

233	*110 × 182 cm.*
234	*107 × 189 cm.*

Both pieces have the typical medallions seen on this large family of Rashwan kilims. Though related in size, the scale of the designs of the field and the border is markedly different; thus plate 233 has three field medallions to plate 234's two. On plate 233 the border patterns blend into the field by means of a crenellated outline; on plate 234 a definite line separates the two. The serrated line that divides field and borders at the top and bottom of plate 233 is replaced on plate 234 with a 'running dog' pattern.

235	*84 × 145 cm.*

An all-over infinite interlocking pattern of diagonally offset diamonds decorates the field of this small kilim. The border design, the end fringe, the texture and the colours are all features common to the small pieces of this group. The row of conjoined diamonds in the centre of the field has an outline that should be compared with the side borders of plates 153 and 180.

236	*82 × 114 cm.*

This light-coloured prayer kilim is unevenly woven and naively drawn but has a charming harmony of muted colours. The prayer arch is of the 'head and shoulders' type and contains at the top a representation which might be that of a standing human figure. At the base of the mihrab is a row of stylized floral motifs, a design feature more common on Anatolian pile rugs than on kilims. The border is of the same general type as those of the last five examples of this group, though it lacks the white trellis pattern which is replaced here with repeat motifs similar to those in the field of plate 235.

237	*no size available*

A larger piece of this sub-group is woven in two halves. As in the Malatya band kilims to which it is closely related (plate 244), each half is an independent, balanced composition. The narrow bands which divide the field into panels contain a repeat design which is also found on a south-east Anatolian kilim (plate 202). The stepped zigzag outline at the sides is a common feature of this group, as are all the small infill motifs.

The Band Kilims of Malatya

These weavings, possibly of Kurdish origin, include some of the longest Anatolian kilims known, their length reaching up to five metres. They are usually woven in two long narrow pieces, for example plates 238 and 239, although there are some one-piece examples, such as plate 240. One example only comprising three identical panels, was once seen in the Kappali Çarsi in Istanbul.

A feature of these kilims is that when they are woven in two sections and each part is often a complete composition in itself (plate 239), unlike most other Anatolian kilims where the two complementary halves join in the middle to form an overall composition (plate 186). Because of this design-independence of the individual panels, such kilims are often found divided; something likely to have occurred at the markets, where they were sold as narrow corridor carpets.

Of all the varieties of kilims examined in this book, these pieces together with Helvacı kilims (plate 101) are the only ones in which a mixture of weaving techniques is a normal feature. Some are woven in pure slit tapestry (plate 239) but most contain bands in pure tapestry weave, alternating with others in a variety of brocading techniques (plates 238 and 241), including weft-floating and warp-wrapping. Their composition consists of parallel bands of design across the entire width of the field, without any borders. Occasionally, however, (as

plate 238) the individual bands of design form long, narrow panels, contained within their own border stripes.

The most distinctive feature of Malatya kilims is a series of four interconnected parallel bands (plates 238 and 239) which form a cartouche-like motif, unique to this type of kilim. Even in the pieces executed in mixed technique, this design always appears in slit-tapestry weave, although sometimes outlined with weft-wrapping.

The patterns and designs are arranged symmetrically along central axes both vertically and horizontally, an unusual feature in long Anatolian kilims, most of which are distinctly directional along a longitudinal axis.

This non-directional approach to design coupled with large size might be an indication of their function. Many of them can be seen on the floors of village mosques in the Malatya region, and one example, hanging horizontally, was seen lining the walls of a small wooden dwelling near Şarkişla.

The overall colour scheme is dark, alleviated in places, especially on the panels containing the four band motifs, by the use of light colours or white. The earlier examples have a warm range of colours which in later pieces becomes cooler with a predominence of dark blues and cochineal reds. The more commonly encountered colours are a deep blue, madder and cochineal reds, various shades of green, dark brown and white.

The material for the warps is wool in natural, undyed ivory white and brown. The warp ends are braided and occasionally plaited (plate 34). The wefts are of wool and natural brilliant white cotton; on later pieces, small quantities of silk and metal threads can be found.

238   *170 × 345 cm.*

This is one of the more finely woven kilims of this group and possibly the most representative of their design repertoire. The composition consists of alternating flatwoven and brocaded bands in the weft-float technique. The brocaded designs arranged within a diamond grid include hooked medallions and lozenges, some of which are set within bands of S-shaped

238

239

240

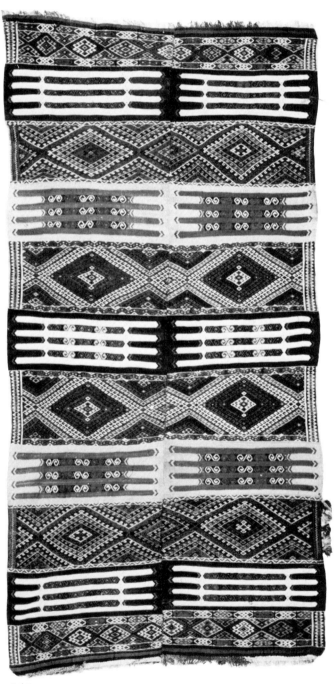

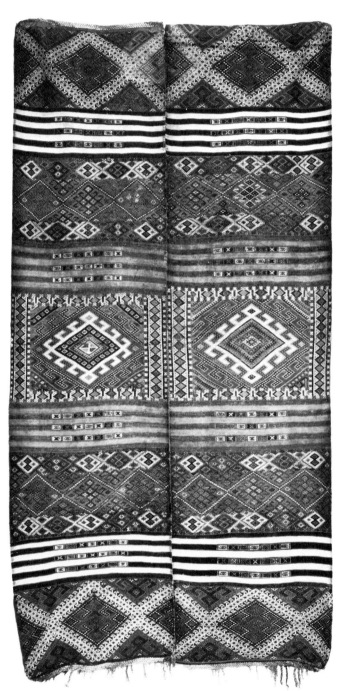

241

242

243

244

motifs reminiscent of early Anatolian carpet designs. The flat-woven four-band motifs between the horizontal bands contain continuous stepped chevron patterns.

239   *186 × 419 cm.*

This is an unusual kilim of its type, for it is woven entirely in slit tapestry. Of all the examples we have seen, this appears to be one of the earliest; it displays the features of the group in their simplest and possibly most archetypal form. The composition consists of five panels separated from each other by means of narrow undecorated bands. In each panel the four-band motif is flanked by narrower bands of geometric patterns. This is a reversal of the format usually found (plates 240 and 241), in which the rows of four-band motifs are used to separate the major, and wider, panels of geometric ornaments.

240   *119 × 436 cm.*

A very elegant, well-drawn and simple example, this kilim is somewhat odd in that it is woven in one piece. It is arguable that it may be only half of a two-part kilim, but the present example is much wider than any separated half-kilim of this group. Furthermore it retains its original overcast selvedges on both sides, a further indication of its completeness.

241   *167 × 342 cm.*

The decoration here is a simplified version of plate 238. The brocaded bands cross the entire width of the field forming panels contained within very narrow borders. Their decoration consists of a series of alternating large and small concentric hooked lozenges.

Note the repeated S-shaped designs within the four-band motifs which replace the more unusual key motif of plate 238. The two pieces have a similar colour range, although here the overall effect is lightened by the extensive use of pale olive green and ivory white.

242   *182 × 343 cm.*

A most striking kilim of this type belonging to the collection of the Islamisches Museum in East Berlin. The drawing, colour and general appearance indicate an early date for this kilim, somewhere near the middle of the nineteenth century. In contrast with the more typical examples, the brocaded panels predominate, especially the central one with its multi-layered hooked lozenges. The four-band motif is relegated to secondary importance and has the appearance of a plain striped background rather than an integral ornament. The visual impact of the piece is accentuated by a play on the scale of the same hooked and brocaded lozenge; it is largest at the centre, framed by rectangular panels, smaller at the top and bottom bands, where it is placed within a wide diamond lattice, with even smaller versions in between the four-band motifs. The braiding of the 'salt-and-pepper' warps is typical of this group and confirms its Kurdish origin.

243   *no size available*

This long narrow kilim is probably only one half of a two-panel piece. It is woven entirely in slit tapestry, most of the designs being highlighted by weft-wrapping or overstitching. The large, intricate, hooked medallions in the shape of flattened hexagons within the rectangular panels each side of the central four-band motif also appear on the following kilim; they are more commonly seen on saddle bags. The design seems to be of a late date, as no example of it seems to predate the second half of the nineteenth century. Through it, this family of kilims is linked with late examples (plate 246) of a more archaic group from the same general area. Notice the narrow borders flanking the four-band motifs. They contain a continuous interlocking spearhead design which can be traced to stone carvings and marble mosaics of the medieval period in Anatolia.

244   *456 × 173 cm.*

This very large kilim is a borderline piece of this group. Like the others it consists of two identical juxtaposed panels with bands of ornamentation. It lacks, however, the characteristic four-band motif. The colour range is very varied and unusual with an emphasis on warm reds, blues, greens, and yellows. Gilt-metal thread is to be found in some of the designs, while others contain yellow and red silk. The wool has a glowing sheen even though the piece shows no evidence of wear. It should be compared with plate 237 which belongs to a neighbouring type.

The Compartment Kilims of Sivas-Malatya

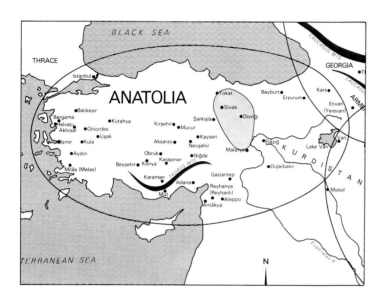

This group of kilims should be attributed to east Anatolia, and they were probably made somewhere in the region between Sivas and Malatya. The reasons for this attribution are many. First, they are related to the band kilims of the Malatya region, the borderline pieces of both groups displaying marked similarities (see plates 243 and 246). Second, they are related in design to the kilims of south-east Turkey (though they do not share either their texture or their colour range) by their compartment composition, also known as 'sandıklı' (see plates 208 and 210) and by a number of shared small-scale infill designs. Third, they link with the kilims to the north-west and north-east of the Malatya area (see plates 252 and 255). Lastly, they show similarities with the kilims of Kayseri-Kirşehir.

Compartment kilims were woven in slit tapestry, and the weft-float brocading of the band kilims is totally absent. All the designs are prominently outlined with loose weft-wrapping.

This is a comparatively early group of kilims, of which we have found no examples with late synthetic dyes. Present knowledge of early kilims is, unfortunately, very incomplete, but we would place this group between the second half of the eighteenth century and the middle of the nineteenth. Their

designs are archaic, and the compositions classical. The colour range is also strongly reminiscent of that of eighteenth-century Turkish village carpets. It displays a richness of shades and a great tonal sensitivity. The resulting visual effect is very harmonious.

The composition of all the kilims of this group consists of a series of juxtaposed compartments arranged in one or more vertical rows which are surrounded by a number of narrow borders (up to four). These compartments are either rectangular, richly decorated panels or prayer niches forming a multiple prayer-arch composition. Narrow bands, similar to the borders, surround the compartments.

The scale of the minor designs is small, producing compositions of rich yet orderly ornamentation. With the exception of plate 246, which is a borderline example of the group, all the known kilims of this type are woven in one piece.

Although we know of four safs belonging to this group, we have been unable to trace small single-arch prayer kilims which we can safely attribute to it. Kilims 231 and 232 are related, but not closely enough to justify inclusion in this group. This is surprising, considering that wherever else multiple-arch prayer kilims have been observed, they belonged to groups where large numbers of single-arch pieces were produced.

245   *189 × 391 cm.*

This very refined kilim displays all the features and colours of the 'compartment' group. It has the full range of border and field motifs, featuring clearly the weaver's *horror vacui* approach to design. Some of the two-layer compartments, separated by multiple guardstripes, contain in their inner layer the stylized carnation pattern which is seen as a principal motif on kilims from the Niğde area (plate 157) and as a skirt design on kilims from the Konya area (plate 142). The diagonal cruciform pattern forming the outer layer of the compartments can be seen on the borders of Obruk prayer kilims (plate 165) and on some south Persian kilims from Fars (plate 410).

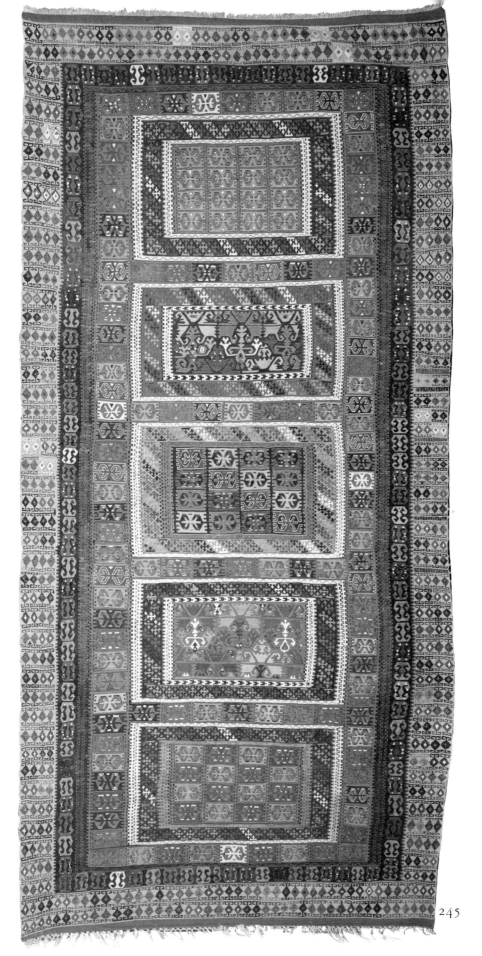

245

246

247

248

249

250

246 *165 × 499 cm.*

This extremely long and narrow kilim has two vertical rows of flattened multi-layered hexagons separated by narrow bands of hooked motifs. The colours, feel, texture and side borders include it within the present group, while the large medallions and the design on the horizontal bands relate it to the band kilims of Malatya. Its colour range is wide and the drawing of the large medallions better executed than in most other related examples.

247 *185 × 370 cm.*

This is a multiple-arch prayer kilim with seven mihrabs, which are contained within compartments surrounded by the inner border. Here we see only two borders compared with the three of the previous piece. It appears, however, that this piece has had an outer border removed. An interesting design feature of this and the following saf is the fact that though the prayer niches point across the width of the kilim, all the minor designs point along the length of the piece.

248 *262 × 409 cm.*

The number of niches in this piece is unusual: six instead of the customary seven. The outer border is like the one seen in plate 245. Unlike the previous piece, all of whose mihrabs have the same infill decoration, we have here a variety of infill ornaments. It is worth noticing that the shape of the niches is more like Turkish tombstones than mosque mihrabs. There is a simi-lar example with six mihrabs in the Textile Museum, Washington, DC, which was published in *Turkish Rugs,* (1968, plate 84). The latter, however, is looser in weave. Its light colours and outer border pattern relate it more closely to the Kirşehir group (plates 253 and 254).

249 *185 × 385 cm.*

The overall similarity of this piece to colour plate 245 is remarkable. On close examination, however, there are a number of differences, though the sequence of borders is the same. This piece has only two rows of small bracketed diamonds in the outer border, to plate 245's four. The compartments here have three concentric layers, while plate 245 has only two, and the shape of these compartments is not as elongated here as in plate 245. Lastly the innermost layers of the panels differ, some in design and the others in pattern; for instance, the same designs are arranged chromatically in different ways to create other patterns.

250 *no size available (Detail)*

This very large piece in the collection of the Museum für Islamische Kunst in West Berlin has two vertical rows of compartments. The border configuration and the design in the panels are closely related to those in the last four illustrations. The handling of the design, however, and the colours, also relate this kilim to the Kirşehir group (plate 251). There is a very similar kilim in the Ethnographical Museum in Ankara.

The Kilims of the Kayseri-Kirşehir Region of Central Anatolia

This variety of kilim is closely related to the pile-woven rugs of the Kirşehir type. The colour range is similar, especially the distinctive pale blue, green and yellow. The texture is flat and silky and the weave very loose, the effect of the slits being most pronounced. If a kilim of this type is put against the light, one can practically see the entire design in outline. They are woven entirely in wool of a shiny and lustrous quality and are made in a variety of sizes, ranging from the very small (plate 253) to the very large (plate 251). The large examples, however, are wider for any given length than most nineteenth-century Anatolian kilims, which are normally long and narrow. This feature is even more remarkable given the fact that all Kirşehir kilims are woven in one piece, indicating the occasional use of looms over three metres in width. Kilims of similar proportions were woven in central Anatolia in the eighteenth century

(plate 62). It may be that these kilims, with their archaic and conservative designs, are late derivatives of earlier pieces.

251   *192 × 285 cm.*

252   *92 × 137 cm.*

The decoration of the compartment and borders of this piece is common to Kirşehir kilims. The outer border is the same as that on plate 251.

253   *135 × 170 cm.*

An example of a small Kirşehir kilim with a single compartment decorated with an expanding, concentric diamond pattern containing hooked motifs. The drawing of these motifs is similar to that on some compartments of plate 251.

254   *135 × 170 cm.*

The field decoration, consisting of vertical bands separated by guardstripes and containing a hooked wavy line, is often found on Kirşehir pile rugs. This field pattern appears in the inner border of plate 253 with which this piece has borders in common. Plates 253 and 254 are the earliest known examples of Kirşehir kilims, displaying their range of colours at its richest. The profusion of small dots in the gaps between the designs is an archaic feature of Anatolian kilims which is common also to the pieces of a previous group (plates 62 and 64).

251

252

254

253

Sivas Kilims

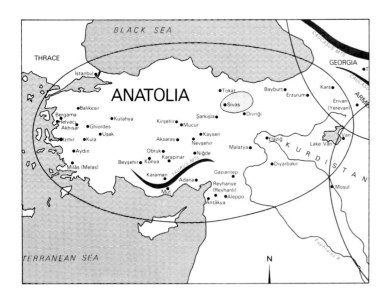

From Sivas all the way to the easternmost reaches of Anatolia, a large number of kilims were made, most of which are believed to have been woven by the Kurds. The majority of kilims made in this region are small prayer kilims. The larger pieces are either multiple-arch prayer kilims or longer and narrow pieces like plates 258, 269 and 270. There do not seem to be any kilims woven in two halves.

The Sivas kilims are the most westerly of this large family. Some of their designs relate to those of the compartment kilims of the Malatya-Sivas region and some to those of Bayburt, Erzurum and Kars. Their colour range is muted and restrained, as exemplified by colour plate 255.

Usually the prayer kilims belonging to what are defined here as the 'Sivas', 'Bayburt' and 'Erzurum' groups have a sequence of three borders: a major border flanked by secondary borders. On comparison of the major borders of all these pieces, a subtle chromatic change can be observed. On 'Sivas' kilims the ground of this border is of a distinctive apricot or salmon pink; on those from Bayburt, ochre (plate 259); and on those from Erzurum, yellow (plate 264). All these prayer kilims have many features in common, and relate to one another in overall

appearance. It is probable that they were made throughout east Anatolia. It would, in fact, be more accurate to consider the present division into three groups as marking a progression from west to east.

The main designs of the kilims of these three groups are largely unrelated to those found on kilims from south, central and west Anatolia. They do, however, have certain similarities with the designs of pile-woven rugs that are generally referred to in vague terms as Yürük or Kurdish.

Sivas kilims are mostly woven on a foundation of natural white wool warps. Their border designs are a distinctive series of abstract geometric motifs, notable among which is a multi-layered 'X' form. The mihrabs have a reciprocal outline, either in the form of a 'running dog' (plate 255), or of a double-hook motif (plate 256). The stepped outline of the arch found on the Bayburt and Erzurum pieces, like plates 260 and 268, does not occur here. Instead the arch is either pointed (plate 255) or 'shouldered' (plates 256 and 257).

255   *115 × 153 cm.*

One of the oldest examples of 'Sivas' prayer kilims, this displays the full range of their colours. The designs are very intricate and finely woven. Some of them link this piece to the previously examined 'compartment' kilims of Sivas-Malatya such as plate 245—especially the small bracketed diamonds of the inner, minor border which compare with those of the outer border of plates 245 and 249.

256   *118 × 170 cm.*

The decoration of this elegant piece is a simplified version of plate 255. The elongated, 'shouldered' mihrab, typical of this group, contains flowers sprouting from a central stem. The two large motifs in the spandrels are often referred to as 'hands'. Given the function of prayer rugs, this term is quite logical as the motifs correspond to the positions where the worshipper would place his hands, his forehead touching the central flower at the very top of the mihrab.

257   *125 × 186 cm.*

In yet another variant of this group of kilims, the designs, though similar to the previous two examples, are on a different scale and placed in different combinations.

258   *147 × 370 cm.*

A long and narrow version of this type of kilim has a red field containing two conjoined and opposing mihrabs, on the principle of the mirror-image. An interesting feature of the piece, emphasizing the double mihrab, is the change in tone in the green ground at the centre of the piece from blueish green to bottle green. In all probability, the prayer-arch motif is only used as a decorative element, and no particular significance should be attached to its double-sided shape.

255

256

257

258

Bayburt Kilims

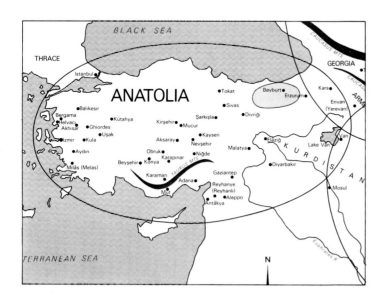

260   *120 × 170 cm.*   **262**   *120 × 187 cm.*
261   *107 × 168 cm.*   **263**   *142 × 162 cm.*

These four prayer kilims have the same repertoire of colours, typified by colour plate 259. While many of the colours are common to other related types of east Anatolian prayer kilims, this group is distinguishable by the olive green of the mihrab, which varies in depth from piece to piece, and even more by the ochre-beige of the middle border. The latter is yellow on the kilims in plates 264 to 269 and apricot or salmon pink on plates 255 to 258.

Kilims of this group have braided warp ends (though these are only visible on plate 262). Some of the designs are executed in gilt-metal threads and silk. All the eleven known kilims of this type are dated, and some have inscriptions. The validity of these dates is questionable. Plate 261 is dated AH 1188 (AD 1774) and plate 260 is dated AH 1290 (AD 1884). Their similarity in colour, texture and design, however, strongly contradicts the possibility that they were woven one hundred years apart. Careful examination of the pieces tends to suggest a date around the middle of the nineteenth century.

The outer borders have an unusual decoration of shields containing plant motifs floating on a dark blue ground. The second border usually has alternating geometric and stylized abstract floral motifs on an ochre-beige ground. Notice the guardstripes separating the various borders which consist of juxtaposed short stepped lines. The green mihrabs, sometimes plain (plate 261) and at other times decorated (plate 262), have a stepped arch crowned by a flower-head which is probably a stylized version of that appearing on plate 69; the sides of the mihrabs are outlined by means of a reciprocal hooked outline, and in the spandrels, abstract floral designs float on a red ground. The similarities among these kilims are very marked but no two pieces are exact duplicates; the minor designs are often interchangeable, the compositional theme being the one that remains constant. It is probable, therefore, that they were all woven in one village or town according to a style that prevailed within a limited period of time.

The attribution of the following pieces to the area around Bayburt is somewhat conjectural but not unjustified. They are related to the kilims of the Sivas region to the west, and also to those of the Erzurum-Kars area to the east. Bayburt pieces have many common characteristics, not least of which is their colour range, typified by plate 259. Other common features include natural brown warps, the use of gilt-metal threads, the form of the mihrab, the decoration of the spandrels and the very common occurrence of dated pieces.

259   *142 × 185 cm.*

Though it is different in design, the general characteristics of this piece place it in the same general group as the following four. The powerful main border is set between a series of small hexagons and a row of large 'S' forms; the sparse decoration of the mihrab provides a good contrast to the bold borders. This kilim is dated AH 1299 (AD 1881).

259

260

261

262

263

Erzurum Kilims

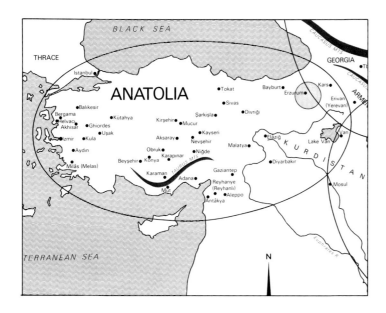

The next five pieces come from the area around Erzurum in north-east Anatolia, where mostly prayer kilims were woven with few, if any, large pieces being known.

The texture is similar to that of Bayburt kilims, with which they also share some minor designs. The main difference lies in the shades of the colours, in particular the yellow of the border which replaces the ochre-beige of Bayburt kilims.

The border designs are especially distinctive. Though there is a variety of these (see plates 264, 266 and 268), two stand out: the 'wing-and-flower' designs found on the minor borders and the stylized tulip and carnation motif of the major borders. The latter is well known from Lâdik pile rugs of the late eighteenth and early nineteenth centuries and derives from designs found on classical Ottoman textiles and ceramics of the sixteenth century (plates 268 and 269). The presence of this border design has led many authors to attribute such kilims to Lâdik; their colours and texture, however, are totally inconsistent with such an attribution.

264   *146 × 190 cm.*

The colours of this kilim are typical of pieces woven in the Erzurum region of north-east Anatolia. The next four kilims belong to the same type, and their colours closely resemble those of this piece.

265   *127 × 152 cm.*

Though closely related to plates 264, 268 and 269 in colour and design, this kilim is more loosely woven and was probably made in the Kars region somewhat further east. The border designs, including the reciprocal red and white outer guard-stripe, are similar to those on plate 269. The piece contains an inscription that is largely illegible and a date that can be read in a variety of unconvincing ways, ranging from AH 1122 to AH 1247 (AD 1710 to 1831).

266   *124 × 170 cm.*

This kilim belongs to the collection of the Textile Museum in Washington, DC. The main border design, consisting of a central stem from which sprout pairs of flowers, is related to that of colour plate 264, but also to borders found on kilims from further west (plates 71 and 72). In the top border a series of small ewers is placed between the adjacent pairs of flowers. Unlike the other examples of this type, the 'wing-and-flower' motif is placed here in the inner border.

267   *126 × 186 cm.*

The tree and plant decoration in the mihrab and the spandrels is similar to that of plate 266. The inner border motif appears to be a stylization of the one on plate 268. In its present form it appears commonly on pile rugs of the region.

264

265

266

267

268

269

268   *124 × 180 cm.*

269   *140 × 345 cm.*

This is possibly the finest example of an Erzurum prayer kilim. The well-proportioned plain green mihrab contrasts well with the orderly floral decoration of the spandrels. The elegantly drawn tulip and carnation border is set between the 'wing-and-flower' outer border and an inner border containing what may be abstract animal forms.

The structure, most of the designs, the colours and particularly the proportions of this kilim indicate an origin from the north-east part of Anatolia, around Kars. Its major border, decorated with stylized carnations and tulips on a yellow ground, is a well-drawn rendering of the design found on Lâdik pile rugs.

The decoration of the main and outer borders is more commonly found on the prayer kilims of the Erzurum-Kars region, this being the only known instance where they appear on a piece of this size.

Kars Kilims

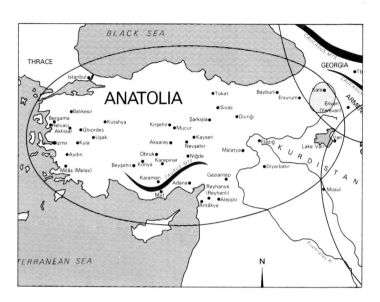

Without exception, the Kurdish kilims of Kars, in common with those of three previous groups, are either long and narrow, or small, prayer kilims. The warps are of thick, natural brown wool, braided at the ends. The texture, loose and pliable, is related to that of early kilims from the Lake Van district, the thick warps producing a noticeable ribbed effect. Early pieces of this group, some possibly dating back to the late eighteenth century (like plate 271), have shiny wool and deep contrasting colours including oxblood red, peacock blue, bottle green, apricot and yellow.

Designs are either of an abstract geometric nature, like plates 270 and 274, relating to ornaments found further east on the Caucasus, or stylized and abstract derivations of classical Ottoman floral designs, like plates 271 and 272. On later examples, none of which is illustrated here, designs degenerate into stiff and misunderstood repetitions of the earlier ones. The colour range is much reduced, consisting mainly of dark colours. Kilims with a large number of synthetic dyes are still produced in the area.

270   *121 × 320 cm.*

The field is composed of three vertical rows of juxtaposed hexagons containing hooked motifs, the spaces in between being filled with star-shaped lozenges. This type of field decoration is not unlike that found on Caucasian kilims, though the handling of the motifs and the colours are very typical of the Kurdish kilims of Kars. The geometric border motif is also a clear indication of its origin. In the field, the second and fourth dotted hexagons at the top of the middle row give a focus to the piece. The colours of this early example display the full chromatic scale found on Kars kilims. Though the designs are executed in a rigid 60-degree grid, the interplay of colours gives a great deal of movement and freedom to the piece, the border appearing to be superimposed on an endless repeat pattern.

271   *142 × 230 cm.*
272   *23 × 61 cm. (Detail)*

Plate 271 and the fragment probably date from the second half of the eighteenth century. The main designs of both pieces are stylized abstract renderings of the large carnation motifs associated with sixteenth- and seventeenth-century Ottoman textiles. On plate 271 the large motifs contain stylized tulips und floral blossoms. For a derivation of this design see the section on designs, patterns and compositions. The carnation motif appears on a number of different groups of kilims across Anatolia (see plates 142 and 157). The Kars variety, however, has its own characteristics, which hark back to very early times, the motif being a combination and derivation of both animal and floral forms.

273   *109 × 136 cm.*

This example of a Kars prayer kilim has deep, harmoniously contrasting colours such as two tones of red, a mid-blue, green

270

271

272

273

274

and yellow. The designs are stylized floral motifs, the inner border containing carnation blossoms related to those found on plates 71 and 72. The effect of colour and design is very charming.

274   *114×152 cm.*

The small motifs of the deep-green mihrab and those of the borders are typical of Kars kilims, and should be compared to those on the borders of plate 271. The dotted ground of the inner border is related to the decoration of the second and fourth hexagons at the top of the centre row of plate 270. The effect of hexagons floating on this dotted ground enhances the attraction of the piece.

The warp ends are knotted to produce a net-like fringe instead of the more common braiding found on Kars kilims.

Kilims from Lake Van

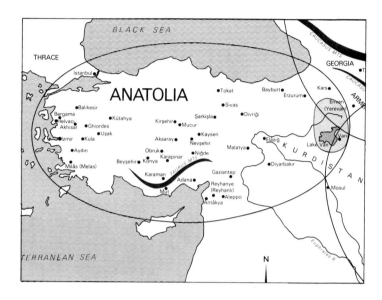

a great variety of designs from all over Anatolia were incorporated in their decorative repertoire, the result being a very rich and varied mixture of traditional designs combined into an endless variety of patterns and compositions.

275   *232×305 cm.*
276   *206×315 cm.*

These two kilims have a similar composition of diagonally offset hexagons surrounded by a geometric border; however, on each piece the design is handled in a very different fashion. On plate 275 the border of small conjoined hexagons appears to blend into the field pattern. On plate 276 the vertical rows of offset hexagons are separated by a narrow band containing S-forms. The border motifs, similar to those of plate 275, are set on a dark brown ground separated from the field by means of a serrated guardstripe. The designs on both these pieces should be compared to those of plates 270 and 274, with which they have elements in common.

277   *180×305 cm.*
278   *186×286 cm.*

These two kilims from the Lake Van region have the same basic cruciform ornament applied to a different field pattern. Plate 277 has a composition (related to that of plate 270) of vertical rows of hexagons, the spaces between which are filled with large diamonds. The outline between the diamonds and hexagons is a reciprocal 'running dog' pattern.

On plate 278 the cruciform star-motifs contained within hexagons are arranged in major and minor horizontal bands. The two end panels form a hooked diamond pattern; the centres of these diamonds contain simplified versions of the motifs found between the hexagons of plate 277.

The region of Lake Van is the source of a great number of kilims. The local weaving tradition survived longer there than almost anywhere in Anatolia. As a result, large numbers of good kilims were produced almost to the present day.

Towards the beginning of this century, however, a number of changes occurred in Van kilims. Early examples, like plate 275 illustrated here, were usually woven in a single piece, while more recent ones are often in two joined halves which seldom match perfectly. Early kilims have a soft pliable texture similar to the Kurdish kilims of Kars, while recent pieces have a hard, shiny texture and a much darker and more limited colour range. It is worth noting that old Van pieces are often significantly wider and shorter than other groups of Kurdish flat-weaves from north-east Anatolia.

The development of design in this group of kilims is fascinating. Early pieces have geometric motifs similar to those of the kilims of Kars, the south Caucasus and some from north-west Persia. From the end of the last century onwards, however,

275

276

277

278

Caucasus

Historical and Ethnographical Notes on the Caucasian Peoples

TAMARA DRAGADZE

The area known as the Caucasus, lying between Russia to the north and Turkey and Persia to the south, remains something of an enigma to Western Europeans, despite its geographical closeness. It is a veritable mosaic of ethnic groups, with at least eighty languages and dialects, and few unifying principles by which to characterize its peoples. A stategic gateway between the East and West, for many centuries it has absorbed and adapted influences from all who have passed through. The great mountain ranges provided shelter both for the original inhabitants, some of whom have preserved their unique languages to this day, and for the many peoples fleeing from troubles or settling in the wake of conquests.

It is possible broadly to distinguish the various Caucasian peoples by ascribing them to large ethno-linguistic groups. In the north Caucasus there are the 'true Caucasians': that is, peoples whose languages belong to no other group outside the Caucasus. In the north Caucasus these are the Abkhaz-Abkhaz, Adighey, Dzhigits, Sumursakans, Tsebalinds, the Cherkess (Circassians) and Kabardians, the Ubykh (now almost extinct in the area), the Chechens-Chechens, Ingush and Bats, and lastly, the Lesghi, under whom can be subsumed about forty languages and peoples—Avars, Andi, Dido, Laks, Dargwa, Samurs, Archi, Udins, Kubans and Khinalugs, to name but a few. The other 'true Caucasians' are the Georgians to the south. The geographical boundaries of these people are not distinct, and often a few villages of one group are in an area mainly inhabited by another. The second large group is of Indo-Europeans, namely the Armenians, Ossets, Talish, Tat, Persians and Kurds. Since the nineteenth century, when the Russian Imperial government settled Cossacks in the northernmost part of the Caucasus, there is a Slav population as well. The third large group of peoples is the Turkish or Altaic. In the north Caucasus there are the Karachai, Nogaa, Kumyks and Balkars, and a few Turkomans and Kirghiz. South of these groups there are the Azeri Turks (of Azerbaijan), the Osmanli Turks and the Karapapaks. To complete the picture, in the north there is a small group of Mongolian Kalmuks, and everywhere there are some Arabs, Aissores and an ancient population of Mountain Jews belonging to the Semitic group.

A simpler grouping of the majority of the Caucasians is by religion: Moslems include most of the north Caucasians and all the Altaic peoples, and Christians, the Georgians and Armenians.

The province of Shirvan (whose main town is Shemakha, or Soumak in some languages) had been part of the land of the ancient, pre-Christian Albanians, a Caucasian people now extinct. In the fourth century it came under the rule of the Sassanid Persians, during the reign of Khosro Nushirvan (whence the province derives its name). It then changed hands many times; first under the Shahs, then under the Arab Caliphs in the ninth century; then under the Georgian monarchs in the twelfth century. Thereafter it was independent or Ottoman-ruled, becoming completely autonomous at the beginning of the fifteenth century, when Emir Ibrahim of Shirvan took all of what is now Azerbaijan, as well as Tabriz and even Isfahan. At the end of the fifteenth century, however, Shirvan fell to the Persians, and its independence came to an end. Then, in the words of a Russian author: 'Little by little, weary of the Persians, Shirvan came under the protection of the Russians.' Comparative peace attracted people of many ethnic groups. In the mid-nineteenth century there were Azeri Turks, Arabs, Persians, Armenians, Jews, Gypsies, Kurds, Talish, as well as a host of resettled mountain tribesmen. In the latter part of the nineteenth century, Shirvan was incorporated into the province of Baku. The whole area of the Caucasus, from the plain of Kuba down to the Persian and Ottoman frontiers, became part of the Russian Empire, although from such examples as the early nineteenth-century Avar, the Mullah Shamil and his Muradic movement, it is clear that Russian attempts at pacification and consolidation did not go unchallenged.

The period which is most relevant to the subject of this study, the second half of the nineteenth century, was one of fundamental political and social change. An influx of Russian administrators and soldiers to the region was accompanied by movements of population: Moslem Caucasians were sent to Turkey and some Greek Christians were moved to Russia. The spread of Islam had taken place slowly in the Caucasus (and indeed, reached some peoples only in the eighteenth century). For the Moslem conquerors, the mountain passes and the Caspian ports of Derbent and Makhachkala had been the strategic centres of control. The Russians gave another port, Baku, particular prominence. Railways were built to link the ports of the Caspian with those of the Black Sea. The most southerly cities of the Empire, administrative town centres such as Gendje (Elizabetpol), Shemakha in the province of Shirvan and Kars, were linked through roads and railway-systems to Central Russia and to Europe. The improvement of transport led to the introduction of mass-produced goods into the Caucasus. At the same time, for political and economic reasons, peasants were forced off the land and into trade and industry, whether they remained in their villages or moved to the newly expanding towns.

Russia now exerted a direct influence on the life of the Caucasian peoples. When the 1861 reform in Central Russia freed the serfs, a similar proclamation was made in the Caucasus, although, like most colonizers who protect their power by ingratiating themselves with local notables, the Russians allowed the north Caucasian feudal lords to grant freedom to their serfs on a charge of 200 roubles per head, plus half of all moveable property.

The type and degree of feudalism and social stratification that existed in the Caucasus varied from group to group. The Circassians, for example, had a rigid social structure ranging from peasants to princes. Their princesses, world-famous for their beauty, were circulated by their captors round the whole of the Middle East in the hope that they would supply the various royal dynasties with fairer children. In some areas of Daghestan, the divisions between rulers and subject were not so distinct, and it was only with the *Jihad* (Holy Wars) of the Murad Moslems against Russia that religious leadership became prominent as a unifying force in the area. In Georgia, with its long tradition of feudalism, nineteenth-century travellers noted that, despite differences in wealth, the life-styles of the rural nobility and peasants were remarkably similar. All sang the same songs, worshipped in the same places, dressed in the same style, and at feasts ate the same sort of food and proposed the same toasts.

In the southern territories, which with Armenia had been under Persian or Ottoman rule, there was a loose hierarchy of foreign-appointed rulers, who were described in the guidebooks on the Caucasus given to Russian administrators as religious leaders (the distinction between political and religious leadership being carefully made). Each rank received dues from the population in the form of money or goods, among which were many types of household woven articles.

'Commander-in-Chief of the Caucasus' was a post of utmost prestige in the Russian governmental hierarchy, and for a long time, was held by the brother of the Tsar himself. The Commander's residence was in Tbilisi (then called Tiflis) in the heart of Georgia. The picturesque and noisy streets of Tiflis were always full of people of many nationalities, who together outnumbered the indigenous Georgian population. Not all works of art made or purchased there were necessarily Georgian: they could be Turkish, or Persian, or Daghestanian or Armenian. But in the lives of the inhabitants there was something held in common, something uniquely Caucasian and recognizable by foreigners. It was an attitude to life, stemming from a variety of conditions, but above all, from the fact that politically, life had always been a struggle.

The ancient kingdoms of Colchis and Iberia—now territories of modern Georgia—were well known for their riches and crafts in the ancient world; indeed, one of the reasons that Jason's Golden Fleece is said to have been found in Colchis is that the land had a unique merino sheep with beautiful wool. Hellenic, Achaemenian, and later Persian, Arabic, Mongolian and Turkic cultures were to make their mark on the peoples of the Caucasus, through trade or conquest; but all benefited in learning from the local craftsmen, who were especially skilled in weaving and metalwork. In the seventeenth century, Shah Abbas I of Persia searched for a genuine Georgian sword which would never fail him in battle. Decorative motifs to be seen on five-thousand-year-old Caucasian pottery, on the stone façades of medieval Christian churches, and engraved on silver and woven into carpets, appear relatively unchanged throughout the ages.

It would be impossible to describe a 'typical' Caucasian household, for there were marked variations among ethnic groups, and between rural and urban populations, and, in the rural areas, between the mountain and valley peoples. Even their artistic expression was different: mountain craftsmen employed geometrical designs, while in the valleys, plant forms were used in all ornamentation.

Social allegiance was to paternal kin. Brothers lived close to one another, and sometimes an entire village would consist of a group of brothers and paternal cousins with their wives and children. So highly prized was brotherly love that it was extended by sworn brotherhood and milk-brotherhood. Sworn brothers made a public pledge of their loyalty by cutting a finger over a bowl of wine; milk-brotherhood followed from

Caucasian ox-cart

the father giving a child to be suckled by a friend's wife, whose children were their milk-brothers. Sometimes members of different tribes become brothers in this way, when marriage links were avoided. When the frequent bitter fighting broke out between these peoples, sworn brothers would never fight one another under any circumstances. Recent historians have pointed out the benefits of this institution for trade and the crafts.

Men and boys pastured the sheep, carried on agricultural work, hunted, and generally defended the family's name. They were expected to be entirely fearless, good marksmen and swordsmen, fine horsemen and graceful dancers.

233

Weddings and funerals were attended by great throngs, and even today, the Caucasians have a reputation for boundless hospitality. In the mountains areas, once anyone had succeeded in crossing the threshold, even if he was a mortal enemy, the host was obliged to feed him and entertain him for as long as he remained under his roof.

In the busy towns, the men carried on the weaving and other crafts in small workshops in the commercial streets. The women led more secluded lives than in the villages. The houses, built of mud-bricks or stone, had balconies on the first floor or large projecting wooden verandas. These verandas were lined with long benches and divans covered in rugs, upon which people spent most of their leisure.

The mountain peoples augmented their livelihood in many ways. Sheep could be bought relatively cheaply north of the Caucasian mountains, in the southern plains of Russia; these were driven over the mountain passes down into the southern Caucasus to be sold where prices were higher. Domestic silk manufacture was carried on in the towns and villages in areas in the south Caucasus such as Shirvan. Throughout the Caucasus, village craftsmen made goods for urban consumption.

Though the spread of Islam into some mountain areas had modified such differences, the inhabitants of those parts usually did not marry close kinsmen. A network of kinship was established by marriage which spread over a large area, as wives were brought in from other villages. Women generally enjoyed great prestige and respect in the Caucasian mountains, especially the mother. In many areas of the Caucasus, the main pillar of the house was known as the 'Mother pillar', and was carved with sun and moon symbols, and held in reverence. It was the custom for a man to step aside when a woman crossed his path, to give her precedence. This chivalry, did not mean however, that women were pampered or helpless; village women would travel miles on foot on errands, in order to spare the men's horses a tiring journey.

The age of marriage varied throughout the Caucasus. The bride's age might be thirteen or fifteen years old, to about twenty-five in some mountain areas. In their father's house girls learned household tasks, spinning, weaving and sewing, and how to look after domestic animals. Cushions and rugs were prepared for the dowry. It was from her mother-in-law's teaching, however, that the girl would perfect her skills. Gradually her husband's family traditions would be imparted to her, most importantly the cooking recipes and weaving patterns. Whenever her work in her husband's home allowed, she would spin and weave, making clothing and saddle-bags, and, in some areas, the long rugs that cover the ox-drawn wagons in which the whole family travels.

Caucasian shop showing kilims

The Caucasian Kilim

The Caucasus, with its rich amalgam of peoples and cultures, produced a large number of kilims, most of which are of fine quality. Despite this ethnological diversity, the kilims of the Caucasus share common designs and colours. The information available at present makes it impossible to ascribe these kilims to particular peoples or regions with any accuracy. We shall endeavour, therefore, to classify them in groups based upon similarities of design and structure.

Some features are common to all Caucasian kilims. In general their composition is based on the principle of repeating geometric ornaments forming patterns. The motifs are mostly arranged in horizontal rows or in diagonally offset formations, or, more rarely, in vertical columns.

For its decoration, the Caucasian kilim relies on rectilinear geometric motifs: sometimes these are simple polygons such as hexagons, lozenges or squares, sometimes more complex designs, reminiscent of animal or vegetable forms.

The majority of Caucasian kilims are woven in one piece like their southern Persian counterparts. There are, however, some pieces woven in two parts with characteristic Caucasian features, but these are likely to lie outside the mainstream of Caucasian kilim production.

The material for both warp and weft is almost exclusively wool, except in some southern examples, probably from north Persia, where undyed cotton is used for the white areas of design, a feature common in the kilims of Fars.

The weave is pure slit tapestry, a technique the Caucasians have mastered possibly better than anyone else, making a virtue out of its limitations and turning the impossibility of weaving simple vertical or diagonal straight lines into a decorative feature with endless variations. Their texture is even and tight, and their thickness does not vary much from group to group.

The designs are very precisely executed. The repetition, which is the basis of all Caucasian kilim compositions, is very accurate and produces stable and orderly patterns. The colour range is rich and varies considerably, but overall the colours are strong and contrasting. The visual effect is one of boldness rather than of subtlety, which is more commonly associated with Anatolian kilims.

The warps are usually either of natural brown wool or of the 'salt-and-pepper' type, a mixture, that is, of white and brown wools twisted together. A characteristic feature of pure Caucasian kilims is the manner in which the warp threads are terminated at the top and bottom. Small bunches of warps are knotted together all along the end of the kilim. The resulting tufts are split in two and each one is knotted to the one adjacent to it. The procedure is then repeated to make four or more rows.

In some southern or western examples, the warps are plaited together along the end of the kilim to produce a multi-layered, flat braid identical to those found in the Kurdish kilims from Kars and Lake Van in east Anatolia, and to those from the north and west of Persia.

In the past, among dealers and collectors, and in the few rug publications in which they appeared, Caucasian kilims (often referred to as 'Palas') were divided into two broad groups: Kuba and Shirvan. Careful examination of several hundred examples soon made it apparent that the diversity of structural and decorative features could not be encompassed satisfactorily within these two groups. A cursory glance at the ethnographical composition of the region is sufficient to demonstrate the impossibility of such a simplification. There are pieces, for instance, which are closely related to Persian weavings and could well be from Azerbaijan or even further south, well into Persia. Similarly, there are examples which have marked Kurdish or even Anatolian features, which may indicate some geographical or ethnographical link with these areas.

Though 'Kuba' and 'Shirvan' refer to important Caucasian weaving regions, evidence that either group of kilims was woven specifically or even predominantly at these locations is scarce. Indeed, there are many surviving nineteenth-century photographs of the so-called Shirvan band kilims showing them being used as covers for ox-carts in the province of Georgia, some three hundred miles to the north-west of their supposed place of origin. Nevertheless, the names have become entrenched in rug literature, and we shall retain them here.

As is always the case when one is attempting to divide oriental textiles into groups based on ornamental or structural features without adequate and reliable evidence, either written or based on local research, the task is awesome. Many pieces have characteristics in common with more than one homogeneous group. Unfortunately for the student of kilims, the Caucasus is rich in such cases. Often kilims with entirely different decoration can be almost identical in colour, structure and texture, a phenomenon which indicates that individual weaving groups were aware of a range of patterns and designs not confined to their immediate vicinity.

The kilims we are about to describe fall mainly into two large families, which are clearly related and yet remain distinct from each other. The first family illustrated has been sub-divided according to ornament. In the second family we have not been able to find such clear distinctions.

'Kuba' Kilims

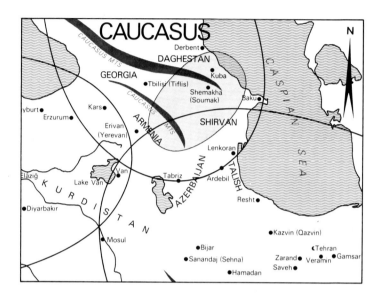

The kilims of this large family are very finely woven and share a unique design feature: the extensive use of large, abstract, geometric ornaments relying heavily on vertical lines. Because of the inherent technical limitation in weaving vertical straight lines in slit tapestry, the weavers alternate the width of these lines at short intervals in such a way as to produce a continuous crenellated effect.

Another distinctive peculiarity of these kilims is the way the designs are formed. The ornaments have definite linear outlines; the spaces between which are filled with colour. In most other Caucasian kilims, however, the motifs are formed by joining blocks of different colours, the outline of the designs being formed by the change in the colours.

Unlike most 'Shirvan' kilims, 'Kuba' pieces are usually enclosed by borders of which there are two varieties: those with repeat designs (such as plates 279 and 284) and those with a continuous 'meander-and-bar' pattern (such as plate 286). The field is decorated with large-scale designs arranged horizontally or diagonally and, more rarely, vertically. The gaps between are filled with a plethora of small minor designs.

While the borders are common to all 'Kuba' kilims, the major ornaments in the field divide them into two main groups—the medallion type and the cartouche type.

It may be argued that the origin of both medallion and cartouche is the same. Furthermore, both vegetable and animal origin can be demonstrated. For ease of identification, however, we shall be using the terms medallion and cartouche throughout the description of the plates.

KILIMS WITH LARGE GEOMETRIC INDENTED MEDALLIONS

The kilims of this type are most prominent among Caucasian kilims. There seems to be an obvious chronological progression indicated by the change in the medallion from a crisp, well-defined and well-spaced directional ornament, to a rigid, symmetrical and mechanical one. However, the convenient and attractive logic of such an hypothesis is somewhat confounded by the fact that occasionally, pieces with what would appear to be 'late' compositions (illustrated at the end of this group) have a beauty of colour and a fineness of texture which suggest that they are at least as old, if not older, than those with the more elegant, and thus supposedly 'early' composition.

It is, perhaps, worth speculating that the origin of the design found on these kilims derives from an earlier group of pile-knotted carpets, referred to here as the 'shield' group (see Ulrich Schurmann, *Caucasian Rugs,* plates 6, 62 and 94). The earliest example of this type is probably a carpet in the Musée des Arts Décoratifs in Paris. F. R. Martin, in his monumental work *Oriental Carpets before 1800,* believed that the origin of the pattern could be found in Ottoman textiles with floral designs. However, the concept of stylized medallions arranged in a series of rows can be traced back to some of the earliest-known textiles.

These medallions could also be interpreted as highly schematic renderings of a motif found in pre-Islamic textiles and on early carpets—that of animals flanking a tree. Lastly, a double-headed eagle derivation can be demonstrated. Today the design is popularly referred to as a 'tarantula'.

279 *174×357 cm.*

The field pattern consists of diagonally offset indented medallions arranged chromatically in horizontal rows. The overall composition follows the typical format of Caucasian pile carpets: field surrounded by a border flanked by guardstripes. Such a composition is confined to the 'Kuba' group of Caucasian kilims.

This piece is one of the finest examples of its type known. The arrangement of the medallions is well balanced. The 'diamond-and-pole' containing a pattern of serrated blocks is typical of the whole group. The triangular form surmounted by a cross, which appears on each side of the medallions, is frequently found on Thracian kilims and is also related to the Turkoman *kochak*, which is assumed to be a stylized representation of a bird's head. The 'hour-glass' border is particularly well drawn and makes an interesting contrast with the more usual 'meander-and-bar' border found on such kilims. This kilim should be compared with one illustrated in *From the Bosphorus to Samarkand*, plate 1, and with an example in *Oriental Rugs in the Metropolitan Museum of Art*, Fig. 241, Cat. no. 179.

280 *139×231 cm.*

The 'kochak' motif noted in the previous example is in plate 280 even more schematic and difficult to recognize; furthermore, the crosses surmounting the medallion 'heads' no longer appear. The space between the medallions, which gives the first piece such a fine compositional balance, is less generous here, and as a result the field has a slightly cramped appearance. The half-medallions do not give the impression of an endlessly repeated pattern, rather they seem to have been used as a space-filling device. Both the main and outer borders are most unusual, this being the only kilim of the group known to us on which they appear. The main border contains hooked stepped cruciform designs seen on carpets depicted in fifteenth-century Flemish paintings by Hans Memling. The design survives on knotted rugs, produced until recently in Anatolia and also in the Caucasus, specifically in the Moghan and Gendje areas. The

outer border, an elegant version of the 'running dog' design, is found on Soumak rugs and on certain Turkoman pile carpets, particularly those of the Yomut.

281 *188×408 cm.*

In this last example of the directional medallion type, the scattered ornaments within the medallions have almost entirely disappeared. The 'diamond-and-pole' here appears as an 'octagon-and-pole'. These octagons contain a serrated motif which is the normal alternative to the pattern of square blocks seen in the previous examples. The individual medallions are less well defined, and the lattice arrangement of the field is far more immediately apparent. The 'meander-and-bar' border is the one most often encountered on kilims of this type.

282 *183×361 cm.*
283 *no size available*

The principal departure of plate 282 from the designs of the kilims illustrated so far is that the composition is no longer directional; that is, the piece may be viewed satisfactorily from either end. The 'kochak' motif, seen most clearly on plate 279, is present at the four corners of the medallions. These are beautifully drawn and have become symmetrical along both the horizontal and vertical axes. They are close and regular, thereby emphasizing once again the lattice-like nature of the field.

The indented medallions of plate 283 show a further stylization of outline. The three-pronged motifs at the sides of the medallions have become clearly stated and are a constant feature on later examples. Note the two small animals at either end of the second row of medallions.

The borders of plates 282 and 283 are obviously related. Both have the 'meander-and-bar' outer border and the 'hour-glass' main border. However, in plate 282 the 'hour-glass' motif has a crenellated outline at either end; this is missing in plate 283, and the latter also has an added hexagon in the centre of the motif.

284–7 *Four Variations on the Same Medallion*

These four kilims are only illustrated in part. Kilims like these have been found with synthetic orange dyes, which would place them no earlier than the last quarter of the nineteenth

279

280

281

282

283

284

285

286

287

century, and probably well into the present century. Such dyes are not present in any of the pieces illustrated, although they show what might be a late development of the medallion type.

284   *147 × 315 cm. (Detail)*

The three-pronged motifs first seen in plate 283 are more pronounced here. The extensive use of scattered ornaments between the medallions is uncommon. This is the only piece of the group in which medallions are not offset but form two vertical rows, although this arrangement is found in pile-knotted rugs and is common in the next group. Plate 284 has unusual stepped-diamond serrations at either end of the medallions and a most uncommon border design: at the ends of each of the principal borders may be seen two variants of the main border motif. These are archaic 'kochak' forms and may be seen drawn in similar manner on some of the famous fragments of early pile-knotted carpets found at Fostat in Egypt. The four unusual versions of the border design, two of which may also be seen enclosed in white rectangles in the lower half of the field, are an alternative renderings of the 'kochak' in which the birds' heads appear to point outwards. The narrow end-borders of this piece contrast with the side borders. They contain alternating blocks of colour separated by diagonal lines; this difference in the borders should not be considered as evidence of pattern degeneration or of a late date. This feature also appears on other kilims illustrated, plates 296, 297, 303, which we do not consider to be late examples.

285   *no size available (Detail)*

The inner border of this kilim appears only on three sides and contains designs similar to those on plate 284, while the outer border frames the piece completely. The handling of the half-medallions relates this piece to plate 280.

286   *155 × 251 cm. (Detail)*

Here we have a different and more complex infill to the centres of the 'diamond-and-pole' motifs. The medallions, on a deep blue field, form a diagonal pattern, but the colours are used at random. The three-pronged motifs of the neighbouring medallions form opposing pairs; these pairs are reminiscent of a typical minor design element found in Anatolian kilims (border of plate 126 and field of plate 186).

287   *165 × 295 cm. (Detail)*

This kilim, yet another variant of the group, contains alternating blue and white horizontal rows of medallions on a red field, seemingly in opposition to the diagonally offset arrangement of the medallions. These have become thinner and the three-pronged elements predominate. The piece bears a close resemblance to a kilim in the Victoria and Albert Museum, London, published by Kendrick and Tattersall, 1973, plate 118B, where the design is referred to as a derivative of the 'sunburst'. Both this piece and the next are somewhat mechanically composed, though their 'meander-and-bar' borders are very elegantly drawn.

288   *160 × 282 cm.*

The last of the geometric medallion kilims we illustrate points to the problem of the relative dating and stylistic development of the whole group. Stylistically, it would appear to represent the last phase in the development of the pattern, with no suggestion of an endless repeat and very static, angular, ornamentation. However, this seeming progression is contradicted both by the extensive and beautiful range of colours and by the texture, each of which suggests a considerably earlier date, and relates the piece to plate 279.

Thus this piece represents the crucial dilemma facing those who seek to date kilims—the weight to be given to the character of the design on the one hand and the quality of the piece on the other. We have avoided dating these kilims although we believe, admittedly with little evidence, that this group may be attributed to the second half of the nineteenth century and the early years of the twentieth. A kilim of the type of plate 286 may be seen among the wares of a Caucasian rug-shop illustrated in *Aspects of the Caucasus* by E. Marcov (Moscow 1904), which we reproduce on page 234.

288

289

290

291

292

293

The three pile rugs on plates 289, 290 and 291 show the geometric medallion designs found on the kilims discussed so far. The transposition of flat-weave designs to pile-knotted pieces, and vice versa, is most unusual.

Plate 289 has a medallion similar to that found on plate 282. However, the 'kochak' motif of the latter is missing from the four corners, being replaced by bars, a format which is closest to plate 288. We have not been able to examine this piece: the photograph is drawn from the archives of the once-famous Perez Company of London; it was attributed by them to the Karabagh region of the Caucasus. The formal arrangement of large medallions and small infill designs of plate 289 is unknown in the kilims of this group, as is this form of the reciprocal 'spear-head' border. One of the most fascinating aspects of this and the following rugs, is the transposition of the crenellations, essential to the creation of vertical lines in slit-tapestry weaving, to pile-knotted pieces, a sure demonstration that this piece is a copy of a kilim. It would also, of course, seem to indicate that the weavers of these carpets had little knowledge of the slit-tapestry technique. It is likely, therefore, that they simply admired the decorative effect of the crenellations and wished to emulate it on the knotted pieces.

The field composition of plate 290 is perhaps closer than that of the previous example to the kilims of the medallion group, and should be compared to plate 283. The small ornaments between the medallions are typical of these kilims. The 'octagon-and-star' within the 'diamond-and-pole' has not been observed so far on flat-woven pieces.

Plate 291 has an unusual composition by Caucasian kilim standards: a single, rigid, vertical row of medallions; the spaces between are filled on each side with the three-pronged elements. There are also scattered animal, bird and floral motifs, including *boteh* (floral clusters in the shape of pine cones), some of which contain 'barber's pole' patterns. These scattered motifs give the carpet a direction which does not stem from the medallions themselves. This design feature is often encountered in carpets with an apparently nondirectional composition. The 'boteh' with 'barber's pole' filling are related to those found on Marasali pile-knotted prayer rugs (see Ulrich Schurmann, *Caucasian Rugs,* plate 78) from the Shirvan district. The minor borders are similar to those on pile-knotted pieces from the Kuba region, while the major border has already been seen on plate 280.

Plate 292 is related to the next group of 'Kuba' kilims illustrated, those with angular cartouches. Both the form of the cartouches and the minor designs between them justify such a relationship. The infills are typical, both in style and layout, of the Caucasian interpretation of the Turkoman *gül,* a feature that we have not found on the kilims. This plate, taken from the catalogue of an exhibition held in 1973 at the Sursock Museum, Beirut, was attributed there to the Shirvan region, and there is little reason to doubt this, though some scholars would prefer an attribution to Chajli, slightly further south.

293   *88 × 162 cm.*

Plate 293 shows the opposite procedure, a pile-rug design woven in slit tapestry, and is the only flat-woven Caucasian prayer rug so far discovered. It appeared in an auction held by Lefevre and Partners in London on 25 November 1977, lot 4. The lattice, niche and ornaments in the spandrels are typical of the pile prayer rugs of Daghestan (see Ulrich Schurmann, *Caucasian Rugs,* plate 125). However, the ornament within the lattice is similar to the inner ornament of the 'diamond-and-pole' of the previous kilims. The major border is found on both kilims and pile rugs, while the inner reciprocal border is quite common on pile rugs from this region and can be found in the kilims of north-west Persia (see plates 338 and 341).

KILIMS WITH ANGULAR CARTOUCHES

A pointed, angular cartouche is the distinctive feature of the following four examples. In two of them the motifs within the cartouches are hooked and angular while in the others they adopt a more scroll-like form.

Certain ornaments appear on all of them, notably the central vertical pole culminating in a 'double kochak' at the centre of the cartouches.

294   *160 × 292 cm.*

In texture and feel this seems to be one of the earliest Caucasian kilims we have examined. It is also one of the most striking. The field decoration consists primarily of two vertical rows of

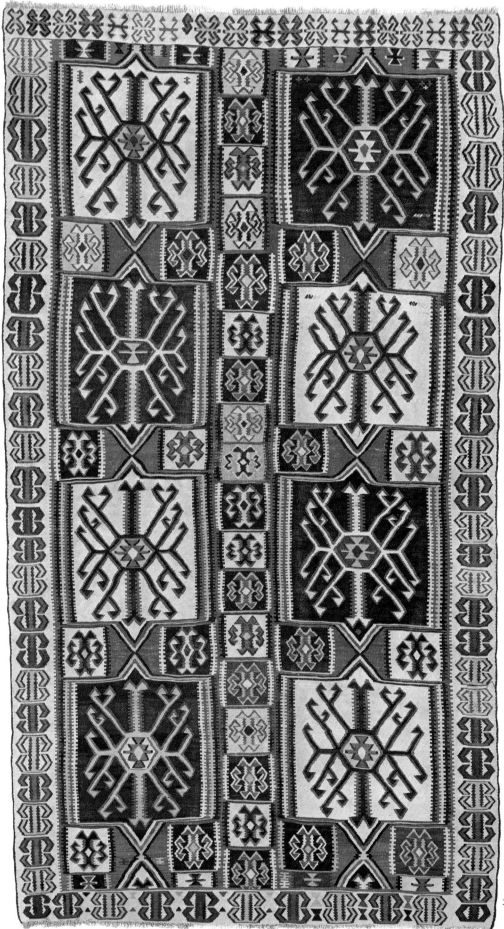

294

295

296

297

large cartouches, separated by a narrow row of small juxtaposed rectangles containing hooked motifs similar to those found in the field of the prayer kilim on plate 293. The elegant border is reminiscent of Turkish kilims; worthy of attention are the contrasting designs of the top border. The 'pole-and-hexagon' at the centre of the large cartouches relates to the 'pole-and-diamond' of the previously discussed group, especially plate 281.

295   *175 × 310 cm.*

With its hooked interior ornament, this kilim is similar to the previous example. However, the compositional arrangement of horizontal rows of three juxtaposed medallions, and the lack of narrow vertical dividing rows creates long cartouches between the medallions; this strict alternation of shape gives the field a more formal or rigid appearance. At either end of the field is the 'hour-glass' motif found in the borders of some of the geometric medallion kilims (plates 279, 282, 283). A small rectangle at the upper end bears the date AH 1322 (AD 1904). In handle, the piece is crisp and finely woven. The red and blue are harsher than on the other pieces of this type illustrated, and there are also small amounts of synthetic orange. These features confirm the lateness of the piece, independently of the woven date.

296   *157 × 254 cm.*

Plate 296 has the same layout of triple medallions and cartouche-shaped spaces, although here, the effect is less rigid, due in the main to the variety of ornaments within the cartouches. This piece has strong, rich colours; the darker medallions have an unusual shade of deep blue-green. Note the simple striped border at the top end of this kilim, a feature already encountered in plate 284 and which will also be seen on the next piece. Simplification of the top border, or even its omission, may be indicative of the weaver's intention to stress the directional nature of his work and could also be dictated by the function intended for the piece.

297   *152 × 305 cm.*

This piece also has vivid colours. The medallions are more

widely spaced than those on the two previous examples, and there is a lively variety of infill ornamentation. Three of the infill octagons in the field contain the hooked cruciform motif discussed in connection with plate 280. A continuous series of small ornaments, similar to those found scattered all over the field, surrounds the two rows of large cartouches. Once again, we see a contrasting striped outer border at one end. A kilim of the present group sold at Lefevre's in London on 25 November 1977, lot 5, had the same main field cartouches as this piece; the areas between, however, were filled with a small version of the indented medallions of plate 284, and its borders were variants of those found on plate 284 and at the top end of plate 294.

The presence of tiny amounts of synthetic dye can often be found on kilims of this group, which would place them no earlier than the last quarter of the nineteenth century. It is known that early synthetic dyes were considered bright and beautiful by Middle Eastern weavers, and that in the early years of their export to the East, they were extremely expensive and considered precious.

KILIMS WITH MIXED DESIGNS

Several kilims contain a mixture of all the design elements of the pieces previously discussed, as well as showing similarities of colour and texture. However, whereas examples of the previous compositions occur regularly, the various types included here are far less common. This should not necessarily be taken as evidence that they were produced in significantly smaller numbers—indeed, since kilims are a traditional art, it is reasonable to assume that many more do, in fact, exist. It is likely that we have still not encountered the full range of compositions of the so-called Kuba kilims. When another example does appear, it will surely have not only design elements previously seen, but chromatic and textural similarities also.

298   *no size available*

The small diamonds within the larger stepped diamonds of plate 298 closely resemble the motifs found within the centre of the medallions on plate 279. The two pieces also share the 'hour-glass' border. It is most unusual in that it is woven in two halves, a feature common to Anatolian kilims, but rare among those attributed to the Caucasus. Its proportions too, are distinctive, its length being very short compared to its width.

299   *163 × 300 cm.*

Plate 299 is more tightly composed, and there is no diamond-within-diamond arrangement. Instead, there is a single motif in the stepped diamonds which is, again, often found in the centres of the geometric medallions. This piece has vertical guardstripes at either side but no borders or end stripes.

300   *195 × 343 cm.*

The composition is formed by major and minor horizontal bands with no borders. Such compositions are the norm in kilims of the 'Shirvan' type, not the 'Kuba'. The ornaments filling the bands, howerer, are standard features of the 'Kuba' family, and the colours are also typical.

301   *175 × 335 cm.*

Plate 301 is composed of vertical rows of indented hexagons containing hooked medallions, and should be included within the 'Kuba' group, even though such a composition is more typical of pieces from the south and south-west Caucasus. Equally interesting is the vertical pattern of conjoined white diamonds, formed by the outlines of the hexagons, which is a feature of a specific group of kilims from east Anatolia (plate 270). The small representations of people suggest that the piece may have been woven as a wedding gift. It bears a date: AH 1315 (AD 1896).

302   *158 × 310 cm.*

The field of plate 302 contains hexagons, common to the 'Shirvan' band kilims. This piece, however, has a typical 'meander-and-bar' border and is also related to the 'Kuba' group in colour. For a particularly close 'Shirvan' comparison, however, see plate 304. Kerimov publishes a very similar example (*Azerbaidzhan Carpets*, Baku, 1961, plate 218, no. 1) which he attributes to Pashali. An interesting feature of this piece is the use of a diamond lattice to form a pattern of hexagons. Notice also the variety of small ornaments at the sides of the kilim, used instead of half-hexagons to terminate the composition.

303   *167 × 296 cm.*

A piece of strong visual presence, this has the appearance of great age. The rectangular blocks found within the 'diamond-and-pole' in the kilims of the indented medallion group we have examined are used here to outline the two vertical rows of large medallions, each one of which contains a typical geometric hooked motif. Unlike the kilims previously discussed, which have a contrasting border at one end only, this example has well-drawn, narrow diagonal band borders at both ends.

A closely related example was published by J. McMullan in the *Catalogue of the George Walter Vincent and Belle Townsend Smith Collection of Islamic Rugs*, plate 25. It has a single vertical row of diamonds surrounded by an 'hour-glass' border similar to plate 283. At the top of the kilim is an ornament which links that piece to a well known type of Shirvan pile rug, an example of which is published by Schurman, plate 66.

298

299

300

301

302

303

'Shirvan' Kilims

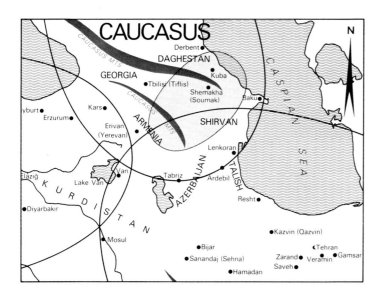

This is the Caucasian kilim *par excellence*. The pieces belonging to this family are the ones most readily identified with the Caucasus; there are large numbers of them and most are of high quality.

In terms of materials they are identical to those of the previous family. Chromatically they are also similar, though occasionally a softer palette is used here. The vertical crenellated line, so predominant in the 'Kuba' pieces, is totally absent, and so are the borders. The weave is fine and even, the resulting fabric being crisp, tight and flat.

The designs are simple, bold, geometric ornaments, more abstract than those of 'Kuba' pieces. There, the medallions or cartouches were large and contained motifs totally unrelated in form to the shape in which they were enclosed. Here, instead, the infills of the ornaments are compatible with their shape and follow the same basic geometry. Both the individual motifs and the compositions are usually symmetrical along the horizontal and the vertical axes, giving these kilims a non-directional appearance.

The majority of these kilims are composed of wide and narrow horizontal bands, in a variety of sequences, going across the entire width of the field. The wide primary bands containing the major ornaments alternate with narrow secondary bands containing minor ornaments. Often the wide bands are flanked on each side by means of very narrow guard-bands.

The major designs are usually hexagons containing either hooked motifs or smaller stepped hexagons. The spaces between these major designs are normally filled with triangles. The minor designs are more varied and can be small stepped diamonds often containing crosses, hooked ornaments of all sorts (often in pairs) zigzags, chevrons and continuous 'S' forms. Occasionally designs normally associated with minor bands are used as major ornaments, as in plate 319, and there are some examples where major bands are totally absent, such as plate 313.

304 *154×323 cm.*

This is one of the few examples of a 'Shirvan' kilim not arranged in horizontal bands. It contains the hexagons usually found in this group. They are capped at both ends with small triangles which turn them into large diamonds. These diamonds are diagonally offset and form a grid pattern, giving the blue field the appearance of a lattice. The composition of this kilim is very similar to that of plate 302 although, in common with the other kilims of this group, it has no borders.

305 *152×300 cm.*

The 'Shirvan' kilim is here in its most typical and complete form. This type, frequently used as the roof of covered ox-carts, often appears in contemporary photographs from Georgia (see p. 233). The hooked motif and diamond containing a cross found within the major hexagons is a common feature; as is the arrangement of the zigzag guard-bands and of the small diamonds in the secondary bands. Note the serrated edge at the sides of the bands.

306   *180 × 370 cm.*

This kilim contains almost the entire range of colours found in this group. The composition is very orderly and follows a regular overall grid-pattern. This aspect of kilim design is discussed in greater detail in the section on designs, patterns and compositions. Notice the richness of minor ornaments between the last hexagons of each band and the serrated edges. Its good state of preservation makes it possible to see the rows of small knots formed by the warps at each end. This technique is also common in the pile rugs of the Shirvan region.

307   *154 × 321 cm.*
308   *171 × 306 cm.*

These two unusual and interesting kilims belong to the 'Shirvan' group in terms of design and also in terms of colour and texture; their difference lies in the presence of a narrow border surrounding the field. The small, simple, repeated diamonds decorating the border are unlike any designs in borders of other Caucasian kilims, but are typical minor ornaments of this family. The compostion is related to that of plates 302 and 304, though here the hooked motifs are not enclosed in hexagons but instead float on the field in a diagonally offset formation with a random arrangement of colours.

The hooked motifs, less elongated than is the norm in this group of kilims, are also on a noticeably smaller scale. The profusion of colours scattered on the field creates a rich and dynamic effect despite the somewhat cool colour range.

The blue border in plate 307 joins the white field by means of a continuous serrated zigzag pattern similar to that found at the sides of plates 305 and 306; the field creates an endless pattern despite the small ornaments filling the gaps at the sides of the composition, which are more varied than in plate 308, where they consist solely of groups of small diamonds.

In plate 308 we have the opposite colour arrangement: a blue field surrounded by a white border. The join of the field and the border is different, consisting of a continuous crenellated outline formed by the juxtaposition of the blue and white, a feature more usually identified with Anatolian kilims. The border designs are more uniform and resemble those at the bottom of the previous piece.

309   *170 × 280 cm.*

This is most probably one of the earliest kilim of this group, and certainly the most attractive. The proportional relationship between the major and minor designs is very harmonious. The bands, both primary and secondary, get narrower as the eye moves from the bottom to the top of the piece, an effect we shall see to such a marked degree on only one other example: plate 336, also of an early date.

The large hexagons in this kilim show an interesting design feature; the figure-ground illusion. The design within the hexagons can be seen either as a hooked diamond or as a star-shaped polygon containing a diamond (see Designs, Patterns and Compositions). The secondary motif between the major hexagons, reminiscent of south Persian kilims like plate 398, may be seen in its complete form in the primary bands of the following three pieces. A charming element of the present piece is the pipe-smoking man with his dog, which appears at the extreme left of the bottom band. A comparable feature is encountered on one of the Qashqai pieces we illustrate (plate 399).

310   *137 × 275 cm.*
311   *144 × 290 cm.*

The exterior of the hexagons on both these pieces has an indented, stepped outline forming a cog-like pattern, which makes an interesting contrast with the designs seen on the previous kilim. Plate 310, however, has the same stepped diamond-and-hook interior as plate 309, while on plate 311 the interiors of the hexagons repeat the exteriors on a smaller scale. On plate 310, the triangular motifs between the hexagons are surmounted by crosses, motifs frequently encountered on Caucasian kilims. At an early stage of carpet scholarship, these were considered evidence of a Christian Armenian origin. Such an hypothesis no longer enjoys the same general degree of acceptance, although there is no absolute proof that it is without foundation. Both these pieces show a variety of ornamentation within their minor borders and have similar decorative elements at the sides. Plate 311 replaces the usual zigzag guard-bands with a series of three plain-coloured narrow stripes.

304

305

306

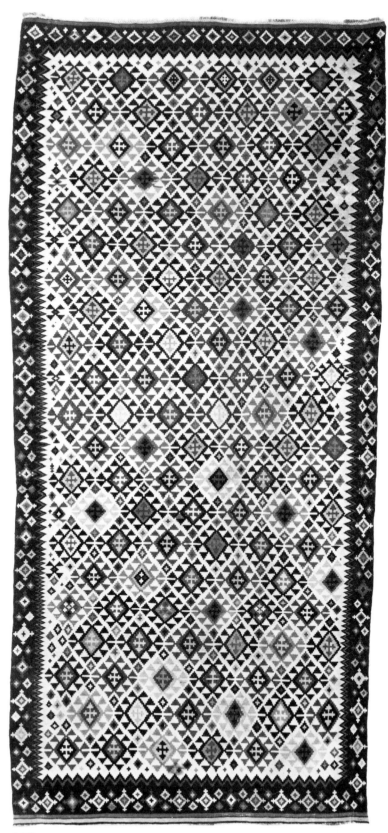

307

308

309

310

311

312

313

314

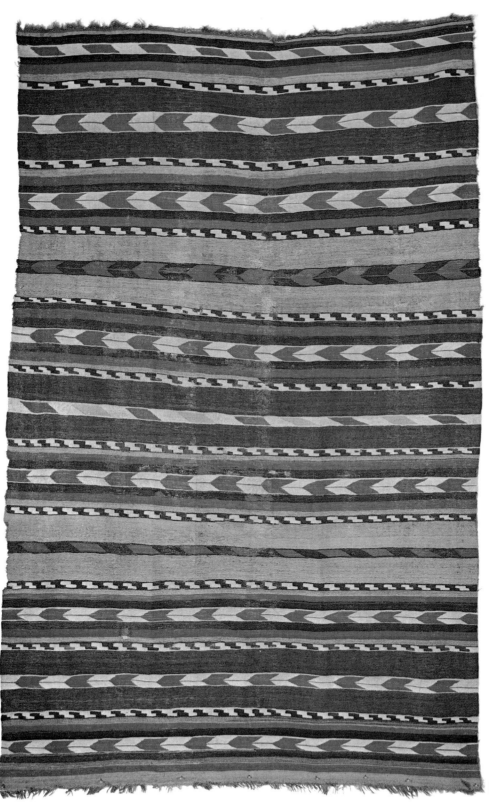

315

316

317

318

319

312   *145 × 320 cm.*

This is a kilim of unusually light colours with excellent chromatic harmony. The designs follow those of plate 311 closely, although the bands have the same serrated edges seen on plate 305. Here the polychrome zigzag guard-bands are very large in scale, almost obscuring the secondary bands, and they contribute largely to the visual appeal of the piece. In texture, quality of wool and colours this kilim differs somewhat from the previous examples, a fact which might indicate a different origin within the same general area.

313   *140 × 270 cm.*
314   *173 × 350 cm.*

These pieces and the following example are composed solely of the secondary bands and the guard-bands seen between the wide bands of the previously illustrated pieces. Plate 313 is a particularly good example of this type. The sense of movement in the meander-and-conjoined-diamond bands contrasts with the static quality of the plain stripes between them. Plate 314, however, is composed only of simple stripes, yet through the use of contrasting light and dark plain bands, it achieves a tremendous sense of space.

315   *158 × 239 cm.*

The principal design feature of this kilim is a series of narrow bands containing continuous 'chevrons' or 'arrowheads'. It is the colours and the proportion of the simple bands which make it so attractive. We have not seen any other similar examples from the Caucasus.

316   *163 × 299 cm. (Detail)*

Plate 316, like plate 304, is an unusual 'Shirvan' kilim with no bands, having instead an overall field pattern of diagonally offset and interlocking star-shaped diamonds. The ivory outline of these diamonds forms continuous intersecting zigzag lines, thus creating a lattice effect.

317   *152 × 254 cm. (Detail)*

In plate 317 the diamonds of plate 316, halved, are placed within bands in a typical 'Shirvan' format; the secondary and guard-bands contain the simple diagonal blocks seen at the top and bottom of plate 316 and in the field of plate 315.

318   *182 × 365 cm. (Detail)*

Plate 318 shows another interpretation of the hooked motif in the interior of the major hexagons. This version is more common in north Persian kilims (like plate 342) and, in fact, a more southern and western origin cannot be excluded for this piece on account of its braided warps. The secondary bands are very pronounced, to the point that the minor designs almost compete with the major ones. The minor hexagons of this kilim occasionally appear elsewhere as major ornaments, and demonstrate yet another variation of this motif. Though none is illustrated in this book, there are examples of 'Shirvan' kilims with alternating primary bands, each containing different major designs.

319   *141 × 300 cm. (Detail)*

Plate 319 illustrates the phenomenon of designs usually associated with secondary bands becoming the major ornament of the piece. The pairs of hooked ornaments again create a figure-ground illusion (see Designs, Patterns and Compositions).

Persia

320

Early Persian Kilims and Their Development

Such has been the fame of the Persian rug that many people not acquainted with the subject use the term generically to embrace all oriental rugs. What is less widely known, is that although Persian carpets have been famed since antiquity, and praised by many contemporary authors, not a single fragment of a Persian pile-knotted rug made before the sixteenth century has survived to the present day. All our information about them comes from texts and paintings. An examination of these paintings, mostly miniatures, suggests that the early Persian carpet was virtually indistinguishable from its Turkish counterpart, sharing with it the same largely geometric decorative repertoire.

Tapestry-weaving, fortunately, has yielded more direct evidence, such as the fabric with the Kufic inscription dating from the Seljuk period (plate 321). That this technique was also employed for large tapestries or rugs is known from literary sources. As mentioned in the beginning of this book, the word kilim, or rather the Persian version *gelim*, appears in texts of the eleventh century, apparently with the same meaning it has today.

What these early kilims would have looked like is not certain. In a fourteenth-century miniature from the *Khalila wa dimna* (plate 320) a textile that could easily be a kilim is shown as a blanket draped over a lady's body. It consists of a series of narrow bands, some plain and some with continuous black and white chevrons. The designs of this blanket bear a striking resemblance to those of Fars kilims like plates 403 and 404, and are identical to the designs on the end panels of plate 382. It is conceivable that the blanket could be of another type of fabric such as a velvet; but considering its function and the marked angularity of the design, it seems more probable that it is some type of tapestry-woven fabric, an early ancestor of the kilims of Fars.

SAFAVID KILIMS

No such scarcity of material, however, exists with regard to Persian carpets from the sixteenth and seventeenth centuries.

321

Carpets and carpet fragments have survived in relatively large quantities, including among them a substantial number of tapestry-woven pieces (about forty). Technique apart, these pieces have little in common with the village and nomadic Persian kilims we know today. They are fine pieces, splendidly drawn and executed in silk and metal thread, decorated in the classical Safavid style created by the artists working for Shah Tahmasp and Shah Abbas, with figural representations, huntings scenes, arabesques and all sorts of complex floral designs (plates 322, 324 and 326). Like all the great Safavid carpets, they were woven in ateliers following detailed cartoons designed by court miniaturists.

These Safavid kilims bear little resemblance in texture to the roughly contemporary Ottoman kilims of the Divriği group (plates 53 to 58), which were much more thickly woven woollen pieces. There are, however, similarities in structure, in that both groups primarily use single-interlock and dovetail tapestry rather than slit tapestry, and also in design, such as the border cartouches on plates 57 and 324. There is, however, one silk and metal-thread tapestry-woven seat cover in the Textile Museum in Washington, DC (plate 323), which has been attributed to sixteenth-century Ottoman Turkey on the grounds of its distinctive shape and designs, notably the hyacinths—a typical Ottoman flower—in the large serrated leaves in the field. If this attribution is correct, it suggests a group of Ottoman tapestry weavings, of which this is the only survivor, that would be almost indistinguishable in colours, materials, technique and texture from the Safavid silk and metal-thread kilims. One should consider whether this may, in fact, be a Persian weaving, and attempt to explain its Ottoman character either as a royal gift, or as an order made for export to the Ottoman market. It could even be that it was woven in Constantinople by Persian weavers.

Whether such relationships are strong enough to suggest a direct artistic connection, involving cross-fertilization of designs, between the master artists in the weaving ateliers of Safavid Persia and Ottoman Turkey, as was certainly the case with paintings and ceramics, is not yet fully established. Certainly, all the available material points clearly in that direction. This is, however, an area where a great deal of research is still required, the results of which will be of crucial importance to our knowledge of early oriental rugs.

In the past, Safavid kilims were generally thought to have been woven in Kashan because of some examples which bear the coat-of-arms of Sigmund III, King of Poland (1587–1632). These are known to have been purchased by the King's

agent, Sefer Muratowicz, who placed the order and had it executed in Kashan. The attribution of the other pieces to Kashan was made in some cases because of their known history, but in others solely on the basis of often-vague stylistic relationships with the emblazoned pieces.

Some authors have long suspected that there are far too many variations among all the surviving examples to support the theory of a common origin. The quality of drawing and execution is by no means uniform, and there are marked stylistic and iconographic differences among them. Some pieces have a decorative repertoire restricted to floral motifs and arabesques, while others have a complex combination of figural representations and floral designs. The royal workshops of Isfahan, the capital of Shah Abbas, were, therefore, suggested as a further source for these tapestries.

Recently, however, a hitherto unknown example of this group was discovered, bearing an inscription which states that it was made in Tabriz (plate 325). This new kilim throws fresh light on the previously known pieces, and establishes that the production of these luxurious silk and metal-thread weavings was restricted neither to a single atelier nor to one centre, being much more widespread than was originally thought.

This family of Safavid kilims can be dated fairly accurately to the late sixteenth and early seventeenth centuries on the basis of King Sigmund's reign; a dating which is corroborated by another piece, in the Kodai-ji in Kyoto, which was made into a coat that belonged to the regent Toyotomi Hideyoshi, who died in 1598.

Two related pieces exist, however, which, on stylistic grounds alone, seem to be the precursors of the others, and probably date no later than the middle of the sixteenth century. One of them, in the W. H. Moore collection (plate 326), is a tapestry-woven rendering of a painting depicting a hunting scene with large-scale figures, and the other, presently in the Los Angeles County Museum of Art (plate 327), has figures, animals and flowers arranged in a complex grid pattern of eight-lobed medallions and eight-pointed stars.

While the classical Safavid style of decoration continued, and survived up to the present day in pile carpets—albeit in a much degenerated form, lacking any of the beauty and splendour of the originals—kilim weaving as a sophisticated court workshop production stopped suddenly in the seventeenth century. The only later kilims of comparable fineness, which may also have been woven in workshops, come from the Kurdish town of Sehna (Sanandaj). The oldest examples of these kilims are not earlier than the end of the eighteenth century,

322

while most date from the nineteenth century (plates 344 to 353). Their delicate floral decoration, consisting mostly of small-scale designs repeated to form endless patterns, is directly inspired by Persian embroideries and brocades of the eighteenth century and bears no relation to the designs of the classical carpets and kilims of the seventeenth century.

The large body of Persian kilims surviving today consists of tribal pieces which have a predominantly geometric repertoire of patterns and designs, arranged in very simple compositions. Their decoration is in no way related to the Safavid style, being much closer to tribal Turkic ornament—not surprising considering how many of the tribes weaving kilims in Persia are in fact of Turkic origin.

Although no example has survived, it is possible that geometric Persian kilims are the product of a long-standing tradition, and once coexisted with the splendid seventeenth-century pieces—or even preceded them, if the blanket illustrated on plate 320 is, indeed, a kilim. Certainly, there are simi-larities in colour and design between some of the glazed-tile mosaics used in architectural decoration in the sixteenth century (plate 328) and some of the typical nineteenth-century kilims from Fars.

These tribal kilims are very dificult to place chronologically and, to some extent, geographically. With the exception of the above-mentioned floral Kurdish kilims from the west of the country, the designs of tapestry-woven pieces usually bear little, if any, relation to the designs of the pile-knotted rugs woven by the same tribes, adding to the difficulty of attribution to places and peoples. Indeed, there is even less information available about nomadic Persian kilims than about their Anatolian counterparts.

Nevertheless, it is these pieces—with their charming, bright and strong colours and infinite varieties of attractive, simple designs, used in all manner of combinations—which define the Persian kilim as we know it today, and which we shall be examining in the following and closing section.

323

324

325

327

328

North-west Persian Kilims

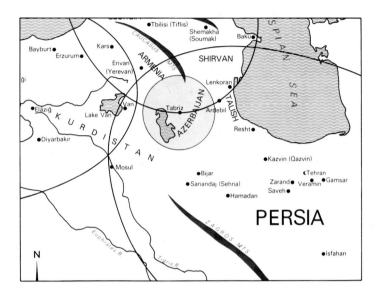

329   *166 × 296 cm.*

This piece is typical of a group of kilims, some of which can be very large. While they are related in design to Caucasian kilims they differ in colours and quality of wool, which here is more lustrous. They have much broader bands; the ornamentation is on a grander scale, and the secondary bands are very prominent. Each design becomes a static individual entity, with no attempt at interlocking within the primary and secondary bands; there is, however, some sense of patterning within the guard-bands. These kilims do not belong to the previously examined Caucasian kilims, they are woven much further south, well into Persian Azerbaijan.

Similar examples have been published by Schurmann, plate 81, who attributes them to Shirvan; by H. Haack, 1960, plate 3; and in *The Undiscovered Kilim*, plate 38. Note that they usually have braided rather than knotted warp ends.

330   *no size available*
331   *208 × 355 cm.*

These two kilims are, at first glance, reasonably similar, although a close comparison of the narrow bands and the infill ornaments demonstrates once again the wide degree of individualism found within what would seem to be a comparatively limited format. Pieces of this type often have all the white areas woven in cotton; such is the case in the two examples illustrated here. They also have, as a usual feature, a reciprocal border that is drawn in a similar way to some pieces from the Qashqai (plate 385). The warp ends of natural brown and white wool are always tightly braided.

332   *207 × 286 cm.*

This piece has braiding along the top and bottom, another feature which is considered to be indicative of a north-west Persian origin. Similar Azerbaijan pieces have in the past been attributed to the Kurds, and some have been called Kazak. The composition is of diagonally offset hexagons, floating on a white field. The hexagons themselves, with their indented outlines, relate closely to those seen on the band kilims. The reciprocal 'arrowhead' border is of the same design as those found on the two previous pieces, though less angular. This overall composition of field and border is occasionally found on *khorjim* (small double bags) and *mafrash* (cradle or packing bags). This piece has been reproduced in colour in *The Undiscovered Kilim*, plate 40.

329

330

331

332

333   *147×340 cm.*

334   *158×368 cm.*
335   *155×390 cm.*

Both these pieces, from the west of Persian Azerbaijan, relate to plate 336 and are woven in two halves. This practice, which is common in Turkish kilims, is restricted to Persian kilims from this area and may be explained by its proximity to Turkey. The two kilims have the same composition: large medallions forming two vertical rows surrounded by a reciprocal border.

On plate 334 the large medallions relate to those on plate 332, having the same indented outer and inner outlines. A row of brocading outlines all the bands, and a number of small motifs are brocaded on the field.

On plate 335 the medallions are more complex, having an outer stepped outline enclosing a hooked motif, which in turn contains a star-shaped polygon. The reciprocal trefoil design in the border of plate 334 has been replaced with a very elegant meandering design, similar to one found on an early Anatolian piece, plate 155.

336   *126×359 cm.*

This piece seems related to plate 332 in terms of both texture and colour. It is worth noting that many of its minor design elements are common on certain south-east Anatolian-'Reyhanlı' kilims, especially the rendering of the continuous 'S-and-bars' motif flanked by a 'running dog' pattern, and the exaggerated crenellated pattern separating the bands of the field from the reciprocal border. The elongated star-shaped medallions in the major bands belong stylistically to north-west Persia, although the overall colour of the piece is, again, closer to Anatolian kilims and to some Kazak pile-woven rugs. However, the narrow polychrome zigzag band below the bottom border of the piece, the knotted warp ends and this type of reciprocal border have never been encountered in kilims ascribed to Anatolia and are all common features of the south Caucasus and of north-west Persia. Interestingly enough, all the comparable Anatolian pieces belong to the second half of the nineteenth century and are believed to have been woven by Circassians who migrated south. There is a possibility, therefore, that this piece, which has considerable age, belongs to the tradition of design which the immigrants transplanted to Anatolia.

333

334

335

336

Nomadic Kilims of West Persia

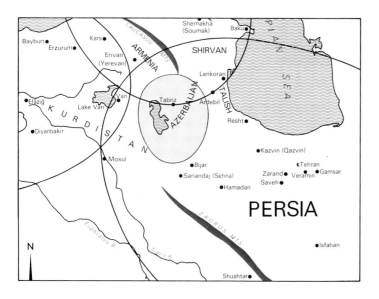

The next group of kilims, of which we illustrate four examples, comes from north-west Persia, where it was probably woven by Turkic villagers and nomads in the area between Qazvin and Bijar.

These kilims are loosely woven in thick wool on a cotton foundation. At the top and bottom, they have rows of two-colour twining, which act both as warp-spacers and as decorative devices. A common design feature is the black and white reciprocal trefoil border. These characteristics are also found on 'Zarand' kilims (plates 364 and 365), which, however, are woven in dovetailed tapestry instead of the slit tapestry used here.

337   *220 × 380 cm.*

The star-medallions on plate 337 are broader, expanded versions of those seen on plate 336, though the colour range is more limited and austere here. The innermost borders, containing bracketed diamonds, and the style of the 'boteh' in the red field are common elements of north-west Persian pile rugs.

These bracketed diamonds are stylizations of the repeated design element in the borders of eighteenth- and nineteenth-century carpets, which are usually referred to erroneously as 'knotted Kufic borders' (see Designs, Patterns and Compositions).

338   *165 × 352 cm.*

The designs enclosed within the hexagons on plate 338 are close to those seen on plates 318 and 330. An unusual feature of the piece is the single large hexagon with a multiple outline in each horizontal row. Overall, the visual impression of the piece is somewhat similar to some south Persian kilims from Fars. Note also the effect created by the successful use of a reciprocal border pattern in the narrow bands dividing the field into panels.

337

338

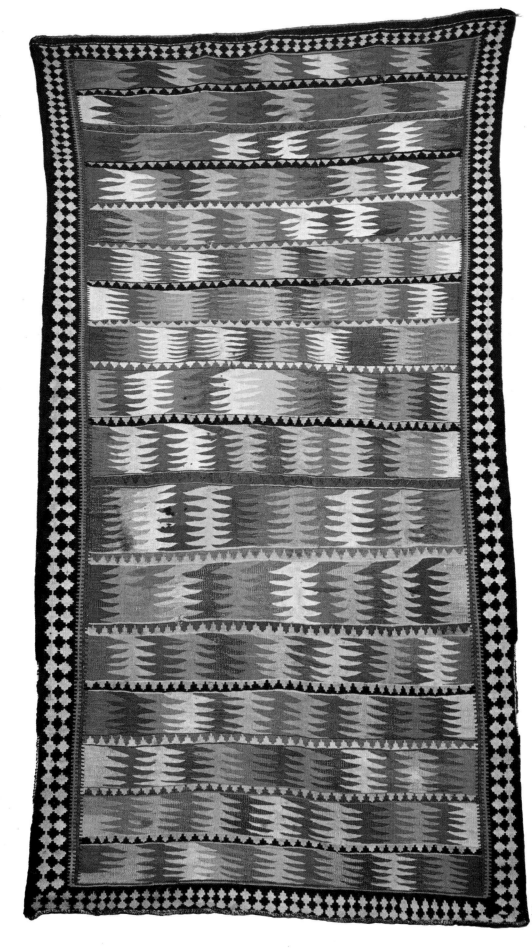

339

340

339   *158×274 cm.*

This is a striking and colourful kilim. Some relationship may be discerned between the interlocking serrated motifs in the bands and those seen on the 'eye-dazzler' kilims of Veramin and south Persia. There is a charming lack of sophistication in the rough, uneven texture and in the variation of scale in the drawing of the bands; note the double reciprocal border. This piece, like plates 338 and 340, has a cotton foundation. The warp ends of this group of kilims normally terminate in the multi-layered flat braid associated with this group of weavings.

340   *174×307 cm.*

In texture, materials and colours plate 340 is related to the previous kilim. The composition, however, is more disciplined. It consists of small serrated star-shaped ornaments placed in a diamond grid on a dark brown ground. The arrangement of colours creates a large-scale chevron pattern, evocative of a prayer arch. Once again we notice the reciprocal border, which is restrained here to a single band.

'Talish' Kilims

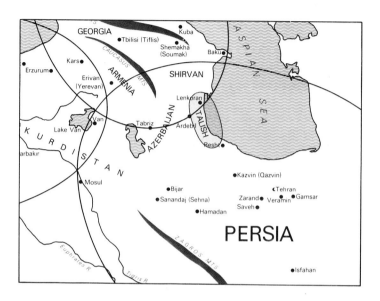

Plates 341, 342 and 343 are related both to Caucasian and to north Persian kilims. A number of them have been found in the bazaars of Ardebil in Persian Azerbaijan. They appear to have been woven in the mountainous area overlooking the Caspian Sea, between Lenkoran and Resht, which is mainly inhabited by Turkish people.

Kilims of this type are as fine as 'Shirvan' pieces, but the wool here is softer and shinier, more like that used by the Qashqai, producing a pliant and soft fabric. The colours, obviously dyed with great care, have a glowing quality and yet are mellow in tone. The resulting visual effect is one of balanced contrasts. A distinguishing feature of these pieces is a red and green narrow border. The brown woollen warps terminate at the ends in parallel rows of small knots.

341   *164 × 400 cm.*

Plate 341 has a pattern of diagonally offset diamonds in a random arrangement of rich and varied colours. This very handsome kilim has a reciprocal trefoil border in red and green, simi-

lar to plate 342, from which, however, it differs somewhat in technique. The slits, normally found at the junction of areas of different colours, do not appear; instead, the wefts overlap, and some of the joins, particularly in the field, are covered with brocading which outlines and enhances the designs. Nevertheless, by reason of both colour and texture, there can be little doubt that plates 342 and 341 are closely related.

The drawing of the main field ornaments is most unusual. The angular indentations at the sides are repeated in the inner layers of the diamonds, at the centres of which are either eight-pointed stars, or small designs reflecting the outlines of the outer layers of the diamonds.

342   *171 × 289 cm.*

At first glance, this looks like a Caucasian kilim. Indeed, with its composition of free-floating hexagons on a dark blue ground it is related to previously illustrated examples, such as plates 302 and 304. However, the principal border and the reciprocal trefoil outer border are indications of a more southerly provenance. A comparison should be made with plates 330 and 331, both of which belong to a related group and have elements of drawing handled in a similar manner but on a different scale. Pieces of the present group, however, are finer in weave and softer in handle.

343   *137 × 290 cm.*

This finely woven kilim is similar in size and scale of design to plate 340, to which it is also related through the field designs. The star-shaped ornaments are once again arranged in a diamond grid, but here the arrangement of colours on the blue ground creates an endless pattern of diagonal bands. In the outer border, the design is unusual, but the green and red colours are typical of 'Talish' kilims, as are the woollen warps.

341

342

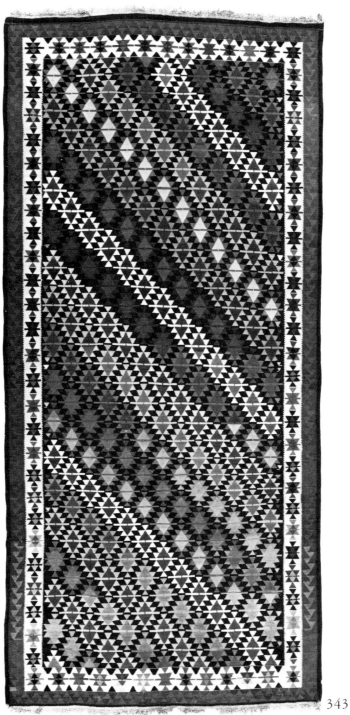

343

Kurdish Town Kilims of West Persia

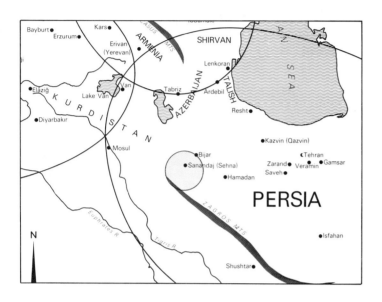

GROUP A

This group of small and finely woven kilims comes from Kurdistan in western Persia. The refinement and sophistication of their designs point to their being woven by townsfolk rather than by villagers or nomads. Their weavers were masters of their craft, producing well-balanced, orderly and yet dynamic compositions. In fineness they rival the kilims of Sehna, with which they are often confused, for the overall visual effect of the compositions and the scale of the designs is similar. Nevertheless, they are quite distinct from each other in terms of design, which is here more simple and geometric. This less naturalistic style of ornamentation shows a certain affinity with kilims woven further north in Azerbaijan, and it seems possible, therefore, that they were produced by Kurds north of Sehna at the limits of Persian Kurdistan. Furthermore, unlike Sehna kilims, which have a variety of field compositions and a more complex weave, those of the present group have either a prayer arch or an all-over chevron pattern, and are woven in pure slit tapestry.

The borders provide a singularly good means of distinguishing between the two groups. It is usual to find more than one major border, occasionally even three, separated from each other by narrow reciprocal trefoil guardstripes. The latter are absent in Sehna pieces, which have one major border flanked by two secondary borders. The border designs consist either of conjoined diamond patterns or juxtaposed hexagons containing hooked motifs.

344   *123 × 161 cm.*

The blue field of this simple and attractive kilim contains diagonally offset small stylized flowers. The colour arrangement creates a repeating chevron pattern evocative of a prayer arch. Here the single hexagon border is flanked by reciprocal trefoil guardstripes: the inner one in red and white, the outer in blue and white. The composition of the piece is related to that of plate 340.

345   *122 × 160 cm.*

The chevron pattern created by the flowers is broken here by the outline of a prayer arch. The field in the niche is blue, while the spandrels are on a white ground. The two main borders are contained within three reciprocal trefoil guardstripes. The angle of the chevron pattern is steeper than on the previous piece; each small flower in the field has two pairs of leaves, while on plate 344 each flower has only one pair.

346   *127 × 157 cm.*

The outer border of this piece contains the hexagons also seen on the three other examples. An interesting compositional feature is the second border of conjoined diamonds which, at the top of the piece, expands to form a pattern of diagonally offset

344

345

346

347

diamonds, covering the spandrels of the simple pointed prayer arch. This diamond pattern, which surrounds the entire mihrab, gives the impression of a window through which the field, containing an endless pattern of horizontal rows of abstract geometric motifs, is perceived.

347   *117 × 152 cm.*

This piece has the same composition as plate 345; the single flowers of the latter, however, are replaced by floral clusters, and the colours in the niche and spandrels are reversed. Note the variation in the drawing of the prayer arch and the three major borders. The floral clusters are similar to some found on Shah Savan pieces, which are brocaded in Soumak on a warp-faced fabric (see J. V. McMullan, *Islamic Rugs*, plate 60).

GROUP B: SEHNA KILIMS

These kilims are named after a city in west Persia which is the principal town of Persian Kurdistan, and which is known today as Sanandaj. Sehna kilims can be extremely finely woven, so much so that the name has become a synonym for fineness. They are usually of small size, though occasionally some very large pieces appear, which are less finely woven on a foundation of woollen warps, while retaining all the other features of Sehna kilims.

The designs are small, very delicate and ideally suited to the fineness of the fabric. They relate closely to brocaded Persian textiles from the Safavid period. The most common are flower clusters, 'boteh', floral scrolls, vines, bees and a repeating abstract floral ornament forming what is known as the 'Herati' pattern. There is a marked deterioration of design in later kilims, some of which have a field-and-medallion composition decorated with a degenerate, stiff version of the Herati pattern, while some others have an all-over pattern of naturalistic flower designs showing Western influence.

Sehna kilims have strong similarities in composition and design to Persian pile rugs; more so, in fact, than any other kilims. The field, which is always enclosed within borders, may consist of repeat designs or overall patterns, medallions with or without corners, series of juxtaposed narrow bands containing floral scrolls, various combinations of the above, and sometimes also a prayer niche.

The major border contains either a repeat ornament, the Herati pattern or a continuous series of narrow diagonal bands of alternating colours. It is flanked by minor borders, usually containing a continuous blossom-and-leaf pattern or a leaf-and-stem pattern.

The warps on the small fine pieces are usually cotton, and on some later pieces with coarser designs, polychrome silk. These later examples often contain architectural forms in the decoration of the field. Woollen warps are seldom used, as wool of the required fineness would tend to be too brittle. The large pieces, however, are on a woollen foundation. At both ends of the kilim, the warps are usually gathered in small bunches and knotted together, often in many layers, creating a web-like effect similar to that found on a larger scale on some Kurdish kilims from east Anatolia. The material for the wefts is mostly wool, but small amounts of cotton and silk are not uncommon.

The weave is basically slit tapestry. However, as some of the refined floral motifs are curvilinear by nature, slit tapestry —which produces stepped outlines—is not the ideally suitable medium. It is common, therefore, to find designs executed in eccentric weft-weave (see chapter on structure). The use of this technique provides yet another means of distinguishing between the kilims of Sehna, and those of the Kurdish group previously discussed, which are woven exclusively in slit tapestry. Nevertheless, the two groups are closely related both geographically and ethnically. They are alone in producing kilims of such fineness; the colour range, texture and quality of materials are very similar. Furthermore, they are the only types of Persian kilims that include prayer rugs, their mihrabs having the same peculiar and distinctive type of outline.

Though none is illustrated in this book, a large number of Kurdish village and nomadic kilims exist, usually of a late date, woven in a variety of sizes, which are coarse in texture and usually repetitive and degenerate in design. Some are known in the trade as Mosul and Bijar kilims, probably because they were marketed there, others as Seraband by reason of their similarity to Seraband pile carpets. A good example of this type of kilim is illustrated in *Tribal Rugs,* plate 11. Worth mentioning also is a type of small Kurdish kilim, rough in weave and naive in design, decorated with large-scale naturalistic floral motifs, animals and people.

348   *129 × 162 cm.*

A main border containing alternating diagonal red and white bands, flanked on either side by a narrow blossom-and-leaf secondary border, surrounds the deep blue field decorated with an all-over repeat pattern of 'boteh'. The attraction of this very old and delicate piece lies in the simplicity of its composition and the refinement of its drawing. A similar piece is illustrated in *The Undiscovered Kilim*, plate 54, and an identical border appears in plate 55 of the same publication.

349   *144 × 168 cm.*

The endless Herati pattern on an ivory field is framed by an abstract border, the flanking bands being similar to those of the previous piece. The border motif resembles that of the prayer kilim in J. V. McMullan, *Islamic Rugs*, plate 36.

350   *144 × 177 cm.*

The field consists of a continuous series of polychrome vertical narrow bands containing 'leaf and stem' designs, vines and floral scrolls. The borders are like those of plate 348. The bright colour range is similar to a related piece published in *Prayer Rugs*, plate XXVII, and to another in *The Undiscovered Kilim*, plate 53. An exquisite prayer kilim with designs related to those of this piece and of plate 348 is illustrated in *Tribal Rugs*, plate 62.

351   *125 × 164 cm.*

The borders of this kilim have the same designs as those of plate

349. The white field on which slits are used to form a herring-bone pattern, contains in the middle a large medallion decorated with the Herati pattern. The corners of the field are cut off with quarter medallions, the outlines of which echo the central medallion on a larger scale.

352   *220 × 550 cm.*

This is a good example of a large Sehna kilim with an all-over Herati pattern, which should be compared with that of plate 349. The main border, containing a leaf-and-blossom motif, is flanked with the typical Sehna minor borders, which in turn are outlined by means of narrow reciprocal trefoil stripes. These are very similar to the ones found on the previous group of small Kurdish kilims, but are never found on small Sehna pieces.

Visually the piece appears more like a carpet than a kilim. In fact, the refinement of the small-scale ornaments is ill-suited to the size of the kilim, its merit being purely in the excellence of the weaver's workmanship.

353   *192 × 560 cm.*

Unlike the previous example, here is an old and large Sehna piece in which the jump from small to large is successful. In plate 352 the designs were identical in type and scale to those on plate 349. Here, instead, the designs, though similar to those of plate 348, have been adapted in scale to suit the large size of the piece. The result is very successful, producing a well-balanced composition. The green-and-red reciprocal borders contrast beautifully with the yellow main border and with the blue field filled with well-drawn 'boteh' motifs.

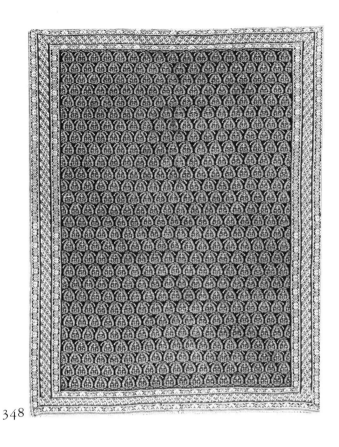

348

349

350

351

352

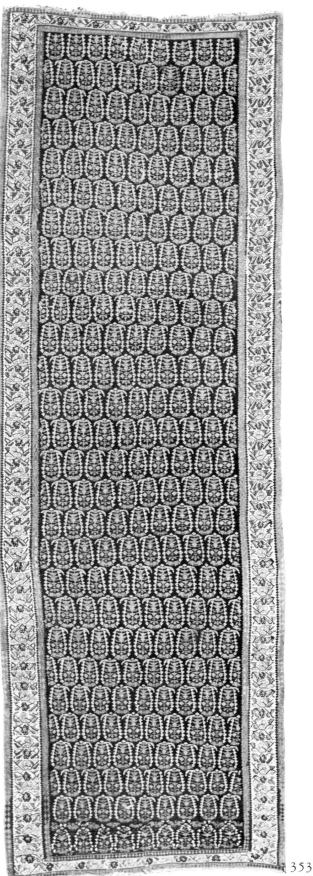

353

A Short Essay on the Kurds

ANDRE SINGER

Divided by the borders of five nations in western Asia—those of Iraq, Syria, Turkey, Iran and the USSR—live over six million people claiming one of the most ancient heritages in the world—the Kurds. The Kurds are a fierce and courageous people who have great pride in their ethnic identity, remaining 'unmixed' by the influx of invading nations. The Macedonians, Parthians, Sassanians, Armenians, Romans, Arabs, Seljuks, Mongols, Turks and Persians, all came and all left their mark on the indigenous peoples of western Asia, but the Kurds in their inhospitable mountainous homeland survived this unending succession of onslaughts. Only today's relentless pressures of modernization and 'civilization' threaten their heritage.

There is dispute over the origins of these tribes before the seventh century BC, and only after the twelfth century AD did the area that they now inhabit become known as Kurdistan. From this time on, individual Kurdish leaders such as Saladin rose to local power, and religious faiths—Zoroastrianism, Christianity, and Islam—held sway, but the Kurds were never united and never formed an autonomous nation-state.

The same problem that plagued the Kurds in the past still continues today—the problem that rigid tribal organization under individual chiefs or Sheikhs makes unity a remote dream. Even in the turbulent decades of nineteenth-century international intrigue, the Kurds were unable to take advantage of the decaying Ottoman Empire to achieve autonomy because of conflicting British and Russian plans for their region; and in the First World War, the Kurds actually supported the Ottomans, and suffered devastating hardships and defeat.

The most serious bid for unity followed President Wilson's Fourteen Points of 1918, when minorities under the old Ottoman Empire were encouraged to seek autonomy. This hope was shattered by the twin considerations of nationalism elsewhere and oil in Iraq. The development of Turkish nationalism under Mustafa Kemal (Atatürk) excluded Kurdish independence in Anatolia, and the British attempt at Kurdish independence in Iraq also failed. Conflict in Anatolia, Iraq and Iran has persisted until recent years.

The main concentrations of Kurds are today found in the following regions: the Jezira district of Syria; along the Turco-Iranian border and around the towns of Bitlis, Erzinjan, Diyarbakır, and Erzurum; on the western slopes of Mount Ararat in Anatolia; in Soviet Armenia; in the Iranian provinces of Kermanshah and Kurdistan, and in north-east Iraq.

Most Kurds subsist by a sedentary farming way of life, or nomadic pastoralism, some groups combining both by living in winter villages but migrating into the mountains to use the spring and summer grass. For the farmers, tobacco, wheat and barley are the most important crops, with a much greater variety where irrigation is available. The nomads naturally rely upon livestock and the products of their sheep and goats. The wool and hair are used mainly in domestic weaving, the former for rugs and kilims and the latter for sacking and tenting.

Traditional tribal organization remained remarkably uniform throughout Kurdistan although, today, it has been changed drastically in many parts by the imposition of differing administrations by the sovereign states controlling the area. In some areas, the traditional hierarchy has survived, and consists of a feudal structure headed by the paramount chiefs—the Sheikhs or Aghas. Sheikh is a traditional religious title, while Agha is a clan leader or powerful landowner. In practice, the two roles are often one and the same. Beneath the Sheikh and Agha are village headmen. Political divisions are not restricted to villages; there are tribal divisions and subdivisions ranging from the Ashirat (confederation of tribes) down through the Tira (members tracing descent through a common ancestor) to the Khel (collection of households or camping units). The blood feuds that used to occur between these groups, or between the nomadic and settled peoples, could only be settled by the Aghas or Sheikhs, upon payment of blood-money. The maintenance of the feudal hierarchy of Agha and peasant or tribesman was based partly on inheritance and was partly economic, with the development of an Agha class through intermarriage and landowning wealth.

The role of the Sheikh families differs somewhat because of the religious powers they inherit. The Sheikhs trace their

354

descent from the Prophet Mohammad, or from various 'saints'. Sects and orders have always flourished among the Kurds, and today some of the strongest surviving unorthodox Muslim sects are to be found there. The Yezidis, the Ahl-e-Haqq and the Dervishes are the most important of these. The Yezidis, living mainly in north Iraq, regard the devil as the creative agent of God, and the peacock as the representation of the devil. The Ahl-e-Haqq and Ali Ilahi's believe in the deification of Ali, the son-in-law of the Prophet Mohammad. The three major Dervish orders, the Naqshbandi, Rifai and Qaderi, that flourish in Kurdistan practise rituals that involve ecstatic trance and bodily immolation, glass-eating, or piercing the flesh with weapons, in order to attain closeness to God. These sects can only operate through the person of a Sheikh, and it is probably because of the hierarchical structure of Kurdish society that such orders thrive. The more orthodox religious functions, connected with birth, circumcision, marriage and death, and feast-days, are presided over by the Mullah, the traditional Muslim functionary.

The Kurds have a relatively austere material culture. The most striking and valuable possession is usually the carpet. More often than not, the wealth and standing of a Kurdish family, whether living in a mud-brick house or a goat-hair tent, can be judged by the quality of its carpets— objects that are displayed for guests and used as dowries or for gifts. Only in recent years have non-Kurdish values penetrated deeply into Kurdistan, and are Western furniture or Persian town carpets regarded as worthy replacements for traditional taste.

354   *95 × 345 cm.*

This simple and bold kilim has well-spread ornaments in contrasting colours. The red border juts into the camel-hair field. The indentations are drawn similarly to those on plate 373, with which, however, this kilim does not relate in any other way. The hooked medallion in the field, the bracketed diamonds of the border and the cotton foundation indicate that it was probably woven somewhere in the large area between Qazvin, Tehran, Hamadan and Bijar in central Persia.

Bakhtiari—Shushtar Kilims

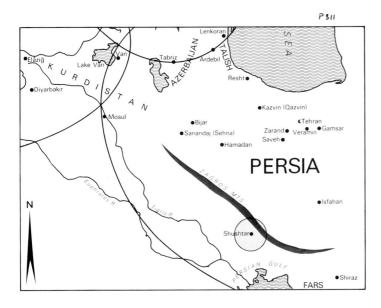

This unusual group of kilims is woven by Bakhtiari tribesmen, reputedly around the town of Shushtar in south-west Persia. The texture immediately identifies these pieces, which do not directly relate to any other kilims. They bear an uncanny resemblance, however, to knotted-pile rugs from the Hamadan area; in fact, the similarities are so striking in terms of composition, individual designs and size that it is most surprising that the two should be woven so far apart.

These kilims are notable for their simple, restrained ornamentation and, particularly, for their wide undecorated surrounds, usually woven in natural, light brown camel-hair. In all other Persian kilims the borders are at the edges of the pieces. Here, the impression created is of borders and field being superimposed, almost floating on a plain surface.

The weft materials are wool, natural camel-hair and cotton, which is not only used undyed for the whites, as is usual in Persian kilims, but also for the light blue, a feature which is unique to the kilims of Shushtar.

The warps are brown wool or a mixture of brown wool and camel-hair. They are clipped at the ends to form a short, loose, single-strand fringe.

The quality of the wool is generally poor; it is brittle and lacks brilliance, as do the cotton and the camel-hair. The woven surface is thus flat and mat.

The colour range, cold and limited, while lacking the warmth found in Kurdish and Qashqai kilims, adds to their overall austere effect, which is the major attraction of these pieces. The main colours are camel-hair brown, white, dark and light blue, a deep rose-red, green and in some of the older pieces, yellow. A fugitive red is often seen, but it looks more like a badly fixed dye than a synthetic one.

The weave is double-interlock tapestry, which produces a single-faced fabric, the reverse side having ridges at the vertical colour-joins. This technique is widespread among the Bakhtiari, but, unlike their other weavings, Shushtar kilims have no selvedges and are very loosely woven, producing a peculiar soft, pliant and very light fabric, too delicate for heavy use. Nevertheless, some of them were used as floor coverings. We know of a set of four long pieces with the same design, forming a typical and traditional Persian carpet arrangement. This consists of a long, wide, centre kilim, the *Mian Farsh*, flanked on both sides by two narrow pieces of the same length, the *Kenarehs*. All three were placed under a head piece, the *Kellegi*, of a length related to the total width of the other three. While most pieces are long and narrow, shorter and wider kilims of *sofreh* size (cloth that was spread out for laying food on) also occur, as do some very small pieces, an example of which is published in *Lori and Bakhtiyari Flatweaves*, plate 52 A.

The field, consisting of either a series of medallions (plate 355) or an all-over repeat pattern (plate 359), is occasionally cut off at the corners, and enclosed within a series of wide and narrow borders. As already mentioned, the entire composition, borders and field, floats on a plain undecorated surface creating a visual impression not dissimilar to that of an illuminated page in a Persian manuscript. This similarity is further enhanced by the horizontal rays stemming from angular brackets in the borders that jut out on to the plain background at short, regular intervals. A comparison should also be made with Persian tooled-leather bookbindings.

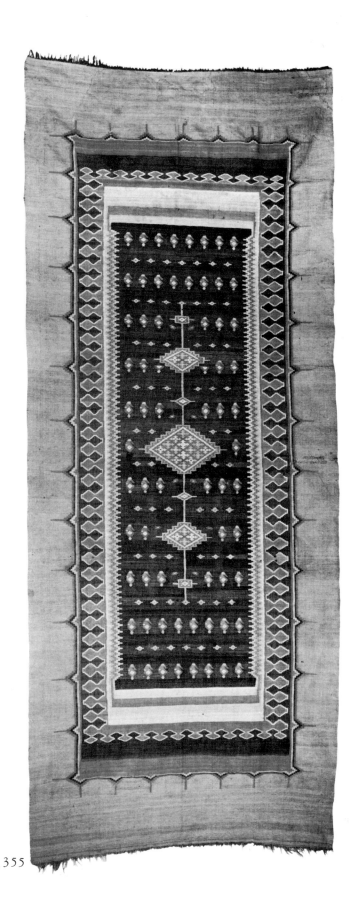

355

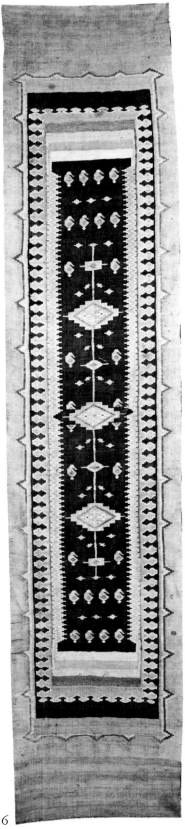

356

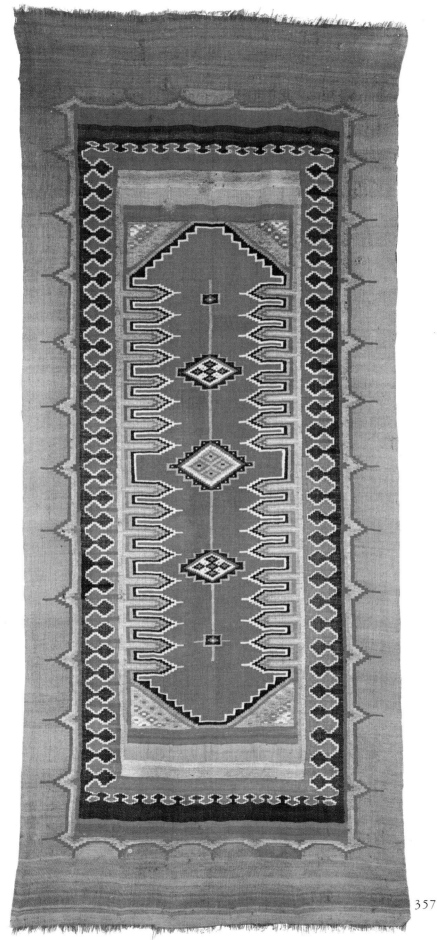

357

358

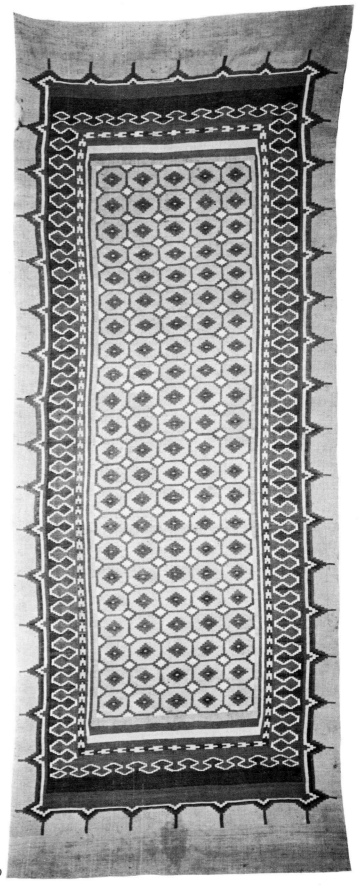

359

A major decorative element is the wide and pronounced reciprocal trefoil border, which is always drawn on a smaller scale at the top and bottom than at the sides. To balance this, the narrow vertical or 'saw-tooth' stripes, flanking the reciprocal side-borders, become much wider at the two ends. The clumsily drawn corners of the reciprocal border designs, a feature common in Kurdish, Qashqai and Lori Bakhtiari kilims, do not occur here. On all the pieces examined, without exception, the same elegant corner solution is used. The side borders terminate at both ends with a complete trefoil motif, as do the top and bottom borders. The gaps created where they join are filled with small floating diamonds, similar to the heads of the trefoils.

355   *198 × 469 cm.*
356   *99 × 467 cm. (One of a pair of pieces)*

These two kilims are identical in colour and decoration and were found together. The larger one is, in all likelihood, a *Mian Farsh,* and the narrower piece, one of two *Kenarehs*.

The medallions float on a blue field decorated with alternating rows of 'boteh' and small diamonds. In the narrow kilim, the centre medallion is the same size as the other two, but is accentuated through the indentations in the 'saw-tooth' pattern that borders the field.

357   *163 × 320 cm.*

The red field of this attractive and boldly drawn piece is cut off at the corners with a pattern of diamonds. The pointed motifs that jut into the field break their continuity opposite the three medallions and, more noticeably, at the centre. Note the change in scale in the drawing of the reciprocal trefoil border.

358   *137 × 508 cm.*

The composition of this narrow kilim is identical to that of the previous piece, but the scale and spacing of the designs is different. Here, the field is of natural camel-hair, as are the areas surrounding the borders.

359   *no size available*

One of the most attractive Shushtar kilims, this is an example with an all-over repeat design decorating the field. The bold pattern of red octagons, floating on a beige ground, is enlivened by the use of yellow, a rare colour in this group of kilims.

Bakhtiari Kilims

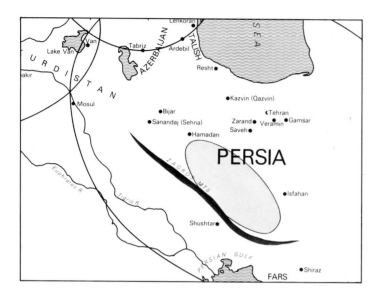

The Bakhtiari weavers of this group of kilims inhabit a mountainous area of west Persia on the Zagros range, overlooking the plain of Isfahan. The inaccessibility of the land, which lies outside the main routes, allowed these ancient nomadic tribes to keep their own way of life for much longer than most, remaining to a large extent uncorrupted by the external influences of the modern world. This survival of tradition until recently is clearly manifested in their weavings, whose patterns are still rich, pure and identifiable.

Like the Shushtar pieces, these kilims are woven in double-interlock tapestry, the resulting absence of slits adding to the durability of the fabric. Here, however, the weave is very tight, producing a hard, stiff, almost leathery texture. These are possibly the most hardwearing and robust kilims, and are very well suited for use as floor coverings.

In proportion, they usually are long and narrow, like those from Shushtar, but a variety of other formats were also made.

Interestingly enough, some are woven in two joining halves. The materials used are wool and cotton, the latter adding to the hardness of the texture achieved through the tight weave. Older examples have rich, strong and contrasting colours, beautifully mellowed with age. However, in common with most other groups of Persian kilims, the number of colours becomes more limited in later pieces, which have two or three hard dark colours alleviated through the contrast with sharp white cotton.

Compositionally they may be divided in two main types: those with a field surrounded by one or more borders, and those with skirts above and below the field. The panels of these skirts are sometimes surrounded by the same borders as the field, while on others, the panels extend across the entire width of the piece.

The ends terminate in a series of narrow bands in weft-float weave, some of which are similar to those found in Qashqai kilims. The sides sometimes have a multiple warp selvedge overstitched in dark wool, and more commonly, a thick cable overcast with polychrome wool forming a 'barber's-pole' pattern.

The decorative alphabet consists of numerous and varied small geometric motifs which are arranged in repeat-pattern formations. The use of double-interlock tapestry makes it possible to weave straight vertical lines, a feature evident in all Bakhtiari kilims, both in the drawing of small field ornaments and, especially, in the long narrow stripes flanking the side borders (plates 360 and 361). The borders have either continuous interlocking designs, such as meanders, swastikas, reciprocal trefoils, 'S' motifs and bracketed diamonds, or narrow sections of field patterns. The fields contain patterns of 'boteh', diamonds, squares, octagons and small crosses, the latter forming a distinctive endless overall pattern, sections of which are commonly seen in the borders of Bakhtiari, but also of Qashqai, kilims (plate 410).

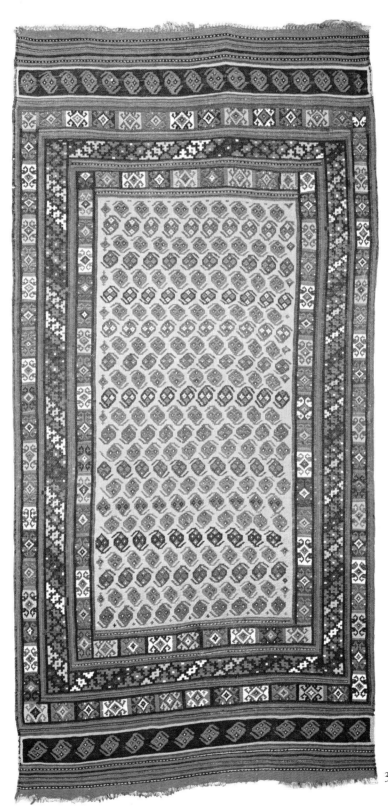

360

361

362

360   *152 × 315 cm.*

361   *152 × 382 cm.*

This well-drawn Bakhtiari kilim has a red field decorated with an endless pattern of small 'boteh' arranged on a rectangular grid. The innermost and outermost borders contain interlocking multi-layered triangular blocks. Of the other two borders, one has a series of bracketed diamonds and the other a reciprocal trefoil pattern similar to those found on Shushtar pieces. The end skirts consist of many narrow bands of double-faced weft-float weave, similar to those found on Qashqai kilims, followed by a series of blue and black plain stripes. Similar kilims are illustrated in *Lori and Bakhtiyari Flatweaves,* plates 39–45.

362   *145 × 380 cm.*

The central field of this kilim is flanked at the top and the bottom by two long and narrow panels. The innermost border of diagonal red and white stripes is similar to those found on Sehna kilims (plate 348); while the next one is the section of a cruciform pattern also seen in central Anatolian (plate 245) and Qashqai kilims (plate 410). The major border has a pattern of continuous interlocking swastikas. The end skirts of this kilim have narrow bands with stepped chevron designs which are also common in Qashqai pieces. Here, however, the designs are executed in double-interlock tapestry like the rest of the piece. The single-cable selvedge is overcast with two-colour wools.

'Zarand' Kilims

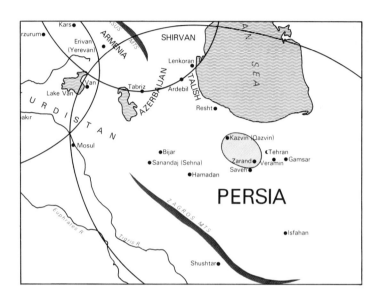

Zarand is a village south-west of Tehran in central Persia. The name is an identification label used by Persian dealers for kilims woven in the area between Qazvin and Saveh. These kilims are woven with thick, heavy wool, usually on a foundation of cotton warps, in a combination of dovetailed tapestry and eccentric weft weave. The latter is extensively used to produce wedges in curvilinear designs and 'lazy lines' in the background. As a result, the fabric has a patterned texture which is further accentuated by the prominent abrash of the colours.

Zarand kilims are heavy and durable, yet pliable. There are no selvedges. Two or three rows of polychrome twining appear at the top and bottom, and the cotton warps are braided along the ends. These structural features are also found on Persian kilims of a previously illustrated group (plates 338, 339, 340). However, such pieces are slit-tapestry woven and differ from Zarand kilims in designs and colour.

The use of dovetailed tapestry, which is the main distinguishing feature of these kilims, allows weavers to use designs with prominent vertical lines (plate 364). The stepped crenellated outline of the borders is, therefore, here a purely decorative feature.

320

363

364

365

The field has either an overall pattern of repeated abstract motifs, known as 'pallang' (plate 365), or an overall composition of large and small medallions (plate 364). The main border contains a series of juxtaposed hooked ornaments or an abstract floral pattern. On some pieces it is flanked by guard-stripes with either a reciprocal pattern or a small repeat motif. The very archaic ornamentation is reminiscent of Caucasian embroideries of the seventeenth and eighteenth centuries and of Kurdish tree rugs of the eighteenth century.

363   *63 × 350 cm.*

This extremely simple, charming and unassuming kilim with the elementary decoration of a toothed pattern jutting into a plain field shows the weaver's ability to create texture and variation. Both the brown of the border and the beige of the field are of undyed natural camel-hair, as are the warps.

364   *147 × 365 cm.*

The field composition of large and small medallions containing

heraldic ornaments is strongly reminiscent of Caucasian embroideries of the seventeenth and eighteenth centuries. This bold and powerful kilim is well drawn, the weaver making full use of the possibilities afforded by dovetailed tapestry and eccentric weft weave. Note the stepped outline of the border, which is a purely decorative feature, contrasting with the straight lines of the large medallions. The outlines of the small medallions are not unrelated in design and method of weave to early Coptic textiles. A similar kilim is illustrated in *Tribal Rugs*, plate 35.

365   *140 × 384 cm.*

Another common type of 'Zarand' kilim, this piece contains bands of plant ornaments in a diagonally offset formation. On other kilims of the same family, the plant ornaments are arranged in vertical rows, and in some cases, a large version of the motif fills the entire width of the field, forming a single vertical column. Note the difference between the hooked designs in the borders of this kilim and those found on plate 364. For another example of this type of kilim, see *Tribal Rugs*, plate 36.

West Persian Kilims with Archaic Designs

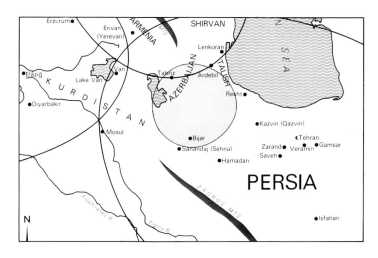

The four pieces in the following illustrations belong to a puzzling group of kilims. The size and proportion of these very long and narrow kilims are consistent with a Persian origin. Furthermore, they have some features in common with northwest Persian weft-wrapped bags and with 'Zarand' kilims with which they share the use of dovetailed tapestry, eccentric weft weave, 'lazy lines' in the plain areas of the background, extensive use of vertical lines in the designs, and also some border motifs. However, instead of the cotton warps, braided at the ends of 'Zarand' kilims, they have wool or mixed wool and goat hair twisted to form a knotted fringe. Peculiarly enough, a piece which appears to be of this group is illustrated in *Decorative Arts of Daghestan*, plate 19, where it is referred to as Avar work from the Caucasus.

The field designs are clearly drawn and well spaced. They are archaic forms, such as classical floral palmettes, abstract medallions, stylized trees and an ornament of combined vegetable and animal forms, somewhat related to the large indented medallions of 'Kuba' kilims. The borders are wide and contain motifs also deriving from earlier Turkish and Caucasian pile carpets. The general impression conveyed by these pieces is that they are of considerable age, and, in decorative terms, much more closely related to earlier carpets than to other kilims.

Three of them have a date, a feature most unusual in old Persian kilims, and one which is more usually associated with east Anatolian prayer kilims. In fact, on all three the date consists of two identifiable numerals: 12.., and some letters which, however, are different on each piece.

366   *158 × 526 cm.*

The mid-blue field is decorated with bands of large floral palmettes, reminiscent of those found on classical carpets. The main border contains alternating animal forms related to those found on very early pile rugs, and rectangles enclosing 'x-and-cross' motifs. The outer guardstripe has a linear design at the sides and a 'running dog' pattern at the ends which is also found on plate 369. The pattern on the inner guardstripe is an elongated small version of the main border decoration of plate 368. The weaver of this beautiful piece has employed effectively the possibility afforded by dovetailed tapestry of using vertical lines in the decoration of the borders and the field motifs. This kilim is dated at the top right-hand corner AH 12 .. (AD 18 ..).

367   *155 × 500 cm.*

Unlike plate 366, where the palmettes are arranged in a diagonally offset formation, the large ornaments here are placed in two vertical rows. The ground of both pieces has a patterned texture created by 'lazy lines'. The large ornaments seem to be an abstract rendering of a floral motif. The small central palmettes are flanked by two black birds. The well-drawn main border, flanked by guardstripes containing interlocking elongated 'S' forms, has the same animal motif as plate 366, alternating with a small geometric medallion. The somewhat rigid and repetitive drawing of this piece, which is the only one not dated, indicates that this is possibly a more recent kilim than plates 366, 368 and 369. It should be compared with plate 19 of *Decorative Arts of Daghestan*.

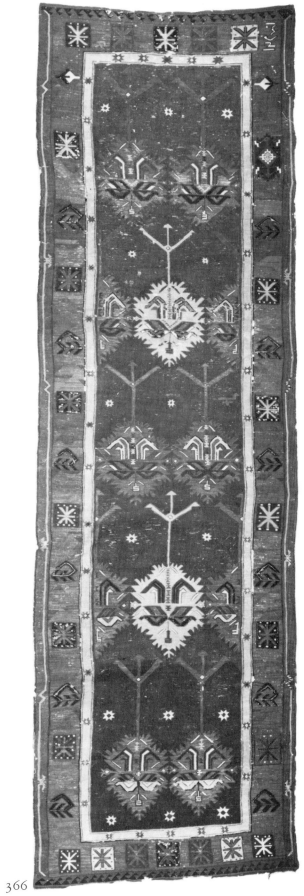

366

367

368

369

368 *155 × 310 cm.*

On the field, horizontal bands of geometric medallions form three vertical rows. The spaces between the medallions contain a variety of ornaments, some of which are stylized animals— snakes, horse with mane and raised legs, and other creatures. Unlike the three other examples of the group, there are no guardstripes here. The changing border, however, is most interesting. It has conjoined linear motifs on one side, related to those on plate 367, but which are also found on 'Zarand' kilims. This same border motif commonly appears on secondary borders of north-west Persian and Bakhtiari weft-wrapped bags. An example appears in *From the Bosphorus to Samarkand*, plate 65. The main field motif of this bag-face is not unrelated to the large medallions of the present kilim. The different border on the other three sides has archaic abstract motifs reminiscent of 'Kufic' borders on Seljuk carpets. Similar 'Kufic' motifs also occur on some Lori-Bakhtiari weft-wrapped bags (see *Lori and Bakhtiyari Flatweaves,* plate 2 A). The date woven at the bottom of the kilim reads AH 128.. (AD 186..).

369 *156 × 430 cm.*

The trees decorating the deep blue field of this kilim are distant descendants of the seventeenth- to eighteenth-century tree rugs of Kurdistan (see Dimand and Mailey, *Oriental Rugs*, fig. 113). The motifs on the red border and the guardstripes differ at the ends and the sides. The alternating animals and medallions with 'S' motifs of the main border become repeat 'x-and-bar' motifs, while the vine of the side guards becomes a 'running dog' pattern that like on plate 366. This piece bears the date AH 12.. (AD 18..) at the top right-hand corner. It should be compared closely with plate 365 as it shows a number of similarities between kilims of this group and 'Zarand' pieces.

Veramin Kilims

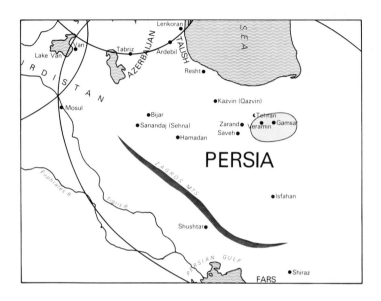

Veramin, a small town in north Iran about thirty miles southeast of Tehran, is an important kilim-weaving centre. It is on the route linking western and eastern Persia, on the path of migrating tribes, some of which settled there. The population, therefore, is of diverse origins, a fact which is reflected in the kilims woven in the area, which are of more than one type. The term 'Veramin' is used here as a generic term, and includes kilims woven around Gamsar, another small town a short distance east of Veramin.

Veramin kilims are durable, hardwearing pieces, tightly woven in thick wool. The weave is in slit tapestry, but as almost all the designs consist of either horizontal or diagonal lines, the slits are not noticeable. The outlines of most individual ornaments, such as hexagons, stars and lozenges, are emphasized by means of weft wrapping. This does not occur, however, in the repeat elements like the serrated blocks of 'eye-dazzler' kilims. Plate 370, only, has warp-wrapped outlines in the stars of the top and bottom border.

A distinctive technical feature of these kilims is the presence of narrow bands in weft-float weave containing conjoined 'S'

forms and, more rarely, other motifs like rosettes. The same technique is used extensively in Baluchi weavings. These bands are placed either at the ends of the piece or, when the composition consists of wide bands, in the narrow stripes separating them (plates 371, 373). The selvedges consist of two or more juxtaposed groups of plied warps forming cables, over and under which the wefts pass normally. This creates the effect of pronounced ridges at the sides of the piece. These multiple-cord selvedges are usually overstitched in wool, forming a double flat piping, either in black or polychrome wools. On older pieces these have worn out, and where they have partially done so, it is the custom at the bazaars to remove them altogether. More rarely, a single thick cable is used at the sides, similar to those found on the kilims of the Qashqai.

The decorative repertoire of Veramin kilims is rich and varied, a phenomenon totally consistent with the diverse origins of the area's inhabitants. The usual compositions are three: a field arranged in bands, diagonally offset motifs forming endless patterns and allover compositions of interlocking motifs such as 'eye-dazzlers'. The latter are woven in large numbers, so much so that there is a misguided tendency by bazaar traders to call all Persian 'eye-dazzler' kilims Veramin. A number of pieces have borders. Usually, these surround the piece on all four sides. They are either reciprocal borders or narrow bands with repeat motifs. Sometimes, however, borders appear only at the top and bottom of the piece, as in plate 370.

The older examples have brilliant deep colours in shining soft wool, prominent among which are blue, red, yellow, a deep green and an attractive peach-orange colour. The most recent examples use harder wool and a more limited dark colour range.

370   *170×336 cm.*

A typical old example of a Veramin 'eye-dazzler'. It is distinguished from Qashqai pieces by the multiple-cord flat selvedge, the two narrow borders at the ends—as opposed to the

370   371

372

373

typical Qashqai reciprocal trefoil border on all four sides—and the narrow bands of conjoined 'S' shapes in weft-float weave. It should be compared to plate 379: the composition is basically the same; however all the colours are different in tone, and the wool of this piece is not as lustrous.

371   *185×317 cm.*

This Veramin kilim has the familiar band composition of Caucasian and Persian kilims. The presence, however, of the narrow top and bottom border containing reciprocal spearheads is a distinctive feature of this group. Between the bands are the rows of conjoined 'S' shapes in weft-float weave already seen on plate 370. This technique and type of design is commonly found on the end skirts of Baluchi pile rugs. The multiple-cord selvedge here retains the original overcasting in dark brown wool.

372   *174×374 cm.*

The hexagons containing star-shaped motifs in the bands of plate 371 are placed here in a diagonally offset formation floating on a dark brown ground. The colour arrangement creates a pattern of diagonal bands. Typically, this piece has the narrow rows of conjoined 'S' motifs of the previous two examples as well as the overcast selvedges. Related kilims are illustrated in *From the Bosporous to Samarkand*, plate 2, and in *Tribal Rugs*, plate 144. The pattern of small conjoined stepped diamonds in the borders is an uncommon example of pronounced slit tapestry in Veramin kilims.

373   *136×230 cm.*

This unusual and colourful kilim is not directly related to the three previous pieces. Nevertheless, its characteristics indicate that it comes from the same general area. The drawing of the bands with their deep indentation is its most striking feature. All the designs are heavily outlined with weft wrapping, and the narrow stripes, separating the wide bands, contain a reciprocal spearhead ornament in weft-float weave. A larger piece, almost identical in colour and design, is illustrated in *Tribal Rugs*, plate 83. This kilim has a single thick cable selvedge with no overcasting.

South Persian Kilims

Most of the kilims illustrated in this section are thought to have been woven by the Qashqai, only one of many nomadic and settled tribes inhabiting the province of Fars in south-west Persia (see p. 372). The principal town in the region is Shiraz. Although the Qashqai are known to have been brilliant and prolific weavers to whom many specific designs can be ascribed unequivocally, the attribution to them of all the south Persian kilims we illustrate is less certain. It is based partly on the evidence of dealers in Tehran, and partly on the similarity of many of the designs to those found on pieces known definitely to be by the Qashqai. Several kilims that are not so obviously Qashqai work may still be linked stylistically with examples of pile-knotted carpets, such as the so-called 'Mecca' Shiraz rugs, regarded by many as the finest examples of Qashqai weaving.

None of the pieces shown was acquired by its present owner directly from the Qashqai, nor indeed from south Persia. Most seem to have been in the West for many years, often for so long that their history has become totally lost.

There are many characteristics that distinguish the kilims of Fars. In design, they are perhaps closest to Caucasian pieces, although there are marked differences in drawing style, and the colours are usually warmer and more brilliant. The overall effect of the south Persian pieces is more light-hearted. Like Caucasian kilims, they are woven in one piece and, as in north-west Persian examples, cotton is often used to give a more brilliant white; this is particularly true of borders with reciprocal designs. These reciprocal borders, it should be added, are among the most specific design features of Fars kilims. The weavers used the contrast between white cotton and ivory wool in a masterly fashion.

On many Fars kilims, there are panels at either end composed of a succession of narrow horizontal bands of different colours; on some examples, these bands are intricately worked in weft-float brocading, although in others they may be in a simple plain weave. The flat woven bands may be designed with a continuous chevron motif. In some cases, plain bands are combined with brocading in zigzags, or with compound brocading forming juxtaposed squares. The sides of most pieces end in a thick cord or cable, which is often wrapped with wool of alternating colours, giving a 'barber's pole' effect (although frequently this has worn away). Occasionally, there are tufts at varying intervals along the sides.

The warps of south Persian kilims are most usually of natural ivory wool; occasionally natural brown wool is used, and more rarely, a combination of both brown and ivory. The warps are knotted at the ends, the knot often being covered in coloured wools. Sometimes the warps are thickly braided, the ends again being tied with coloured wools. Warps are also found which have been braided and then plaited.

The borders of south Persian kilims are superimposed on the designs like the frames of windows. They do not, in other words, only define the central composition but also curtail and limit it, focusing the attention on one area of it. The most common border design is a continuous reciprocal trefoil or arrowhead, a design also found on glazed ceramic tiles used in the domes of Persian mosques. The corners are never carefully drawn, the turns being haphazard. The design may also appear in one, two or three layers. Some south Persian kilims have a variety of different borders, while others (like many from the Caucasus) are designed without borders.

The characteristics outlined in the previous paragraphs, particularly the design and techniques of the end panels, occur on so many examples that it is tempting to consider them as indicative of a particular village or sub-tribe. For the moment, however, this must remain an hypothesis; despite careful analysis, no consistent pattern linking end panels to field designs seems to emerge. The present study of Fars kilims is limited to forty-two examples, although many more have been examined. Nevertheless it has proved impossible to establish sub-groups conclusively, so prevalent are the variations in patterns, designs and compositions.

In illustrating the pieces, we have tried to place them in groups based on similarities in design, ornament and colour. Although the order of groups, and of particular pieces within groups, is subjective, it is hoped that by grouping pieces with subtle variations on single themes, the reader may be made aware of the great vitality and imagination displayed by the weavers. Kilims are essentially a folk art, and folk art the world over tends to be governed by a traditional set of rules. But the greatness of any folk art, whether it be Japanese pottery, African sculpture or Middle Eastern kilims, rests on the ability of the craftsmen to create individuality within the framework of traditional art.

Group 1: Kilims with Patterns of Serrated Motifs

This first group of kilims shares a common field ornament—a small square with serrated sides. This ornament can be combined in several ways, chromatically or geometrically, to create different patterns. It is an interlocking motif which can be repeated horizontally, vertically or diagonally with contrasting or repeating colours. It employs no vertical lines, and consequently the kilims on which it appears have no slits and are as a result more durable.

This design element has a long history and can be found on Safavid pile-knotted carpets. The outer minor border of a fragmentary late sixteenth- to early seventeenth-century medallion rug with split-palmette arabesques has diagonally drawn serrated motifs in red, blue and yellow alternately on three sides, and similarly coloured motifs in a chevron pattern on one of the ends. This piece, now in the Metropolitan Museum of Art, New York, was once in the collection of Joseph V. McMullan and is illustrated in his *Islamic Carpets*, 1965, no. 20. (Note that there is some confusion over the numbering of 20 and 21 in the McMullan catalogue; the number here refers to the illustration, not to the text, where the carpet is described as no. 21). The motif also appears in the minor inner border of a fragmentary 'single-plane lattice' vase-technique carpet in the Burrell Collection, Glasgow (illustrated by May Beattie, *Carpets From Central Persia* 1976, plate 56).

374   *152 × 270 cm.*
375   *141 × 222 cm.*

On plate 374, the serrated elements are combined to form cruciform blocks or three-layer, stepped diamonds, each layer

being of a different colour. These ornaments are arranged in diagonal rows on a rose-coloured ground. In each row, the ornaments are repeated in the same colour-combination, thus giving the diagonal direction to the pattern. The long sides of the field are lined with simple stepped diamonds which have the effect of stopping the pattern laterally. The awkward cornering of the reciprocal border is a normal feature.

Plate 375 is an example of a rare group of kilims with plain undecorated centres. We have located only a few examples attributable to Fars, five with yellow fields and two with ivory. Such a feature is more frequently encountered on kilims from south-east Anatolia. We have decided to illustrate two examples with plain yellow fields, since it is possible thereby to compare the treatment of two different weavers working within narrowly defined compositional limits. In plate 375, the pattern, formed by the juxtaposition of the interlocking elements surrounds the field, giving the composition a well-balanced unity. The border is finely executed, being large and open; as is usual, its function as a frame is emphasized and strengthened by the inclusion of brilliant white cotton.

376   *137 × 262 cm.*

The colour of this open-field kilim is similar to that of plate 375. Here, however, the pattern of interlocking elements appears only in the corners—a seemingly less successful, more encroaching, compositional approach. The border is considerably more rigid than that of plate 375, giving a mechanical appearance to the composition as a whole. The plain expanse of yellow in the field is broken by a central line of multi-coloured tufts of wool, a device not often found in Persian kilims. It has been suggested that the tufts are placed there as amulets, good luck charms for specific occasions such as weddings.

A close comparison with plate 375 suggests that plate 376 may be a later example. This, however, is a purely subjective opinion. Since we have little knowledge of the exact age of any kilim, it is impossible to establish a structured chronological sequence based on style. The composition of this piece seems to be less well thought out than that of plate 375; the field appears too long, thus making the end panels seem like casual additions rather than integral parts of a unified composition.

These two pieces use the theme of large diamonds as their principal decorative motifs. Plate 377, with its golden-yellow field, is one of the most beautiful of all the Fars kilims we have encountered. The interlocking elements are used to form a double configuration in the lower diamond, and appear as the outlining device in the upper one. They are also used along the vertical sides of the field in a zigzag which follows the outline of the central medallions, thus forming wide, plain-coloured channels surrounding the medallions; this is a composition well known from classical pile-knotted carpets. The centre of each medallion is deep red and contains small slit-tapestry stepped diamonds. The reciprocal trefoil border and the end panels are both well composed. We also have here the concept frequently encountered in Fars kilims, of a space surrounding the field, creating a gap between the border and the principal composition. Note too the wide space between the actual border and the four sides of the kilim.

In plate 378 the corners and side-pieces follow exactly the structure of the central medallion, thereby creating an endless repeat pattern of diagonally offset multi-layered large diamonds. It is possible that this was also the original intention of the weaver of the previously described piece. As in plate 377 we have a frame surrounding the field, but in this instance the space contains another decorative device frequently encountered in Fars kilims: a row of juxtaposed and multi-layered stepped half-diamonds. The design on the end panels consists of brocaded rows forming a pattern of alternating blue and white rectangles.

379   160×260 cm.

The use of the serrated element as an all-over composition covering the entirety of the field is striking in plate 379. Once again the composition suggests an endless repeat pattern of diagonally offset vertical rows of diamonds, each consisting of multiple layers of different colours. The diamonds blend into one another, thus covering the entire field. The border cuts the field vertically in the centre of the side rows of diamonds.

The side border consists of a zigzag pattern formed by the vertical repetition in one colour of the serrated elements. The top and bottom borders are formed by a series of small, solid half-diamonds. Although this border is simpler than those found on the kilims illustrated previously, it should be noted that it is made up of the same basic design element found in the field, while at the same time remaining a reciprocal border with the same symbolic role as the trefoil border.

Kilims of this type are often attributed to Veramin, a town just south of Tehran. However, the similarity of both the design and the wool to those found on the two previously described examples justifies an ascription to Fars. The suggestion of a Veramin origin may have arisen, as is so often the case with many different types of oriental weavings, because a marketing town in which some similar pieces were found was assumed to be the place in which they all were woven. The overall design on this kilim seems to have been used by many tribes in west Persia.

The effect made by the serrated motifs arranged in this overall design is very close to that of a group of Navajo Indian blankets. The North American pieces are usually referred to as 'eye-dazzlers', and it is perhaps worth noting that the Navajo and the nomads of west Persia lived on the same latitude, with similar climates and seasonal temperatures. Although such an analogy may seem a little far-fetched, an added coincidence is that although kilims are woven in many diverse areas of the world from South America to China, only two groups—the Navajo and the nomads of west Persia—are known to employ this decorative ornament in this way.

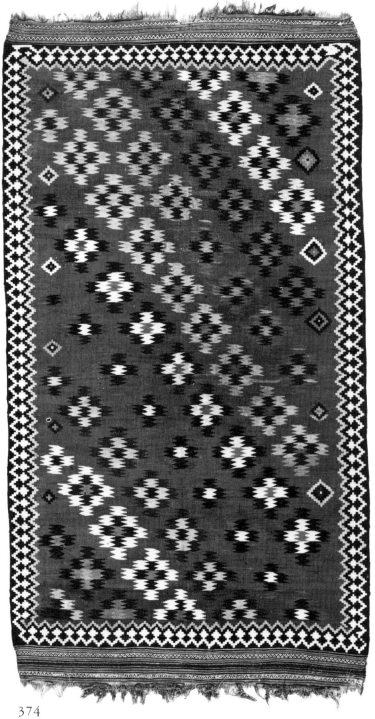

374

375

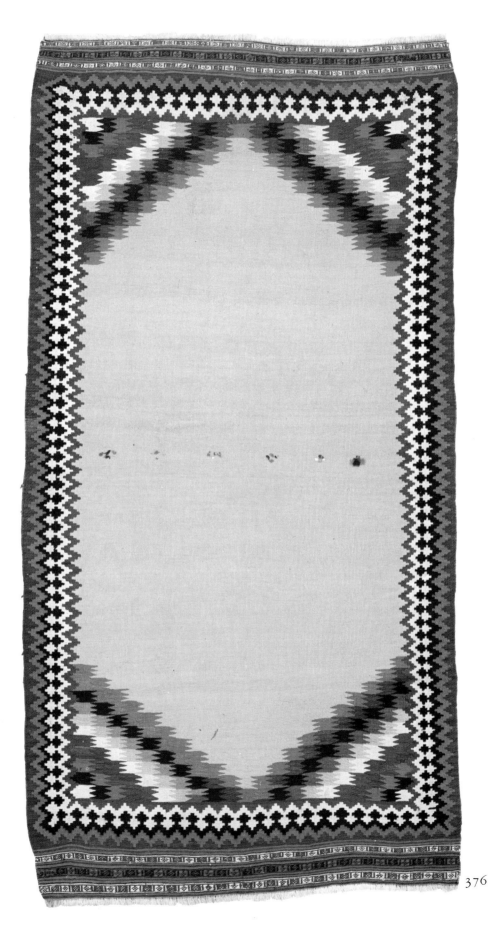

376

377

378

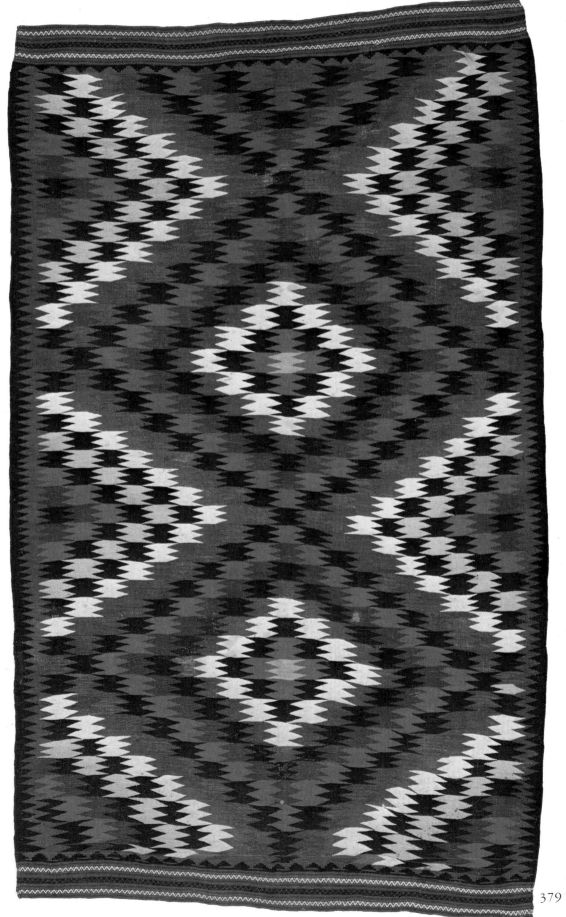

379

Group 2: Kilims with Parallel Stepped Lines

This is a group of kilims in which the principal means of decoration is the use of many parallel stepped bands. This device is ideally suited to tapestry weaving, and the Qashqai demonstrate their mastery of weaving by the richness of the decorative effects they achieve by such comparatively simple means.

380   *153 × 350 cm.*
381   *168 × 350 cm.*

Once again we have a central field composition of three large conjoined diamonds. However, although plate 380 employs the serrated element as a basis for the pattern of the central row of diamond medallions, it has sides and corners consisting of a series of parallel rows of multicoloured stepped lines, the principal decorative motif of this group of kilims. This piece thus makes an interesting and logical link between the first two groups.

The pattern of stepped lines on the sides of plate 380 forms large half-diamonds. The corner devices, however, join at the bottom and the top of the kilim, thus containing the overall composition. The field itself acts as a frame placed between the central composition and the reciprocal borders, as has been seen on other pieces.

In plate 381, which follows the composition of the previous example, the serrated ornament has completely disappeared, to be replaced on the central diamonds by the parallel stepped lines. Unlike most similar looking kilims, this is not woven in the slit-tapestry technique; here, the coloured wefts loop the adjoining warp, sewing up the slits. This form of tapestry-weaving is also known as single-interlock. The wool used to weave the madder ground of this piece was not dyed in one batch, causing the marked variation in shade. This phenomenon, quite commonly encountered on pile-knotted rugs, is considered aesthetically desirable and is known as abrash. Both this piece and plate 380 are fairly long, and have similar brocaded designs on their end panels.

382   *135 × 231 cm.*

This is one of the most outstanding of all Fars kilims, supremely accomplished in both craftsmanship and composition. The open field is of natural ivory wool with subtle variations in tone. The soft harmonious effect that this creates is emphasized by contrast with the brilliant white cotton used in the decoration. A similar example was illustrated in the catalogue of an important exhibition of carpets in Frankfurt and Hamburg during 1971–2, plate 97.

383   *86 × 216 cm.*

Plate 383 is a small kilim of fine quality, with a field woven entirely of white cotton. The principal motifs in the field, small hooked medallions, are arranged diagonally. Such ornaments are frequently encountered on kilims of this group. The same stepped-edge half-diamonds containing hooked motifs encountered on the previous piece are seen here flanking the sides of the field. In addition, a group of four complete motifs can be seen at either end of the field. These medallions are common on Persian, and especially Kurdish, weavings but are not confined to that country alone; they are found on pieces woven from the Aegean to the Afghan borders. The corner panels of the present kilim are similar to those of the previous five examples.

384   *105 × 145 cm.*

In plate 384, the stepped line becomes a secondary element in the overall composition. The piece may be related to plate 383 through its minor ornaments, although a closer relationship may be seen by comparing both with two kilims illustrated in *The Undiscovered Kilim* (plate 52), and *From the Bosporus to Samarkand* (Fig. 11). Both these latter have the same corner and side devices as plate 383, and an arrangement of small ornaments surrounding a diamond medallion similar to plate 384. The corner and side patterns of plate 384 contain small stepped diamonds, a decorative design seen also in plate 386; the latter has in addition the same tiny squares within the reciprocal trefoil border.

380

381

382

383

384

385

386

385   *168 × 252 cm.*

Among the pieces illustrated, this kilim appears to be one of the earliest. The stepped lines have become heavier and bolder and are once again predominant. The colours are strong and brilliant, the composition is well balanced, and the reciprocal borders are large and clearly drawn. The two large diamond medallions culminate at their four corners in smaller conjoined diamonds containing hooked motifs, a device used in one of the longer kilims previously illustrated. The centre of each large medallion is emphasized by the use of a vivid white cotton. The brocaded end panels are close in design to those of plate 379.

386   *165 × 280 cm.*

The present piece contains many of the motifs and elements of design found in the kilims discussed so far. Indeed, it is almost an anthology of Fars kilim design, although the many unresolved elements demonstrate what happens when a weaver works within a tradition but lacks a proper understanding of its meaning. The composition is squashed, and the drawing often haphazard. The series of border designs are particularly fussy. Once again, the stepped line has become a very minor decorative element. It has no organic function within the composition, but is used only to outline designs in the manner of a child who draws an outline and then fills in the spaces.

Group 3: Kilims with an Overall Diamond Lattice

387   *176 × 274 cm.*

This is a powerful composition in which the field, almost completely covered, shows through as a lattice beneath a polychrome diamond pattern. The white cotton of some of the diamonds makes a startling contrast to the dark blue of those adjacent. The reciprocal half-diamond motifs surrounding the field relate back to some of the pieces in other groups and, like the reciprocal borders, are large and well drawn. The diamonds, containing eight-pointed stars enclosed within small octagons, constitute the elements of the field pattern. They are themselves arranged in an overall series of large conjoined-diamond formations, suggesting an endless repeat. They may also be seen to form an enlarged version of the trefoil element which forms the usual Qashqai reciprocal border.

388   *178 × 244 cm.*

This piece, apparently one of the oldest of the Fars kilims illustrated in this book, is unfortunately missing its end panels. In contrast to the previous piece, where the colour-arrangement of the diamonds suggested larger ones, here the formation of the small diamonds suggests a purely diagonal pattern (although this is not immediately apparent). The random arrangement of colours in an almost patchwork effect—an unusually free handling—results in a strange paradox: an incredible harmony of strongly contrasting colours. There is no secondary field surrounding the main pattern, as in the previous example, and the reciprocal border is drawn in its most pure and simple form.

389   *176 × 281 cm.*
390   *no size available*

These two pieces still use the overall concept of a diamond lattice, but in a way that contrasts strongly with the two previous pieces. This contrast is a clear demonstration of the extraordin-

ary imagination of tribal weavers and their ability to create endless variations on apparently limited themes. It is an ability which has a particular fascination for twentieth-century Western painters—one need think only of Joseph Albers, Morris Louis, Kenneth Noland or Frank Stella.

The field of plate 389 consists of a central area contained within large, irregular, stepped-edge half- and quarter-diamonds. The overall effect is one of bold areas of colour upon which float individual diamond medallions of various sizes and designs. The two large central examples are series of diamonds within larger concentric diamonds. Such pieces are often irregularly drawn and look naive. However, they display a harmonious use of colour, and in the best of them there is an instinctive feeling for compositional balance. Plate 389 appears to be the oldest example of its type, although kilims with the same features are still made today. A common feature is the simple two-colour reciprocal border. To date, we have found only one example of this type of kilim using the border device of reciprocal arrowheads seen on the majority of Fars kilims illustrated in this book. However, one peculiar feature of this piece is the design of its end panels, which are related to the Shushtar group of kilims.

In plate 390 the two large indigo diamonds of subtly differing shapes give the kilim great dramatic impact. Unlike that of the previous piece, the composition is symmetrically arranged, although there is a similar naiveté of drawing. The indigo corners effectively frame the central design. The end panels differ in design from the previous piece.

391   *145 × 275 cm.*

Like plate 390, the composition is formed from the simplest of elements: plain, multicoloured, stepped diamonds arranged in a diagonal lattice or grid without the inclusion of any minor ornaments. A sense of space, and the achievement of an harmonious colour scheme, seem the principal aims of the weaver of this piece. Brilliant white cotton is used to form the field upon which the diamonds float, which highlights their soft but glowing colours. The diagonal pattern is disturbed by the row of gaps in the field near the top, and by the infilling of certain of the half-diamonds at the top and on the sides. Note the uneven end panels, with three rows at the top and two at the bottom.

387

392   *146 × 229 cm.*
393   *142 × 246 cm.*

Plate 392 is a less interesting example of the naively drawn degenerate diamond type, with a weak sense of colour. The colours of the side panels repeat diagonally, giving an unbalanced quality to the design. The use of the standard reciprocal border is somewhat incongruous, even though it is well drawn. Plate 393, however, is more exciting; at each corner of the ivory field are four extraordinary wedge shapes containing small diamonds, and in the field itself float a variety of diamonds and other ornaments. The composition as a whole is most unusual, and, once again, is a demonstration of a lively, original mind working within an established tradition. Notice the double border design.

394   *147 × 242 cm.*

Although this piece is not an outstanding example of its type, the colours are bold and dramatic. The central design is once again framed by a section of the red field, and there is a particularly pleasing three-colour interlocking border design, obviously a simplification of the reciprocal trefoil border. The outlines in the field show a curious and interesting combination of small- and large-scale stepped lines.

395   *143 × 253 cm.*

This is almost certainly a late piece. It is coarsely woven and rough to the touch. The vivid colours, however, are all composed of natural dyes. This is a particularly rare design, relating to the diamond and channels of the previous pieces and also

to those pieces with strong axial designs, such as the diagonal pieces we illustrate next. It is possible that the weaver may have intended to create a three-dimensional illusion with this design, although this hypothesis perhaps leans too heavily on Western concepts of modern art; painters such as Vasarely come to mind. The contrasting designs of the two end panels is another very unusual feature.

396   *148 × 299 cm.*

Plate 396 and the next example illustrate designs based on diagonal bands. Plate 396 is not an altogether successful composition. The pattern of decorated bands is framed by a zigzag border contained within a two-colour rectilinear band, outside which is the standard multi-layered reciprocal arrowhead border. The overall effect is a little crowded and mechanical. The stepped swastika motifs relate this piece to plate 394. Notice that here it is not the designs that form the diagonal pattern, but clearly defined bands outlined with the same device as plate 394.

397   *173 × 246 cm.*

This very finely woven piece has a most unusual green ground; the motifs are arranged in diagonal rows but without the framing bands of the previous piece. There is, therefore, a greater freedom and fluidity of movement. The stepped medallion contained between a pair of hooked ornaments is, in various forms, almost a universal motif on Middle-Eastern kilims. On this piece, note the interesting reciprocal effect of the spaces between the hooked designs and those found within them. This gives a perfect sense of balance to the design.

388

389

390

391

392

393

394

395

396

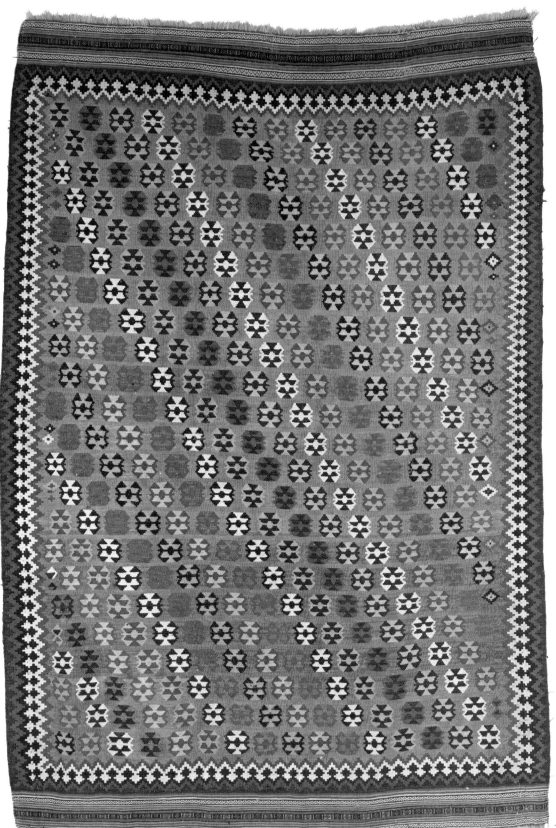

397

Group 4: Kilims with Horizontal Bands

The composition of horizontal bands, the major bands flanked by minor stripes, was greatly favoured by weavers of Fars kilims, although it is, perhaps, more often associated with Caucasian pieces. The Fars pieces are of two principal types: those with framing borders and those in which the bands continue to the edge.

398   *178 × 317 cm.*
399   *152 × 281 cm.*

Plate 398 has an exceptional and unusual colour range. The horizontal bands all in turquoise, red, natural dark brown, greyish-yellow, dark blue, white cotton, natural light brown, yellow and aquamarine blue. It is unusual to find natural brown wool in Fars kilims; here it appears not only in the bands but also in the outer part of the border.

The design within the bands is often found on Caucasian kilims and is probably of north-west Persian-Azerbaijan origin. The meandering wavy bands are common to the weavings of the Turkic peoples in the nineteenth century, although this is one of the most ancient of textile designs.

Plate 398 is exceptionally finely drawn and has a superb range of colours and was shown in 'The Qashqai of Iran', an important exhibition held in various museums in England throughout 1976 (catalogue no. G 18, colour plate 4).

Plate 399 may appear to be something of an interloper in this group. The diagonal centre bands hark back to pieces such as plate 396, but the end panels relate it to the present group. The motifs which appear in these two end bands are especially close to those found on the next kilim illustrated. Note the single small human figure walking up the fifth band. Although such apparently humorous quirks are found on Qashqai pile weavings and very occasionally on Caucasian kilims, this is the only appearance known to us on Fars kilims.

400   *143 × 312 cm.*

The overall proportions of the field in this piece are more satisfactory than those of plate 398, with which it has a close affi-

nity. It is, however, more restrained in its colour range, and the border design is stiffer, with less carefully composed drawing. The stepped interlocks of the vertical border once again illustrate the phenomenon of a design created by the nature of the kilim technique. The field design is a rectangular version of the diamonds of plate 398.

401   *147 × 318 cm.*
402   *153 × 279 cm.*

Plate 401 and the following three examples share with the previous three the principal composition of horizontal bands separated by minor stripes. However, there is one major difference: the horizontal bands extend to the sides of the kilims, there being no borders. Many types of south Persian kilims, and several from the Caucasus, are borderless, and there are many other points of similarity in the various ornaments between the south Persian and Caucasian pieces. In style, however, they are entirely different. The kilims from the south can be distinguished easily by their end panels, often brocaded, a feature not known on Caucasian pieces.

Plate 401 has a balanced and harmonious colour combination, with a predominant bluish tinge which gives the piece a slightly cool appearance. Plate 402 is more vivid, with reds, yellows and browns predominating; it is also much more finely woven. Indeed, a close physical comparison between the two pieces demonstrates that, despite stylistic similarities, they are totally different in texture and colour range. Both kilims display a very rich vocabulary of design.

403   *145 × 260 cm.*
404   *140 × 272 cm.*

Both these pieces show a simplification of the band composition, with chevrons alternating with well-spaced geometric ornaments. Plate 403 is related to plate 402 through its end panels, and plate 404 is closer to plate 401. The composition of plate 404 is obviously a further simplification of the design of plate 403, particularly in the transmutation of the complex geometric motifs in the alternate bands into single diamonds, of which only two bands appear. The diamond ornament is frequently encountered on Caucasian pieces. Plate 404 is similar to pieces woven in north-west Persia.

398

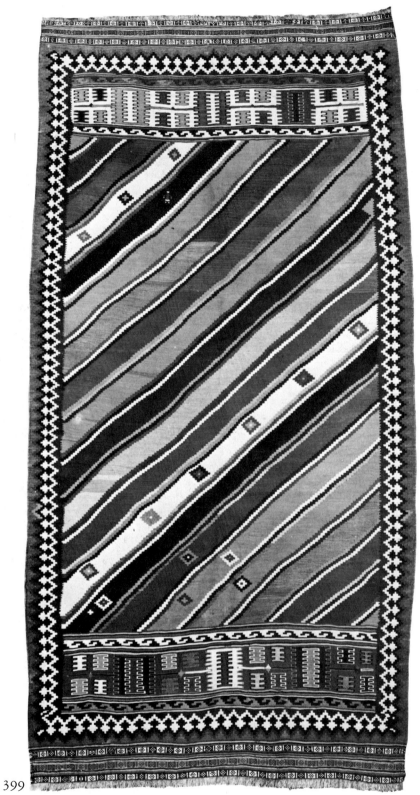

399

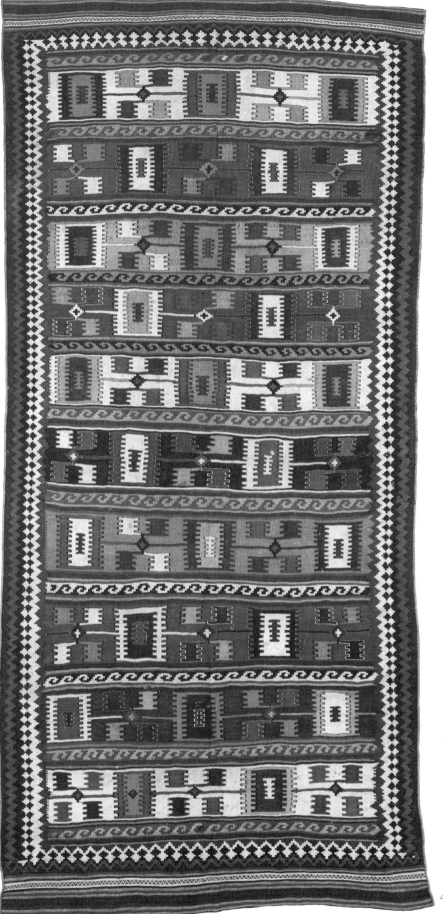

400

401

402

403

404

405

406

405   *152×218 cm.*
406   *no size available*

With these two pieces we return to the composition of horizontal bands contained within borders. The motifs in the major and minor borders of both pieces are typical of Caucasian kilims, although had these pieces been woven there, the bands would almost certainly have been wider and of more complex ornamentation. The border design of plate 405 is close to that of previously discussed Qashqai pieces, particularly plates 384 and 386. Plate 406 has the chevrons found on plates 403 and 404 and the alternate band ornaments of plate 405. The single bracketed diamond ornament found on the far left of the central band of plate 406 can be found as a major ornament on plates 401 and 402.

365

Group 5: Kilims with Centralized Designs

The following eight pieces have designs which focus on the field, and in many cases, on the centre of the field.

407   *no size available*
408   *155 × 254 cm.*

In plate 407 the chequered square draws the eye inexorably to the centre of the extraordinary deep tan-red field. Only the white cartouche, containing the inscription, acts as a diversion. The main border consists of juxtaposed small diamonds on a white ground arranged vertically and horizontally to form a square grid pattern. The alternation of colours creates the impression of square blocks. Many types of oriental carpets have blank, or almost blank, fields; among the best known pile-knotted examples being the 'Talish' rugs from the Caucasus. Baluchi weavers from the Persian-Afghan border made pile carpets with plain kilim centres called *sofraes*. Plain-field kilims, however, as already discussed, are comparatively rare.

The well-spaced field ornaments of plate 408—stepped lozenges—are more often encountered on Caucasian kilims. Of particular interest is the border design of both these pieces, especially that of plate 407, in which the tight diamond bands are broken by blocks of alternating colours. These borders seem to relate to the so-called 'frozen' border design of late pile-woven carpets in the vase technique from central Persia.

409   *137 × 275 cm.*
410   *162 × 260 cm.*

Both these pieces are comparatively late: plate 410 contains a synthetic orange. They show an overall degeneration in colour, drawing and general composition. In plate 410, there are two secondary borders, one light and one dark, flanking the main border of conjoined diamonds: an arrangement typical of late kilims.

411   *152 × 272 cm.*

Notice the extraordinary depth given to this piece by the contrast between the cream wool of the field and the vivid white cotton used in the borders and in the star motifs within the squares. This kilim and the two following examples illustrate another popular Qashqai composition. which might be described as a 'floating squares' or tile pattern. The present piece is noteworthy for the dramatic central indigo square. A further example of this type is illustrated in *European and Oriental Carpets* by Jack Franses (London, 1970, colour plate 11).

412   *no size available (Detail)*
413   *99 × 148 cm.*

Plate 412 is a late piece, and the red in the borders of plate 413 shows very slight bleeding, which may, in this instance, be due to over-dyeing or harsh cleaning, rather than to the presence of aniline. Plate 413 is exceptionally small and very finely woven. Plate 412, like plate 411, uses indigo as a contrast, in this instance in the two squares in the top left and bottom right corners.

414   *178 × 241 cm.*

This variant of the previous pieces has the ubiquitous hooked hexagon ornament contained within the floating medallions. The 'broken jigsaw' pattern of the inner border of this and the previous piece relates to certain Turkish village pile-knotted rugs (specifically those from Ezine and Bergama), and to the compartment kilims of Malatya (such as plates 245 and 249) and the prayer rugs of Obruk (such as plates 163 and 165).

407

408

409

410

411

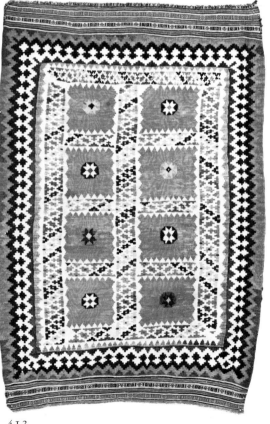

412

413

414

Ethnographical Notes on the Qashqai

JOAN ALLGROVE

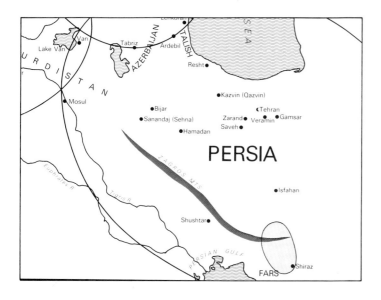

The difficulties encountered in the classification of rugs and kilims from the province of Fars in south Iran reflect a complex political, economic and ethnic history, particularly over the past one hundred and fifty years. The study of any tribe must consider the exchange and borrowing of patterns brought about by war, emigration, settlement and the merging or fragmenting of groups; all circumstances that counter the tribe's natural instincts for conservatism.

The two major tribes now in Fars, the Qashqai and the Khamseh, present peculiar problems, since they are political rather than ethnic entities. The Qashqai have received some attention from Western writers such as M. Ullens de Schooten and V. Cronin—and passing references from travellers and historians like Dora Curzon, who noted austerely, 'The sympathetic and not too squeamish will like them.' Two pioneering articles by Dr. O. Garrod, published in 1946, remained among the few serious works until 1974, when P. Oberling's historical account *The Qashqai Nomads of Fars* appeared.

Following this, the exhibition catalogue *The Qashqai of Iran* was the first attempt by an anthropologist and an art historian

to study the textile crafts in the context of the life of the tribe. It will be appreciated, therefore, that work on the classification of tribal and village weaving is still in its infancy.

The term 'Shiraz' was commonly used in the West until 1976 to cover several large groups of rugs and flat-woven textiles; nineteenth-century Europeans habitually named types of weaving after the place in which they were marketed. Although Shiraz was known for its pile-knotted rugs in mediaeval times and as late as the eighteenth century, very little weaving was done there over the past century until the recent government-sponsored revival. 'Fars' or 'south-west Persia' are now preferred as generic terms, although they take us no further towards clarification, since they make no distinction between tribal and village products.

Most of Persia consists of a high, central desert plateau; an estimated five-eighths of its land is uncultivated, tapering down to the flat southern coastline of the Persian Gulf. Throughout history, its settlements have had something of an oasis character. But in Fars province—virtually the cradle of Persian civilization—the Zagros mountains running from north-west to south-east give a series of hill valleys. The higher, though unpredictable, rainfall creates pastures that have made this perfect nomad country, while on the plains, corn, citrus fruit and even vines can be grown.

This duality is of great antiquity: beyond the hills which surround Shiraz the Marrdasht plain, now more fertile under government subsidized irrigation, is the scene of increasing agricultural activity, while farther along the road today's nomads migrate past stone reliefs of people who may have been their remote ancestors from Central Asia, offering gifts of horses and textiles to the great King Darius I.

The pastoral nomads of south-west Iran have in the past played a more important role in the area's history than their numbers might suggest, since they have formed well-organized, if mobile, groups which have tended to avoid incorporation into the structure of central government. Indeed, they were frequently at odds with each other and with the administration up to the 1950s. Their numbers have always been difficult to calculate; the nomad population has been estimated in terms of 'tents', i. e. families, but there is no firm agreement as to the number of people living in a tent, figures varying between five and ten. In 1972, the Qashqai, the largest tribe in Fars, were estimated by the Department of Tribal Education to total about 141,000 persons, of which possibly thirty-three per cent were settled.

Their neighbours to the north are Kurds, who spread over into Iraq and Turkey; further south are the Persian-speaking tribes, the Zurs and the Bakhtiari, the latter spreading across the area towards Isfahan. Also to the north-east, towards Kerman, are Afshars; in southern Fars, the nearest neighbours of the Qashqai are the Khamseh tribes who share part of the Qashqai's migration routes.

In an area with so complex a history, the problems of the historian and anthropologist are obvious. Tribes may be classified either according to the political unit with which they identify themselves or to the ethnic group of their original core. Either method has its pitfalls. The Qashqai are predominantly Turki speakers (although many of them are bilingual), using a dialect related to that spoken in the Caucasus and Azerbaijan, where it is known as Azeri Turkish. However, there are other Turki-speaking people in Fars, notably the Ainalu and the Baharlu, two of the five Khamseh tribes, of which the other three are the Arabic-speaking Sheybani and Jabbareh, and the Persian-speaking Basseri.

The Khamseh confederacy, its name derived from the Arabic word for 'five', was set up in 1865, under the leadership of Shiraz-based traders, as a political antidote to Qashqai power. This echoes to some extent the circumstances under which the Qashqai tribe itself is thought to have originated.

No mention of the Qashqai is known prior to the reigns of Shah Abbas the Great (AD 1587–1629), when Jani Agha Qashqai was given authority over the various tribes already in Fars. Among these were Turki-speaking groups including the Farsi Madan, still one of the major Qashqai *taifeh* or divisions, whose name means 'those who speak no Persian'.

Jani Agha Qashqai appears to have founded a loose confederacy of tribes that flourished under his able descendants, so that the considerable political and economic power of the Qashqai during the nineteenth century was identified with what was in practice the hereditary ruling family of *ilkhanis*. There has been movement among the various groups, however; some have declined in number or shifted political allegiance; and others, including people of Persian, Zuri, Bakhtian and Afshar origin, joined the Qashqai when it seemed expedient to

do so. In 1876 fifty-seven named groups of the Qashqai were listed by Fasa'; six major divisions *(taifeh)* are now recognized: the Shesh Boluki, the Farsi Madan, the Darrehshuri, the Keshkuli Bozorg, the Keshkuli Kuchek and the Amaleh. These incorporate smaller named groups *(tireh)*; especially the large Amaleh group, as the *taifeh* and the ruling family attracted a large number of smaller *tireh* to its ranks.

The Qashqai who, among other nomads, were forcibly settled by Riza Shah, resumed their migratory habits on his abdication in 1941. Their political power, however, came to an end when the confederacy was officially disbanded by the Iranian governmen in 1956 and the roles of the *ilkhan* and of the chieftain *(kalantar)* of the *taifeh* were made obsolete. However, the people have survived as a tribal entity, due to their own determination and to the successful realization of the tribal education scheme conceived by Mohamed Bahman-Begi, himself a Qashqai. This not only provides education for tribal children but also teaches weaving at the tribal weaving school in Shiraz. The Qashqai still constitute the largest migratory tribe in Iran, and have preserved much of their old lifestyle.

Persian traditional costume was banned by Riza Shah who, like Ataturk, believed that the people must wear European dress if they were to identify with the West. Now both townsmen and tribesmen alike wear ready-made clothes of drab European cut, the Qashqai men distinguished only by their hat, the *kotah* or 'cap with two ears', a round high-crowned hat of felt with flaps that turn down to protect the ears in winter or the eyes from the sun's glare in summer. It is of modern design, however, being reputedly an innovation of Naser Khan Qashqai, the last *il Khan,* in the 1940s. The women still cling wholeheartedly to their costume of multifarious ankle-length frilled petticoats under a gathered skirt of patterned fabric, often lurex brocade, a long tabard and a tight waist-length jacket, perhaps of velvet. The fabrics are bought in the bazaars where customers can often be seen shopping in family groups.

Silk fabrics are made up by the women themselves or taken to a bazaar tailor. They are fond of jewellery, notably necklaces that they string according to taste, using coins, beads, stones and charms, also purchased in the bazaar. The most characteristically Qashqai ornament is the *sanjagh* (chin pin), a silver or gold fibula with pendant discs, coloured stones, coins or lucky fish that fastens the sequin-trimmed head kerchief under the wearer's chin. These voluminous clothes are everyday wear, and the swinging skirts with flash of lurex are a notable feature of the migration, although the best finery is reserved for festivities.

415 Migration

The carefully planned migrations take place twice a year. The spring migration starts in mid-March at about the time of Ro-Ruz, the Persian New Year. The tribes move towards the summer quarters on the Kuh-e-Dinar, part of the Zagros chain west of the Shiraz-Isfahan road, a journey of about six hundred miles from the plains near Firuzabad to which they return in September. They travel in small, orderly groups (plate 415), the components of which move at a different pace, supervised by their leaders and the heads of families.

Each day starts before dawn when the animals are loaded. Those who are able to ride do so, including the women, who generally travel with the donkeys; the latter carry household equipment and the young lambs, goats and chickens. The men take charge of the heavily laden camels (plate 416). The slowest are the flocks and the men and boys who drive them.

They may be on the move for anything up to half the day, depending on the weather and the terrain. If it is not too hot, however, a camp site is chosen by early afternoon, and the rest of the day is spent in pitching camp, preparing food, tending the animals and waiting for the latecomers to arrive. The men and boys act as shepherds, but chores like packing and unpacking and milking the animals are shared.

All tribal women are hard-working, and those of the Qashqai are no exception. They have considerable standing and influence in the home, where polygamy is rare. They used to ride and shoot and, according to Mohamed Bahman-Begi, were known in the past to participate in tribal politics. They alone spin and dye the wool and carry out weaving.

A feature of this type of pastoral nomadism is the complex relationships with settled people. In the past the nomadic tribes

374

416   Group of camels migrating in the
       vicinity of Firuzabad Gorde

417   Tent and family with Tribal School tent
       in the background

had been inclined to look down on those settled villagers whose economy was based on agriculture; quarrels over land and water were endemic. However, in Fars a substantial proportion of the village population is of tribal origin. It is quite common for some members of a family to live in a village or in Shiraz while others are nomadic. In any case a number of the necessities of a nomad's life have to be obtained either from town or village bazaars or from itinerant pedlars. Such goods, including flour, tea, sugar, metalware and cloth, are bought or exchanged for wool, skins, rugs or milk products. Richer nomads, owning a piece of land, may pay villagers to till and plant it for them and collect the crops on a later migration; the very wealthy are able to own houses in Shiraz and send their sons to foreign universities.

Among nomadic groups the wool preparation and weaving are practised when the people are relatively immobile; the period spent in summer quarters in the Zagros mountains is one of great activity. The Qashqai favour the rectangular black tent generally used in this part of Persia; its cover, made by the women of rather loose black goat-hair cloth, can both be water-repellant and provide insulation against the summer heat. The structure and size of the tent varies according to the wealth of the owner and the season. In the severe winter, it is enclosed by a wicker lattice supported by mud and stones, but it is seen at its best in the summer quarters, when it will be open invitingly along the front to reveal the family's possessions (plate 417).

There is a strong element of ritualization in many tribal activities: a group of tents, for instance, will be formally aligned to face south if possible, in a hollow that provides protection against bad weather and wild animals. Such tent groups are generally based on kinship or economic dependence. The senior member will choose his camping site first, while the others accept an established order of precedence.

In the past textiles and rugs were made for home-consumption, and a variety of storage bags—of pile, slit tapestry or other flat-weave techniques—is still necessary to hold household articles and serve as furniture in the tent. Large bags containing bedding, clothes, dry foodstuffs, etc. are stacked with immaculate precision on a line of stones placed along the inner wall at the back of the tent. Some are made in slit-tapestry technique, the sides patterned and the bases plain, with leather bindings and straps added to give strength. Bags are made in pairs for convenient loading on the animals, and such heavy burdens are usually carried by camels (plate 416).

418   The tent of a Darrehshuri Khan

419   Inside a Khan's tent near Ardakars, 1944

376

420 Spinning

Other articles like the hammock-shaped cradles are often made in tapestry weave, and among the variety of finishes added to pile or flat-weave bags, slit tapestry can appear as the back or as the ends, where it facilitates the lacing of cords to fasten the opening. Large kilims are an essential feature of tent furnishing. The line of bags along the back wall of the tent forms a divan-like structure on which one can recline, and over these, temporarily obscuring their kaleidoscopic colours, may be flung one or several kilims (plate 418). They are also used as floor coverings, although pile rugs are preferred. Old kilims form the underlay for pieces in better condition. The best examples will be kept rolled up, being brought out with the cushions and the tea when guests arrive (plate 419).

Most of the wool preparation and weaving processes are common to the tribes in Fars. The Qashqai, who raise a breed of broad-tailed sheep well-suited to migratory life and famous for its strong, glossy wool, differ only in their practice of shearing the animals once, and not twice, a year. This is done in May or June after the animals have been washed; the goats are also combed at this time to obtain their hair.

The wool is given a further wash in hot water and potash or bicarbonate of soda to remove excessive lanolin; after combing it is spun. Spinning is women's work and village men who perform this task are despised. It is most carefully done and, since it is laborious, the women and girls carry the simple wood and metal hand-spindles about with them (plate 420), the coil of fibres being tucked under their arm or into a sleeve. The spindles come out whenever there is a spare moment as they walk, and even while riding on the migration.

Wool of different consistency and ply will be required for tent-cloth, for warps, which usually consist of a mixture of

sheep's wool and goat's hair, and for the dyed wefts of a kilim. The finest quality wool, from the shoulder area of the animal, is reserved for pile-knotting.

Most of the dye-plants used are common to the rest of Persia, but the recipes of the Qashqai women, as well as their skillful juxtaposition of shades in the weaving, have made their colours justly famous. Apart from indigo, imported from the Indian sub-continent since antiquity, plants have generally been gathered during the migration and used in small quantities to make up batches of dye. Madder is the ubiquitous red dye, the addition of pomegranate skins giving the sharp clear red associated with this tribe.

The pomegranate has several other useful functions, producing a yellow that deepens to apricot with the addition of small quantities of madder. It also acts as a mordant (as does yoghurt), though alum, which is mined in north-west Persia and sold in the bazaars, is the most widely used fixing agent. The wool is immersed in it for a day before being put into the dye-bath. Certain colours, notably a strong cerise pink of which the Qashqai are nowadays fond, have for a long time been purchased in the bazaars, where chemically dyed wool can be seen alongside undyed fibres and wool coloured with vegetable dyes, the latter brought in and offered for sale by tribespeople and villagers (plate 421).

The horizontal loom associated with the nomads of Persia is of simple structure and can be easily rolled up and packed during the migration. Two beams, generally of plane wood, to which the warps are attached, are held in place by wooden pegs driven into the ground at each corner, holding the warps taut. No heddles are needed for weaving articles like kilims in the slit-tapestry technique. The weaver makes a shed by lifting alternate warps by hand to the width required and inserting wefts with a shuttle loaded with coloured wool.

This simple loom can be adapted for the weaving of more complex techniques by the addition of a heddle rod supported by a tripod. In the villages and at the Tribal School, the loom frames are of metal and permanently *in situ,* but still of the horizontal type. Weaving is a convivial activity, women working together when they are not otherwise occupied with household chores or tending the animals. Skill is passed on from mother to daughter or grandmother to grandchild. Some wealthy men have been accustomed to set up a tent and loom and provide a team of women with food and materials while

421 Wool-sellers in Shiraz bazaar

422   Teachers at the Tribal Weaving School, Shiraz, weaving a kilim

they have worked on a large piece. The two old ladies shown in plate 422, who now teach slit-tapestry weaving at the Tribal School, were once famous for the kilims they produced for the *ilkhanis*. Such commissions, among nomadic groups and in the villages, account for some at least of the larger rugs and kilims which seem to contradict the often repeated statement that tribal pieces are generally of small size.

A few patterns have been identified with certain of the tribes; however, the problems of attribution are formidable. Where certain *tireh* are largely settled in villages while a small percentage remain nomads, the distinction between a 'tribal' and a 'village' product becomes a very narrow one. It may also become necessary to re-attribute certain pieces to the Khamseh, who have shared a common tradition with the Qashqai but whose work has been studied hardly at all.

Not until recent anthropological work was focused upon the pastoral nomads was there much fundamental understanding of their way of life, and they have always had a poor reputation, owing to their predatory raids on their more settled neighbours.

It is almost inconceivable to urban dwellers that a people should wish to use a natural environment only to the extent of their own limited demands without exploiting it to maximum efficiency, or that they should defend fiercely the freedom to be nomads while all around them are the manifestations of rapid technological development. This freedom is, however, a central feature of their culture, as are the highly developed sense of tribal identity and the ties of family. This latter is strongly influenced by the women in whom are also vested the tribe's aesthetic traditions.

Appendices

Bibliography

ALI, Ibrahim Pasha, 'Early Islamic Rugs of Egypt or Fostat Rugs', *Bulletin de l'institut d'Egypte*, vol. XVII (1934–35).

The Arts of Islam, Hayward Gallery, London 1976.

BACHARACH, J. and I. BIERMAN, ed., *The Warp and Weft of Islam*, Seattle Art Museum 1977.

BAUSBACK, Peter, *Alte Orientalische Flachgewebe*, Mannheim 1977.

BEATTIE, May H., 'Coupled Column Prayer Rugs', *Oriental Art*, vol. XIV, no. 4, 1968.

— *The Thyssen-Bornemisza Collection of Oriental Rugs*, Castagnola, Switzerland 1972.

— 'The Present Position of Carpet Studies', *Apollo*, vol. CIII, no. 170 (1976).

BENNET, Ian, ed., *The Country Life Book of Carpets and Rugs of the World*, Feltham 1977.

BLACK, David and Clive LOVELESS, ed., *The Undiscovered Kilim*, London 1977.

BODE, Wilhelm von and Ernst KÜHNEL, *Antique Rugs from the Near East*, London 1970.

DENNY, Walter B., *Oriental Rugs*. Part of *The Smithsonian Illustrated History of Antiques*. New York 1979.

DICKIE, James, 'The Iconography of the Prayer Rug', *Oriental Art*, vol. XVIII, no. 1 (1972).

DIMAND, Maurice S., *The Ballard Collection of Oriental Rugs in the City Art Museum of St Louis*, St Louis 1935.

— and Jean MAILEY, *Oriental Rugs in the Metropolitan Museum of Art*, New York 1973.

ELLIS, Charles Grant, *Near Eastern Kilims*, Textile Museum, Washington, DC 1965.

— 'The Ottoman Prayer Rugs', *Textile Museum Journal*, vol. II, no. 4 (1969).

ENDERLEIN, Volkmar, 'Zwei Ägyptische Gebetsteppiche im Islamischen Museum', *Forschungen und Berichte, Staatliche Museen zu Berlin*, Band 13 (1971).

ERDMANN, Kurt, *Seven Hundred Years of Oriental Carpets*, London 1970.

— *The History of the Early Turkish Carpet*, London 1977.

ETTINGHAUSEN, Richard, 'Interaction and Integration in Islamic Art', *Unity and Variety in Muslim Civilisation*, ed. von Grunebaum, Chicago 1955.

—, M. S. DIMAND, L. W. MACKIE and C. G. ELLIS, *Prayer Rugs*, Textile Museum, Washington, DC 1974.

FRANSES, Jack, *European and Oriental Rugs*, London 1973.

FRANSES, Michael, *The World of Rugs*, London 1973.

GRABAR, Oleg, *The Formation of Islamic Art*, New Haven and London 1973.

HAACK, Herman, *Oriental Rugs*, London 1960.

HAWLEY, Walter A., *Oriental Rugs*, New York 1937.

Katalog wystawy kobierców mahometańskich ceramiki azjatyckiej i europejskiej, Cracow: Museum Narodwe (1934).

KENDRICK, A. F. and C. E. C. TATTERSALL, *Handwoven Carpets, Oriental and European*, New York 1973.

KRUIZHANOVSKY, B., *Ukrainskīe ī Rumuiskīe kīlīmui*, Leningrad 1925.

LANDREAU, Anthony N. and W. R. PICKERING, *From the Bosporus to Samarkand, Flatwoven Rugs*, Textile Museum, Washington, DC 1969.

— ed., *Yörük, the Nomadic Weaving Tradition of the Middle East*, Museum of Art, Carnegie Institute, Pittsburgh 1978.

McMULLAN, Joseph V. and D. O. REICHERT, *Islamic Rugs, Smith Collection,* Springfield, Mass. n.d.

— *Islamic Carpets,* New York 1965.

MARTIN, F. R., *A History of Oriental Carpets before 1800,* Vienna 1908.

MIGEON, G. and H. SALADIN, *Art Musulman,* Paris 1907.

MIGEON, G. and M. J. GUIFFREY, *La Collection Kelekian, Etoffes et Tapis,* Paris 1908.

— *L'Orient Musulman,* Paris 1922.

Near Eastern Art in Chicago Collections, The Art Institute of Chicago, Chicago 1973.

POPE, Arthur U., 'The Art of Carpet Making, History', *A Survey of Persian Art,* ed. A. U. Pope, vol. III, Oxford 1939.

SPUHLER, Friedrich, *Islamic Carpets and Textiles in the Keir Collection,* London 1978.

—, KÖNIG and VOLKMANN, *Old Eastern Carpets,* Munich 1978.

VELEV, Dimitri, *Bulgarian Kilims,* Sofia 1960.

WIET, Gaston, *Exposition de Tissus et Tapisseries du Musée Arabe du Caire (VIIe–XVIIe siècles) Periode Musulmane,* Musée des Gobelins, Paris 1935.

WORREL, W. H., 'On Certain Arabic Terms for "Rug"', *Ars Islamica,* I, 219 (1934).

TECHNIQUE

ACKERMAN, Phyllis, 'Persian Weaving Techniques', *A Survey of Persian Art,* ed. A. U. Pope, vol. III, Oxford 1939.

COLLINGWOOD, Peter, *The Techniques of Rug Weaving,* London 1968.

EMERY, Irene, *The Primary Structure of Fabrics,* Washington, DC 1966.

JACOBY, Heinrich, 'Materials Used in the Making of Carpets', *A Survey of Persian Art,* ed. A. U. Pope, vol. III, Oxford 1939.

TATTERSALL, C. E. C., *Notes on Carpet Knotting and Weaving,* London 1969.

THOMPSON, Jon, 'The Anatomy of a Carpet', part 1, *Turkish Carpets,* ed. Lefevre & Partners, London 1977.

— 'The Anatomy of a Carpet', part 2, *Caucasian Carpets,* ed. Lefevre & Partners, London 1977.

— 'The Anatomy of a Carpet', part 3, *The Persian Carpet,* ed. Lefevre & Partners, London 1977.

WHITING, Mark, 'Dye Analysis in Carpet Studies', *Halı,* vol. 1, no. 1 (1978).

SYMBOLISM

ARDALAN, Nader and Laleh BAKHTIAR, *The Sense of Unity,* Chicago 1973.

ARNOLD, Sir Thomas, 'Symbolism in Islam', *The Burlington Magazine,* vol. LIII (1928).

BURCKHARDT, Titus, *Alchemy,* London 1967.

— *Sacred Art in East and West,* London 1967.

— *Art of Islam,* London 1976.

CAMMAN, Schuyler, 'Symbolic Meanings in Oriental Rug Patterns', *Textile Museum Journal,* vol. III, no. 3 (1972).

— 'Paradox in Persian Carpet Patterns', *Halı,* vol. 1, no. 3 (1978).

COOMARASWAMY, Ananda, *Christian and Oriental Philosophy of Art,* New York 1956.

CRITCHLOW, Keith, *Order in Space,* London 1969.

— *Islamic Pattern,* London 1976.

D'ALVIELLA, Count Goblet, *The Migration of Symbols,* London 1894.

ELIADE, Mircea, *Myth and Reality,* New York 1963.

GUENON, René, *Symbolism of the Cross,* London 1958.

— *Symboles fondamentaux de la science sacrée,* Paris 1962.

— *The Reign of Quantity and the Signs of the Times,* Baltimore 1972.

— 'Initiation and the Crafts', *Journal of the Indian Society of Oriental Art,* vol. VI (1938); reprint, Ipswich, Suffolk 1974.

LINGS, Martin, *Ancient Beliefs and Modern Superstitions,* London 1965.

— *What is Sufism,* London 1975.

LOSSKY, Vladimir, *Essai sur le Théologie Mystique de l'Eglise d'Orient,* Paris 1944.

NASR, Seyyed Hossein, *Islam and the Plight of Modern Man,* London and New York 1975.

PAPADOPOULO, Alexandre, *L'Islam et l'art Musulman,* Paris 1976.

RUMI, *Mathnawi,* London 1925–40.

SHABISTARI, Sa'd al-Din Mahmud, *The Garden of Mystery,* London 1880.

SCHUON, Frithjof, *Light on the Ancient Worlds,* London 1965.

ANATOLIA

ACAR, Belkis, *Kilim ve Düz Dokuma Yaygılar,* Istanbul 1975.

— 'Yüncü Nomad Weaving in the Balıkesir Region of Western Turkey,' *Yörük,* ed. A.N. Landreau, Pittsburgh 1978.

ARSEVEN, Celal E., *Les Arts Décoratifs Turcs,* Istanbul 1952.

ASLANAPA, Oktay, *Turkish Art and Architecture,* New York 1971.

— *Turkish Arts,* Istanbul, n.d.

— and Yusuf DURUL, *Selçuklu Halilari,* Istanbul, n.d.

BEATTIE, May H., 'Coupled Column Prayer Rugs,' *Oriental Art,* vol. XIV, no. 4 (1968).

— 'Some Weft-float Brocaded Rugs of the Bergama-Ezine Region,' *Textile Museum Journal,* vol. III, no. 2 (1971).

— *The Thyssen-Bornemisza Collection of Oriental Rugs,* Castagnola, Switzerland 1972.

— 'Some Rugs of the Konya Region,' *Oriental Art,* vol. XXII, no. 1 (1976).

BLACK, David and Clive LOVELESS, ed., *The Undiscovered Kilim,* London 1977.

BRECK, Joseph and Frances MORRIS, *The James F. Ballard Collection of Oriental Rugs,* New York 1923.

ÇETINTÜRK, Bige, 'Les tapis de palais à Istamboul jusqu'à la fin du XVIᵉ siècle,' *Communications of the First International Congress of Turkish Art, Ankara 1959* (Ankara 1961).

DENNY, Walter B., 'Ottoman Turkish Textiles,' *Textile Museum Journal,* vol. III, no. 3 (1972).

— 'Anatolian Rugs: An Essay on Method,' *Textile Museum Journal,* vol. III, no. 4 (1973).

DIMAND, Maurice S., *The Ballard Collection of Oriental Rugs in the City Art Museum of St Louis,* St Louis 1935.

— and Jean MAILEY, *Oriental Rugs in the Metropolitan Museum of Art,* New York 1973.

DIRIK, Kâzim, *Eski ve yeni Türk haliciliği ve cihan halı tipleri panoramasi,* Istanbul 1938.

DODDS, Dennis R., 'Anatolian Kilims from the Sivas Region,' *Halı,* vol. I, no. 4 (1978).

DURUL, Yusuf, 'Halı ve Kilimlerde Kız Motifleri,' *Türk Etnoğrafya Dergisi,* no. 1 (Ankara 1956).

— 'Türkmen, Yürük, Afsar Halı ve Kilim Motifleri Üzerinde Araştırma,' *Türk Etnoğrafya Dergisi,* no. 2 (Ankara 1957).

ERDMANN, Hanna (ed.) and Kurt ERDMANN, *Orientteppiche, 16.–19. Jahrhundert,* Kestner Museum, Hanover 1966.

ERDMANN, Kurt, *The History of the Early Turkish Carpet,* London 1977.

FRAUENKNECHT, B. and K. FRANTZ, *Anatolische Gebetskelims,* Nürnberg 1978.

GÖNÜL, Macide, 'Türk Halı ve Kilimlerinin Teknik Hususiyetleri,' *Türk Etnoğrafya Dergisi* no. 2 (Ankara 1957).

— 'Türk Halı ve Kilimlerinde Sembolik Kuş Şekilleri,' *Dil ve Tarih Coğrafya Fakültesi Antropoloji Dergisi* (Ankara 1965).

İŞLEK, Sevim, 'Ankara Etnografya Müzesindeki nomad karakterli halılar.' *Vakıflar Dergisi,* VIII (Ankara 1969).

ITEN-MARITZ, J., *Turkish Carpets,* trans. by Richard and Elizabeth Bartlett, New York and Tokyo 1977.

JONES, H. McCoy and Ralph S. YOHE, ed., *Turkish Rugs,* Textile Museum, Washington, DC 1968.

LANDREAU, Anthony N. and W. R. PICKERING, *From the Bosporus to Samarkand, Flatwoven Rugs,* Textile Museum, Washington, DC 1969.

— 'Kurdish Kilim Weaving in the Van-Hakkari District of Eastern Anatolia,' *Textile Museum Journal,* vol. III, no. 4 (1973).

LEFEVRE & PARTNERS, ed., *Turkish Carpets,* London, 1977.

MACKIE, Louise W., *The Splendour of Turkish Weaving,* Textile Museum, Washington, DC 1973.

McMULLAN, Joseph V. (Intro.), *Turkish Rugs, The Rachel B. Stevens Memorial Collection,* Textile Museum, Washington, DC 1972.

MOSTAFA, M., *Turkish Prayer Rugs,* Cairo 1953.

Near Eastern Art in Chicago Collections, The Art Institute of Chicago, Chicago 1973.

ÖZBEL, Kenan, 'Cicim ve Sili,' *El Sanatlari Dergisi,* Ankara 1947.

— 'Anadolu kilimleri,' *El Sanatlari Dergisi,* Ankara 1948.

PETSOPOULOS, Yanni, *In Praise of Allah, Prayer Kilims from the Near East,* London 1975.

PITCHER, Donald E., *An Historical Geography of the Ottoman Empire,* Leiden 1972.

REINHARD, Ursula and Volker, 'Notizen über Caucasian Webteppiche, insbesondere bei Süd- und Südwest-Turkischen Nomaden,' *Baessler-Archiv,* vol. XXII (1974).

REINHARD, Ursula, 'Turkic Nomad Weaving in the Döshemealti (Antalya) Area of Southern Turkey,' *Yörük,* A. N. Landreau ed., Pittsburgh 1978.

RIEFSTAHL, Rudolph M., 'Primitive Rugs of the "Konya" Type in the Mosque of Beyshehir,' *Art Bulletin,* XIII (1931), pp. 166 ff.

Samples of the Old Turkish Carpets and Kilims, Istanbul 1961.

WALKER, Daniel S., *Oriental Rugs in Cincinnati Collections,* Cincinnati Art Museum, Cincinnati 1976.

YETKIN, Şerare, 'Türk Kilim Sanatında Yeni Bir Grup Saray Kilimleri,' *Belleten,* vol. XXX (1971).

— 'Hekimoğlu Ali Paşa Camiinden Hayvan Figürlü Bir Türk Kilimi,' *Vakiflar Dergisi,* vol. IX (1971).

— 'Divriği Ulu Cami'inde Bulunan Osmanli Saray Sanatı Üslübundaki Kilimler,' *Belleten,* vol. XLII, no. 165 (1978).

— 'Zwei Türkische Kilims,' *Beiträge zur Kunstgeschichte Asiens. In Memoriam Ernst Diez* (Istanbul 1963), pp. 182–192.

CAUCASUS

BLACK, David and Clive LOVELESS, ed., *The Undiscovered Kilim,* London 1977.

CHIRKOV, D., ed., *Daghestan Decorative Art,* Moscow 1971.

DIMAND, Maurice S. and Jean MAILEY, *Oriental Rugs in the Metropolitan Museum of Art,* New York 1973.

Exhibition of Oriental Carpets, Nicolas Sursock Museum, Beirut 1963.

FRANSES, Michael, *Palas, Kilims from the Caucasus,* London 1974.

KERIMOV, Lyatif, *Azerbaidzhanskii kovyor,* Baku-Leningrad 1961.

— *Folk Designs from the Caucasus for Weaving and Needlework,* New York 1974.

LANDREAU, Anthony N. and W. R. PICKERING, *From the Bosporus to Samarkand, Flatwoven Rugs,* Textile Museum, Washington, DC 1969.

LEFEVRE & PARTNERS, ed., *Caucasian Carpets,* London 1977.

SCHURMANN, Ulrich, *Caucasian Rugs,* London, n. d.

TSCHEBULL, Raoul, 'Northwestern Iran and Caucasus', *Yörük,* ed. Anthony N. Landreau, Pittsburgh 1978.

PERSIA

ALLGROVE, Joan, J. A. BOYLE, and Mary BURKETT, *The Qashqā'i of Iran,* Manchester 1976.

BEATTIE, May H., *The Thyssen-Bornemisza Collection of Oriental Rugs,* Castagnola, Switzerland 1972.

— *Carpets of Central Persia,* Mappin Art Gallery, Sheffield, London 1976.

BLACK, David and Clive LOVELESS, ed., *The Undiscovered Kilim,* London 1977.

DE FRANCHIS, Amedeo and John WERTIME, *Lori and Bakhtiyari Flatweaves,* Tehran 1976.

DIMAND, Maurice S. and Jean MAILEY, *Oriental Rugs in the Metropolitan Museum of Art,* New York 1973.

EDWARDS, Cecil A., *The Persian Carpet,* London 1975.

GARROD, Oliver, 'The Qashqā'i Tribes of Fars', *Royal Central Asian Society Journal,* XXXIII (1946).

GLUCK, Jay and Sumi Hiramoto GLUCK, ed., *A Survey of Persian Handicraft,* Tehran, New York, London and Ashiya, Japan 1977.

HOUSEGO, Jenny, *Tribal Rugs,* London 1978.

— 'Northwestern Iran and Caucasus', *Yörük,* ed. Anthony N. Landreau, Pittsburgh 1978.

LANDREAU, Anthony N. and W. R. PICKERING, *From the Bosporus to Samarkand, Flatwoven Rugs,* Textile Museum, Washington, DC 1969.

LEFEVRE & PARTNERS, ed., *The Persian Carpet,* London 1977.

MAŃKOWSKI, Tadeusz, 'Some Documents from Polish Sources Relating to Carpet Making in the Time of Shāh 'Abbās I', *A Survey of Persian Art,* ed. A. U. Pope, vol. III, Oxford 1935.

Near Eastern Art in Chicago Collections, The Art Institute of Chicago, Chicago 1973.

POPE, Arthur U., ed., *A Survey of Persian Art,* London 1939.

STRAKA, Jerome A. and Louise MACKIE, ed., *The Oriental Rug Collection of Jerome and Mary Straka,* New York 1978.

TSCHEBULL, Raoul, 'Northwestern Iran and Caucasus', *Yörük,* ed. Anthony N. Landreau, Pittsburgh 1978.

WALKER, Daniel S., *Oriental Rugs in Cincinnati Collections,* Cincinnati Art Museum, Cincinnati 1976.

WERTIME, John, 'The Names, Types and Functions of Nomadic Weaving in Iran', *Yörük,* ed. Anthony N. Landreau, Pittsburgh 1978.

WIET, Gaston, *Exposition d'Art Persan,* Musée Arabe, Cairo 1935.

WULFF, Hans E., *The Traditional Crafts of Persia,* Cambridge, Mass. 1966.

Location of Kilims Illustrated

The Textile Museum, Washington, DC 100, 114, 175, 266, 323, 346
Thyssen-Bornemisza collection, Castagnola, Switzerland 322
Edouard Totah collection, London 97, 172, 201, 364
Raoul Tschebull collection, Frankfurt 298
Türk ve Islâm Eserleri Museum, Istanbul 126, 200
Mrs Ullman collection, London 253, 254
Ulu Cami, Divriği 54, 55, 56, 57, 58
Victoria and Albert Museum, London 1, 63, 64, 71, 190
Vigo Sternberg Galleries, London 301
WHER S. A., Panama 268

Neil Winterbottom collection, London 68
Georgie Wolton collection, London 124, 128, 131, 134, 152, 210, 259, 263, 269, 296, 297, 299, 302, 358
Tassos Zoumboulakis, Athens 230, 240, 244
Samy Zubaida collection, London 243, 286
Private collections: Athens 279; Athens 353; Bonn 8, 59, 153, 255, 294; Cologne 121; London 135; London 139; London 142; London 325; London 361; 362; U.S.A. 171, 283; U.S.A. 314; U.S.A. 326
Present location unknown 75, 176, 338, 410

Photo Credits

Victoria and Albert Museum 2, 21, 33, 38, 39
Walter Denny 55, 56, 57, 58
The Fine Art Society, page 136
Ernst J. Grube 320
Connoisseur 368
Mary Burkett 415
Peter Wallum 416, 417, 420, 421
Feridoun Darrehshuri 418
Oliver Garrod 419
Joan Allgrove 422

Index

This book was printed in February 1982 by Imprimerie Paul Attinger S.A., Neuchâtel
Filmsetting: Febel AG, Basle
Binding: Mayer & Soutter, Renens (Lausanne)
Maps: Ronald Sautebin
Editorial: Barbara Perroud-Benson
Design and Production: Franz Stadelmann

Printed in Switzerland

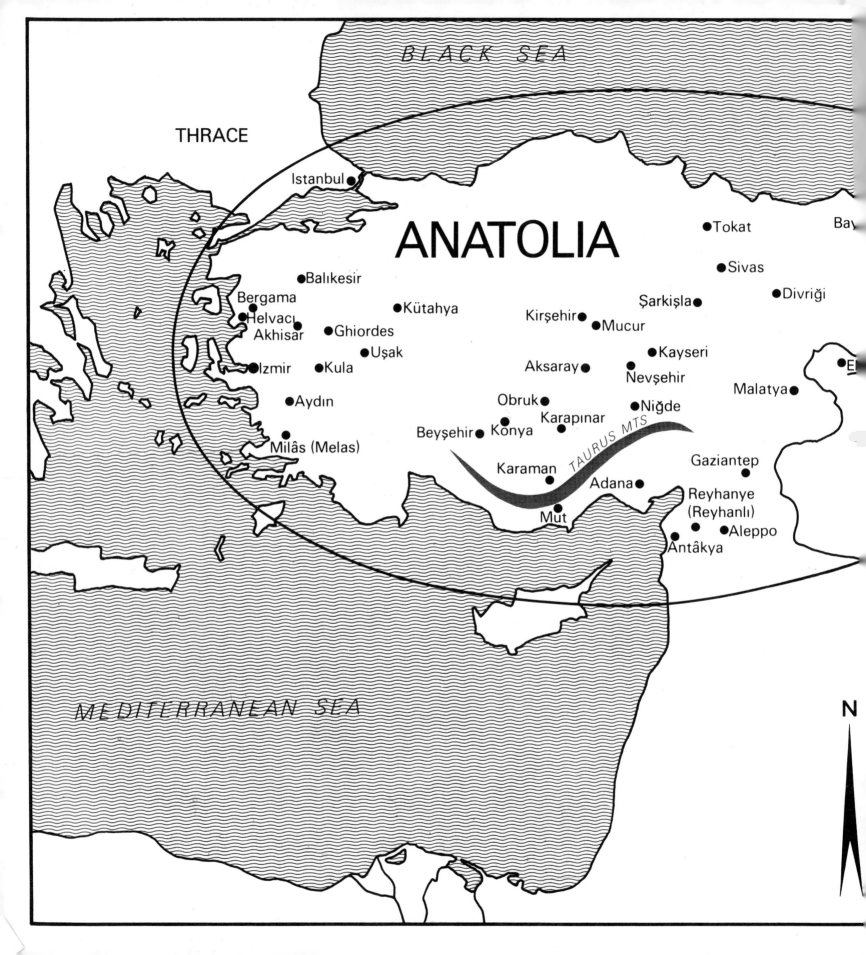